RELIGIOUS TRANSFORMATION
IN WESTERN SOCIETY

RELIGIOUS TRANSFORMATION IN WESTERN SOCIETY

The end of happiness

Harvie Ferguson

London and New York

First published in 1992
by Routledge
11 New Fetter Lane, London EC4P 4EE

Simultaneously published in the USA and Canada
by Routledge
a division of Routledge, Chapman and Hall Inc.
29 West 35th Street, New York, NY 10001

© 1992 Harvie Ferguson

Laserset by LaserScript, Mitcham, Surrey
Printed and bound in Great Britain by
Biddles Ltd, Guildford and King's Lynn

British Library Cataloguing in Publication Data
Ferguson, Harvie
Religious transformation in western society: the end
of happiness.
1. Religion
I. Title
306.6

Library of Congress Cataloging in Publication Data
Ferguson, Harvie.
Religious transformation in western society: the end of happiness
Harvie Ferguson.
p. cm.
Includes bibliographical references and index.
1. Happiness – Religious aspects. 2. Religion and sociology.
I. Title.
BL65.H36F47   1991
306.6–dc20   91-13665
                                                  CIP

ISBN 0–415–02574–5

FOR SOPHIE

CONTENTS

Acknowledgements   viii
Introduction: the end *of happiness*   ix

1 HAPPINESS: BEYOND THE SOCIOLOGY OF
  RELIGION   1

2 FAITH: HAPPINESS PROCLAIMED   34

3 BELIEF: HAPPINESS OBSCURED   69

4 MORALITY: HAPPINESS POSTPONED   102

5 PASSION: DESIRE FOR HAPPINESS   135

6 SENSUOUSNESS: HAPPINESS RECLAIMED   170

Conclusion: the end of happiness   204

Notes   212
Bibliography   246
Name index   263
Subject index   266

ACKNOWLEDGEMENTS

I have tried to acknowledge all my principle debts in the Bibliography. However, as my intention has been to range as widely as possible and to pay little regard to disciplinary boundaries, I have no doubt failed to note many publications that played a part in what follows. For those omissions let me apologize in advance.

What cannot appear in any bibliography and yet, without which, no book of this sort could possibly be written is the library upon which the author has depended for so much source material. At a time when Glasgow University Library, like so many other academic libraries, is faced with declining resources and arbitrary cuts in its acquisitions, it is important to realize that future generations of scholars will find it increasingly difficult to carry out the kind of research which I have had the good fortune to attempt. I have benefited from an academic tradition which I fear has already come to an end.

What does continue and is a pleasure, therefore, to acknowledge is the tireless and friendly service of the staff of Glasgow University Library; after I had developed a realistic fear of its unreliable lifts, they made my repeated journeys to its seventh floor the easier to bear.

I would also like to thank my students, who bore my enthusiasms with considerable fortitude. I hope this will answer, somewhat more adequately than I was able to at the time they were asked, the awkward questions with which they interrupted my lectures.

INTRODUCTION
The *End* of Happiness

To speak of Happiness is to invite ridicule. It is not just an outmoded concept, superseded by an entire vocabulary of technically more precise terms; it invokes a vanished and degraded world. Even advertisers seem embarrassed by the word, and in offering every imaginable human good they yet remain shy of promising Happiness. This, surely, rather than indicating any residual good taste or modesty on their part, betrays something deeply ambivalent in the notion of Happiness itself. The modern commodity, the advertiser knows, cannot afford to be associated with the past. And the idea of Happiness, as Happiness itself, is undeniably old.

The word is, seemingly, an anachronism. The meaning it expresses no longer has behind it the compulsion of an undeniable reality. It retains, apparently, a purely lexicographical significance. Even so, persisting by inertia, it continues to carry with it the burden of undischarged meaning. It has refused to be translated into some innocuous modern equivalent; pleasure, satisfaction, fulfilment, are labels we attach to particular segments of experience and lack the radical inclusiveness of Happiness (and its related spiritual terms, Bliss, Joy, Ecstasy), which designates a completely autonomous mode of being. Yet a sufficient trace of such a world remains (in memory or in imagination) to make of Happiness a disturbing idea. It is a world we pretend no longer exists, but whose existence we readily confirm in the faintly embarrassed reaction with which we greet its occasional disclosure.

This is all, no doubt, a little exaggerated. In terms of everyday language who would not, after all, still assent to Augustine's simple declaration that 'We all certainly desire to live happily'?[1] There is no difficulty so long as we leave everyone to define 'happily' for themselves. Indeed, it is wholly characteristic of the modern, degraded

ix

notion of Happiness, that it should be defined subjectively and privately; that is to say, not defined at all. Augustine, however, had no wish to leave important terms unmolested. He goes on at once to point out (what he in fact believed to be self-evident) that 'no one can be happy who does not enjoy what is man's chief good, nor is there any one who enjoys this who is not happy'.[2] Happiness, he explains, can be given a precise meaning which does not depend on unexaminable states of mind or feeling: 'Happiness consists in the enjoyment of a good than which there is nothing better, which we call the chief good'.[3]

Now the chief good of man cannot be 'bodily pleasure, not absence of pain, not strength, not beauty, not swiftness, or whatever else is usually reckoned among the goods of the body'.[4] All these are the satisfaction of changing states, the enjoyment of which depends upon something other than themselves, namely the soul. And as 'virtue gives perfection to the soul',[5] Happiness is uniquely a qualification of a spirit obedient to an orthodox way of life. The soul is the precondition of every specific and limited good; and Happiness is the enjoyment of the soul's own perfection. Augustine, again uncontroversially, points out that the soul's inner tendency towards its own perfection is obscured in the pursuit of a host of lesser goods. Everyday enjoyments and pleasures are, in fact, obstacles to the attainment of authentic Happiness. The soul can only acquire its own perfection by the submission of the body and spirit to something other than themselves. Happiness, the soul's enjoyment of itself, is known uniquely as a relation with God: 'The perfection of all our good things and our perfect good is God'.[6] And virtue, which disposes the soul towards its authentic end, is 'nothing else than perfect love of God'.[7]

Happiness is a term used exclusively in relation to the experience of a transcending reality, and ought not to be confused with any limited, or conditional, or relative enjoyments of whatever sort. For Augustine the matter is clear: 'to reach God is Happiness itself'.[8] Augustine is not alone in this view. Boethius, writing from prison while awaiting execution, expresses himself in very similar terms: 'In all the care with which they toil at countless enterprises, mortal men, travel by different paths, though all are striving to reach one and the same goal, namely, Happiness, which is a good which once obtained leaves nothing more to be desired'.[9] And since the conception of such surpassing goodness is nothing other than the idea of God, then 'God is the essence of Happiness'.[10] And Aquinas tells us unequivocally that as 'Happiness consists in gaining our last end', and as 'manifestly man is destined to an end beyond himself, for he himself is not the supreme good', then human Happiness is the 'perfection of soul' wrought by the contemplation of God.[11] Or to take a more modern example, Pascal, equally, believes that human beings are 'made' for Happiness. 'Despite their afflictions', he writes, 'man wants to be happy, only wants to be happy, and cannot help wanting to be happy'.[12] And, equally, he holds that, to be happy, 'we must love God alone'.[13]

It is just this proximity to God that makes us uncomfortable. God and Happiness, it seems, are indissolubly linked. Interestingly, however, in abandoning the language of Happiness, we have not simultaneously renounced the privilege of talking about God. Para-doxically, since He was pronounced dead, the ceaseless philosophical chatter in His honour has been carried forward with undiminished vigour. God is continually rediscovered as an urgent and novel object of intellectual curiosity. Modern philosophers would be lost without Him, and modern scientists, as much as modern novelists, delight in His quirkiness.[14]

The paradox, formally speaking at least, is easily resolved. Happiness is a personal relation to God; but God *is*. Whether or not we seek Happiness we can acknowledge the necessary existence and essential characteristics of God. God is greater, in other words, than our rejection of Him. This is just a further demonstration, in fact, of one of His attributes; namely that aspect of His creation we call human freedom, or, in an older vocabulary, sin.

The difficulty, however, is not purely formal; it is also historical and sociological. In the formation of the west (which is no longer a grandiose or vacuous term),[15] Christianity played a central role. In proposing a novel conception of God it sought to unite two funda-mentally different ideas: God as creator, as the first cause of all material things; and God as personal salvation, as the end for which human existence was contrived. The ultimate significance and fate of the individual was thus linked, necessarily and essentially, to a cosmic principle. Human Happiness was found in the love of that which, as both *terminus a quo* and *terminus ad quem* of all existence, stood apart from and superior to our immediate experience of the world.

Superficially at least it seems as if our resolve to do away with God is half-hearted. Or, rather, it is a gesture made wholly with the heart but not with the head. It is the promise of personal salvation, and not the God of natural necessity, that we have foregone, or would like to forego. This seems to be a somewhat perverse version of the conventional view of the development of modern society as a process of secularization. Since the scientific revolution of the seventeenth century, and more particularly since the rationalist attack on religious belief that it inspired during the eighteenth century, it has become a commonplace to claim that God is 'an hypothesis of which we have no need'.[16] The notion of God, that is to say, far from adding to our understanding of the world in which we find ourselves, in fact tends to constrain the operation of purely human, natural reason. Religion, where it does persist, does so in answer to an unquenchable appetite for personal salvation; it offers Happiness, not Enlightenment.

Whatever view of such a process is adopted the coherence of Christianity, in any event, is fatally compromised. Its view of the indivisibility of cosmological and existential elements has been challenged by the experience of modern life as well as the development of modern thought. Sociologists, as heirs (reluctant or otherwise) to the Enlightenment, have tended to view the problem of religion in modern society from a cosmological viewpoint. Even where they have considered the personal element of Christianity to be important they have done so in the context of an individual's beliefs. The persistence of religion can then be assimilated to the general question of explaining irrational beliefs.

Happiness, however, does not fit into the sociologist's categories. For a time its challenge is easy to avoid (since it is, by convention, unreal), but it is difficult to ignore completely. In what ways, then, might it still make sense to talk about Happiness? Has the association between specific ideas about God and the notion of personal salvation been irretrievably broken? Has Happiness, like an outworn theory of the world, simply disappeared? It may (one hopes) be somewhat indecent to raise such issues. Certainly there is little prospect of discovering any simple answers. The ambiguity deliberately invoked in the title is intended, therefore, as rather more than a rhetorical flourish. 'The End of *Happiness*' asks, quite simply, whether the inner reality traditionally defined by that term any longer exists; has Happiness, in fact, ceased to be a part of human life in modern society? If so, when and how was it abolished? 'The *End* of Happiness', seeks to understand western society in terms of the ultimate values which have informed the development of its social life. Are human beings best understood as animals who spontaneously seek an end beyond themselves? And if so, is Happiness uniquely the end which is sought in western society? These two questions are linked, substantively as well as linguistically, in the actual development of Christianity in the west. Any attempt to answer these questions therefore exploits our existing understanding of this development.

In its initial stages at least, such an enquiry amounts to little more than an unorthodox (perhaps even perverse) approach to the sociology of religion, or more specifically to the sociology of salvation within the context of the development of Christianity in the west. Something rather wider than this, however, is intended. The particular focus of this study is not belief systems or ritual practices or ecclesiastical organization or any of the conventional subject matter of the sociology of religion, but, in a rather broad sense, human subjectivity. Its main contention is that the spiritual history of the west provides the sociologist with an enormously rich source of material for such a study; that, simply put, the history of Christianity is a history (if not *the* history) of human subjectivity in western society.

The series of transformations which have been undergone, and which make up this development cannot, of course, stand on their own. Insightful and breathtakingly clever as it is, Hegel's *Phenomenology* cannot supply the model for such an essay. The various forms of human subjectivity are not self-generating or self-explanatory. They can be understood only as aspects of social relations, the forms of which exist in the soul and the mind as much as in the exchange of goods or the spectacle of battle. Yet, a direct approach in terms of conventional sociological categories is all too likely to leave the soul altogether out of account. Those particular aspects of social relations, in becoming internal and subjective, fall under a modern prejudice which tends increasingly to their being neglected or explained away as the epiphenomenon of some more real presence.

By approaching the nature of subjectivity in terms of its end, and more particularly through the notion of Happiness as its unique *telos*, religious and spiritual categories will be forced into the foreground and made the organizing principle of the discussion. Happiness is not, that is to say, a fixed and unchanging condition, or part of a universal human psychology. It is not simply a matter of social conditions making accessible, or in turn constraining, a common human good which is itself unaffected by history. The very nature of Happiness, and the means through which it is sought, are subject to radical transformation.

This raises a familiar, but quite serious, methodological dilemma. In describing a process of change we might assume the persistence of something essentially unchanged which gives to the succession of differing states a substantial and identifiable unity. From the perspective of the present argument it might seem that the west or western civilization is accorded this somewhat dubious metaphysical privilege, and the arrangement of its subdivisions and stages is merely the reappearance in different forms of what is in reality held to be its underlying and changeless spirit. Alternatively we might suppose each stage possesses a substantial unity of its own, separating it radically from anything preceding or succeeding its peculiar actuality. The obvious difficulty with such a view is that history (in the sense of meaningful continuity) is abolished, to be replaced by an irrational sequence of unconnected phenomena. We might then be able to understand ancient society or feudalism or capitalism, but be unable to make any sense of the various transitions among them. This difficulty cannot be resolved here. All that can be attempted is to repeat other people's errors, and claim (as they do) the virtues rather than the limitations of both approaches.[17]

Happiness, thus, will be taken to be, from one point of view, the constant tendency of western subjectivity, dissolved and reformed according to the tendencies of succeeding social formations. This is, however, a somewhat abstract and formal unity which conceals important historical shifts in the character of human inwardness itself. The means by which Happiness is procured, the manner in which it is finally experienced, and the relation of these to other aspects of the social world require a more refined vocabulary. The changing characteristics of Happiness can be distinguished in terms of the predominant religious preoccupations and techniques of a particular society. The justification for these distinctions depends less upon the prior acceptance of any particular sociological theory than on the sympathetic reconstruction of each type from its own point of view. It is not a matter simply of contrasting the modern secular world with a pre-modern and putatively religious age. Any such dichotomy – which is plausible, if at all, solely in relation to the cosmological dimension of religious thought – fails to do justice to the radical transformations in personal religious life undergone in *both* pre-modern and contemporary western society. From the advent of Christianity to the Enlightenment, after all, can hardly be regarded as a religiously homogeneous era. The distinctions and transitions within it are as radical and as profound as we would like to think the difference between our own world and *any* religiously conceived mode of existence. In fact this latter distinction, it will be argued, is no different in kind to the categorical divisions born of earlier and more self-consciously religious phases of the western tradition. The characteristic secularization of the modern age, however it is evaluated, need not be viewed as the 'decay of a former capacity for transcendence'.[18] That capacity, rather, has to be seen as prolific of much that is new in the modern age.

To ask whether modern society is more or less religious than it was at any arbitrarily chosen point in its past is meaningless. The following will argue that modern society is religious in a new way, and that the religiosity of the modern age can only be perceived in a comparative historical perspective. Just as in the past, the social transformations which constitute the development of western society continue to be embedded in and expressive of a particular form of religious life. The particular and characteristic type of religious life in modern society – the novel form of the continuing search for Happiness which seizes its members – is bound up with just those social and cultural changes more usually designated by the term 'secularization'. It is not that religion has somehow persisted into the modern age; it is, rather, that, viewed within the proper perspective, everything that is new in modern society can be understood, simultaneously, as an original form of religiosity.

To grasp the religious reality of modern life it is necessary first of all to establish the social character of western Christianity as a whole. After discussing some of the theoretical issues this involves, therefore, an attempt will be made to characterize primitive Christianity. From this theoretical and descriptive starting point a series of social and religious transformations will be outlined.

Happiness in the western world, it will be asserted, has been construed in terms of five fundamental modalities: Faith, Belief, Morality, Passion and Sensuousness. These dimensions of Happiness, continuously present in varying proportion and in differing combination, lend to each period in the development of western subjectivity its characteristic 'colour'. The stages in the development of human subjectivity might be approximately traced in the movement from one predominant modality to another. Spirituality, that is, can be conceived initially as Faith, then primarily as a matter of Belief, before becoming ethical and Moral, and then in a modern form crystallizing as Passion before dissolving into Sensuousness. As opposed to other world religions, which have their own specific psychological characteristics, Christianity has embraced, in turn, each of these elements as a source of absolute and unconditional value. The individual's relation to this variously conceived and symbolized other, beyond all immediate experience but upon which all experience depends, and in which all experience is grounded, is regarded as the only foundation of Happiness.[19]

These distinctions cannot be made on the basis of cold logic alone. In order to grasp their significance – to realize the depth and extent of their own inner world – we have to surrender, albeit temporarily, to *their* visions of existence. Suitably provoked, however, a sociology of religion provides an appropriate medium for the reception, and ordering, of these differentially coloured visions of human salvation.

The sociology of religion, that is, already offers many partial insights into the nature of Happiness. No single text or author can serve as an exclusive model. Each, rather, offers insights appropriate to one or other particular aspect of the problem, one rather than another period or stage of its ambiguous development.

In attempting to establish the study of the irrational on a scientific foundation the sociology of religion was of key significance in the formation of sociological thought in general.[20] In this initial ambition it failed. But it is just this failure which now prompts fresh sociological interpretations of the *religious* character of modern life.

1

HAPPINESS: BEYOND THE SOCIOLOGY OF RELIGION

An ideal of personal Happiness is not rooted in human life by necessity. In the perspectives of world history, or the comparative evolution of cultures, it appears exceptionally as a collective aspiration towards a *perfect* society. We would like to think that, with the advantage of living in an apparently post-religious society, the temptation to trace Happiness to an invariable (if hidden) truth of the human condition can now be seen for what it was: an ethnocentric conceit of the western mind. And we need no longer, therefore, spend our energies in its vain pursuit, or become anxious over its elusiveness. Along with its family of similarly fictitious absolutes (Truth, Reality, Beauty . . .), we believe that Happiness has become a harmless concept, no more than a useful means through which we can protect the present by cleansing it of its *past*.

To understand the allure of Happiness we must place ourselves in the midst of a world for which, rather than appearing as a veiled and ambiguous possibility, it bore the incorruptible value of reality itself. Happiness, in this sense, can be discovered only, and then not always directly, within the religious tradition of the west. Rather than turn directly to the major spiritual sources of that tradition, therefore, many of which, even where they have remained superficially familiar, have become psychologically opaque, we have to make an elliptical approach through the distorting lens of sociological theory. It is not necessary, however, to reconstruct (if that were possible) the analytic framework of the sociology of religion as a whole. It is, or was, a particular aspect of western religiosity which provokes, or provoked, the longing for Happiness, and in proposing a sociological understanding of Happiness the major classical sources of the sociology of religion are best used selectively. The original aims of, for example, Emile Durkheim, or Max Weber, were clearly more comprehensive

1

and systematic than the limited ambitions of the present essay, which seeks to illustrate, rather than to criticize, certain strands of their arguments.

The study of religion, in fact, played a central role in the development of sociological theory. This was partly, and obviously, because modern society appeared to be wholly or almost wholly secular. It was also a result, in a somewhat less obvious way, of sociology's critical response to the cruder forms of rationalism that had been popular throughout the eighteenth century. If religion had indeed disappeared, it was difficult to believe that it had done so merely as a consequence of these intellectual assaults. And, more importantly, the long centuries during which some form of religious belief and practice had formed an indispensable part of the organization of social life could not be lightly dismissed as the history of error or deception.[1]

Religion, therefore, whether or not it would persist, deserved to be interpreted positively; however absurd its outward forms and explicit content, it must have some 'real foundation' in the life of society.

EMILE DURKHEIM: THE SOCIAL MEANING OF THE SACRED

In defining Happiness, provisionally at least, in a theistic fashion, it would seem that we have placed ourselves altogether outside the most general formulation of the sociology of religion – that found in the work of Emile Durkheim. Durkheim was concerned above all with 'elementary' phenomena, that is with the characteristics of society as such. He therefore makes clear, at the outset of his famous work, that religion cannot be conceived narrowly within the western tradition of monotheism, or indeed within the generally civilized but historically and ethnologically limited field of the great world religions.

It is, in his view, one of the characteristic faults of the scientific studies of religion in his own day that, in confining themselves to its more advanced forms, they came to regard what were in fact only the most highly developed types of spirituality as universal phenomena.[2] Durkheim insists, rather, that 'Religion is more than the idea of gods or spirits, and consequently cannot be defined exclusively in relation to these latter'.[3] Even advanced religions, such as Buddhism, are conspicuously lacking in spiritual elements in the sense of either a deified natural power or a hypostatized personality.

Durkheim believed religion, in his own sense, to be genuinely universal and to be defined by a single common characteristic, namely a 'division of the world into two domains, the one containing all that is sacred, the other all that is profane'.[4] This distinction is, he admits, peculiar. It is not simply that the profane is in some sense subordinated to the sacred; they comprise, rather, radically heterogeneous classes. 'In all the history of human thought', he claims, 'there exists no other example of two categories of things so profoundly differentiated or so radically opposed to one another'.[5] They are not subdivisions of an inclusive category, but 'two worlds between which there is nothing in common'.[6] And they are conceived, therefore, not merely as distinct, but as antagonistic realms.

The radical heterogeneity of the sacred is defined primarily in spatial terms. The sacred is that which is 'set apart' and 'above' the profane, and which profane things 'must not touch'.[7] All objects, all beings, real and imagined, *must* fall into one category or the other. Now religious beliefs are simply 'the representations which express the nature of sacred things and the relations they sustain, either with each other or with profane things'.[8] And a religious rite is just 'the rule of conduct which prescribes how a man should comport himself in the presence of sacred objects'.[9]

Durkheim, additionally, insists on distinguishing religion by its communal aspect; it is 'an eminently collective thing'. And it is, therefore, by virtue of their essential character that 'the really religious beliefs are always common to a determined group'.[10] He has in mind here the significance of the distinction between magic and religion. He wishes to preserve this difference, but, in denying the purely spiritual character of the latter, he has denied himself one conventional means of maintaining such a categorical distinction.[11] Magic is wholly lacking, he claims, in that binding force which makes of all believers a 'moral community'; the feeling of union which comes 'from the simple fact that they have a common faith'.[12] Indeed, 'there is something thoroughly anti-religious in the doings of the magician',[13] but this has little to do with the nature of the beliefs common to either system. Magic is characterized by a 'technical and utilitarian' disposition which discourages speculation, and supports at best an *ad hoc* and impermanent form of social organization. Magic, that is to say, has little influence on social life beyond its own narrowly conceived boundaries.

The definitional strategy has moved from the logical presupposition (the distinction between the sacred and profane) to the universal consequences (the formation of a moral community) of religion. Neither method appears logically sound and Durkheim apparently compounds the difficulty by deriving both from different aspects of what he originally claimed to be a single, elementary phenomenon. His subsequent efforts to maintain the coherence and unity of this phenomenon have failed to convince many commentators.[14] Even ignoring the embarrassment of beginning with a tautology, these conceptions of religion seem, to common-sense observation at least, to be both empirically, and analytically, separable. It appears, therefore, that Durkheim will be forced to develop two linked, but distinct, theories of religion. Indeed it is possible to view the very different traditions of contemporary social thought which draw their inspiration from Durkheim's work as diverging at just this point. The first, developed by Durkheim's own students before absorbing fresh insights from linguistic studies, was transformed into structuralism.[15] The second, which remained particularly influential in Britain and America, took Durkheim's functionalism as its guiding principle.[16]

Partly, perhaps, to maintain the illusion of unity, and partly from a conviction (widespread at the time he wrote)[17] that the elementary features of universal religion could be more easily observed in primitive societies, Durkheim chose to illustrate his thesis by examining the totemic beliefs of Australian Aborigines. There, more than anywhere else, Durkheim was convinced the underlying *social* reality of religion was manifest. In Aboriginal society the classification into sacred and profane is a direct expression of social 'solidarity'.

The community of the clan, the fundamental organizing principle of the society, is defined *both* as a relation of kinship, *and* as a universal classificatory principle. All the members of the same clan, that is, are held to be related by bonds of kinship, and each clan represents this cardinal principle in the form of totemic beliefs and practices.[18] Together with its subdivisions (phratries and marriage-classes), each clan adopts, as it were, some definite animal or plant species in relation to which special prohibitions are observed. Members of the same totemic group cannot use the totemic species in an everyday manner. They may not normally, for example, eat it, or wear its skin, or make tools from its bones.

The crucial point, for Durkheim, is that both kin groups and totemic classes have something fundamentally arbitrary about them. The members of a clan, or totemic division within it, 'consider themselves united by a bond of kinship', but it is a bond which springs simply from their bearing the same *name* and 'does not come from the fact that they have definite blood connections with one another'.[19] Kinship, that is to say, is, in part at least, a matter of conventional definition and does not correspond in any definite and systematic manner to indisputable facts of nature. It is just because of this arbitrariness that it can, indeed it must, be *represented* emblematically. The totemic species, similarly, has a purely conventional boundary, and a purely conventional relation with the group it represents. Both kin group and totem, that is to say, are socially constituted as *classes* of similar objects. The totem is primarily a logical class introduced to simplify and order the facts of nature, while the kin group is an organizing category of social relations. Now Durkheim is quite clear in saying that 'the idea of class is an instrument of thought which has obviously been constructed by men'.[20] He goes on at once, however, to argue that in constructing such classes 'we had need of a model', and 'it is hard to see where we could have found this indispensable model except in the spectacle of the collective life'.[21] He seems, in fact, to suggest a direct causal relation between the two, which again leaves him open to criticism on a number of empirical and analytic grounds. Can such an association between forms of classification and forms of collective life in fact be observed? And where do these latter forms come from in the first place?[22] He has already argued, however, that kinship relations are classificatory in the same way as totemic groups, and it is similarity rather than causality that he is trying to establish. Somewhat later, for example, he reaffirms that 'totemism and the clan mutually imply each other', and that the unity of the clan 'comes solely from their having the same name and the same emblem'.[23]

The nature of this mutuality emerges more clearly in his interpretation of totemic beliefs. Totemic decorations are used in religious ceremonies. But it is not primarily for this reason that 'it is the very type of sacred thing'.[24] Its religious character is just as marked in the interdictions regulating its everyday relations to the group. Nor does its religious nature rest upon some primordial or degenerate mythic conception of the world. It cannot be founded upon an error. It is not a particular animal or plant species that is worshipped, but the 'anonymous and impersonal force' represented by these sacred objects. The emblem of the species is thus more potent and dangerous than its living counterpart, its name still more so. This force, indeed, 'is so completely independent of the particular subjects in whom it incarnates itself, that it precedes them and survives them'.[25] The totem is 'only the material form under which the imagination represents this

5

immaterial substance, this energy diffused through all sorts of hetero-geneous things, which alone is the real object of the cult'.[26]

This force has a conspicuously 'moral character' and is, in fact, 'the source of the moral life of the clan'.[27] Now, since the totem is merely the symbol of some vague and indefinite force, Durkheim feels he is in a position to reveal the real foundation of such a force. With another characteristic lurch in the logical ground Durkheim argues that: 'In a general way, it is unquestionable that a society has all that is necessary to arouse the sensation of the divine in minds, merely by the power that it has over them; for to its members it is what a god is to its worshippers'.[28]

It is the necessity of perpetual dependence which links the fact of social life with the idea of religion. It is a dependence which, by virtue of its interiority, is quite unlike that of our subordination to nature. It is intimate and less fearful, amounting to respect rather than dread. [29] The force of society is felt from within, as moral compulsion. And it is this force of which the totem is emblematic. In an almost pure state it appears in the 'effervescent social environment' of primitive rituals, where, 'feeling himself dominated and carried away by some sort of external power', the clan member may 'become a new being'.[30] The sentiments provoked in such ritual become detached, as it were, from the specific ceremonial context and are subsequently associated with the symbols of collective arousal. In them each member of the clan carries with him an image of the whole society. Religious belief is, therefore, primarily 'a system of ideas with which the individuals represent to themselves the society of which they are members and the obscure but intimate relations which they have with it'.[31]

It is from the relation of individual to society that the fundamental religious notions spring. The intuition of Happiness is, in fact, well founded and may indeed be universal, for there is a very real sense in which society, existing independently of any of its particular members, can only be expressed in the vocabulary of transcendence. Durkheim, therefore, concludes that 'If religion has given birth to all that is essential in society, it is because the idea of society is the soul of religion'.[32] Religion is, therefore, an essential aspect of social life as such. It follows from this that the specific character of Happiness in the west must be sought in the peculiarity of its becoming in the 'post-axial' age a 'personal value' rather than in the general conscious-ness of society as a superior and external force.

It is perhaps clear by now, from the welter of illustration, the inter-related definitions, and the tendency to tautology, that it is difficult to extract from Durkheim's marvellous book any very precise account of what he understands by religion. His theory follows necessarily from his definition, which itself cannot be supported by additional, independent argument. He appears at times to account for religion as some kind of logical necessity, at other times as the outcome of social activities which, presumably, have some other (non-religious) foundation. Society is invoked as both cause and effect of the religious life; and religion appears, equally, to be the cause and effect of society. These criticisms are, from one point of view, wholly justified.[33] Yet Durkheim was himself a trained philosopher and taught philosophy before turning to sociology. He expected consistency and rigour in argument, and was highly critical of its absence in others. If he was driven to offend against this training it is at least plausible to suppose that the insights he was attempting to elucidate were of such a kind as to defy the constraints of logical or scientific analysis as these were generally conceived in his day.

Rather than choose between a structuralist and a functionalist reading of Durkheim's analysis of religion, therefore, it is worth trying to recover the intuitive unity which lies beneath the variety of apparently conflicting and even contradictory arguments deployed at various points in his work.

It should be recalled, first of all, that *The Elementary Forms of the Religious Life* stands at the end and not at the beginning of a productive life. His intellectual starting point is not 'primitive' society, but modern, complex, 'organic' society. It is one of the leading characteristics of such complex societies that they are secularized. What creates the coherence of such societies is simply their high level of differentiation. Each individual has become dependent on an extraordinarily large number of other, unknown and unseen individuals. The consequential links of mutuality and dependence generate moral forces from within the necessary social relations which even the minimal requirements of comfort and companionship require. There is no particular need for anything to be superimposed on top of this organic unity. The existence of complexity is self-perpetuating, and modern society persists by forces generated from within itself.[34]

Durkheim's real intellectual problem begins when he asks what holds society together in the absence of a complex division of social labour. Even the simplest society must be regarded as a reality *sui generis*. Indeed, even less than is the case with modern contractual relations can the order of a simple society be reduced to the rational pursuit of individual interest. And as Durkheim accepts the prevailing mythology of the biogenetic law of development, he imagines that contemporary primitive is equivalent to archaic, both of which are inherently simpler than modern, complex societies. In terms of social organization the division of labour is the essence of complexity. So simpler, archaic societies must be 'less divided' than complex modern ones and, by implication, the former must have emerged at some indeterminate point in the past from a wholly undivided 'social protoplasm'.[35] It is this assumption which forces Durkheim to postulate the existence of a 'collective or common conscience', a system of 'representations' which he conceives as 'the totality of beliefs and sentiments' which are common to the members of such an undivided society and form 'a determinate system which has a life of its own'.[36]

In simple, undivided, or minimally divided, societies relationships are generated and maintained solely by the force of a *conscience collective*. In terms of gaining the essentials of life, the members of such a society are not interdependent. The practical difficulty facing such a society is to arouse the 'sentiments' which will find expression in acts of co-operation. Durkheim's view, in fact, is one of the relatively few fully developed expressions of an asocial conception of primordial man.[37] Society, in his view, is not founded upon necessity; it is at least conceivable that human beings could have survived outside of society. The mere *existence* of society, in other words, does not explain its actual presence. There is no instinct of sociability that prompts man naturally to form the conventional bonds of social life.

Paradoxically, then, it is easier to understand a highly complicated modern society than to understand the simplest of original societies. Indeed, the simpler one imagines it to be, the more difficult it is to conceive of its social nature. Durkheim's solution is an act of desperation. The *conscience collective* is conjured from nowhere and amounts, in fact, to another description of just that phenomenon he is purportedly explaining. The *conscience collective* must be the result of social interaction, to be nothing other than society itself. For primitive society to exist the *conscience collective* must spring up overnight. Society, we might say, presupposes itself.

The descriptive difficulty is obvious, but Durkheim is, in one sense at least, surely correct. The transition from a condition of natural indifference to a state of social organization is an impossible requirement of any evolutionary theory of society. However Durkheim approaches the problem he is forced into logical difficulties; it is the problem, however, which lies at the heart of *The Elementary Forms*.

8

The functionalism in Durkheim's argument, therefore, is of a peculiar sort. It is not that religious rites serve to perpetuate a social totality which might otherwise disintegrate into atomistic chaos. It is, more profoundly, that religious rites *create* that social totality out of which subsequent functional relations emerge. Religious rites affirm the existence of something which is, otherwise, without basis. It is not religious belief which it affirms but the reality of the society posited in such belief. It should not be supposed that Durkheim is suggesting that primitive religion, in its ritualized form of interaction, provides the glue without which the essential life of the society could not be carried on. Nor does he suppose that primitive religion is in itself the essential basis of social life. Both functional and causal interpretations are aspects of the *representational* power of religious forms. It cannot be too often stated that the distinction between the sacred and the profane is a purely conventional one. There is no necessity underlying any of its particular instances. It is only the act of classification itself which is necessary and, therefore, universal. Society begins, that is to say, with an arbitrary act, the making of a division which has no rationale beyond the mere assertion that such a thing is possible. The division of sacred and profane has no meaning beyond itself, beyond stating that society has been brought into existence in an ungrounded act. Society is created, we might say, *ex nihilo*. What the primordial act of distinction establishes is the *conventionality* of society. All social relations are matters of convention; they are not formed from nature but belong exclusively to the realm of culture.

This is not to say that rational purpose, or utilitarian ends cannot be met through the medium of society. Indeed they cannot be met in any other way. The rationale of society, from the individual's viewpoint, is just its capacity to fulfil needs which begin in nature. But such needs are satisfied in society only through activities regulated by convention; and conventionality is itself conventional. The conventional, in other words, might not have existed; man might have lived (or more likely died) outside of society. Nothing, however, should conceal the fact of its arbitrariness, its wilfulness, and therefore its deep inexplicability. The distinction between the sacred and the profane stands before all difference. It is the presupposition of society, the beginning of the social logic which, without ever freeing itself from this original act of separation, will give rise to all subsequent forms of life. It is a distinction which is continually encoded and re-encoded in all subsequent social divisions, a difference essential to all others. The fundamental religious dichotomy is, then, an unnecessary but essential division which makes possible all the necessary but inessential distinctions particular to each specific society.[38] This is no more than a radical statement of Durkheim's objection to the utilitarian tradition in modern social thought.

Society emerges, then, as a religious phenomenon, not in the evolutionary sense that its earliest forms were the most religious, but in the purely logical sense that it can exist only in and through the establishment of that absolutely arbitrary division which defines the religious life. Durkheim had begun by asking (rhetorically) whether religion, which he took to be a universal human phenomenon, could be without foundation. His argument has led him to the conclusion that, in one sense, the foundation of religion is society. But in another sense it is just because religion is itself without foundation that it can serve as the foundation of society. The social efficacy of religion is due less to its capacity to form pre-existing divisions into an artificial unity, than to its being the primordial classificatory act from which flow all subsequent divisions.[39]

The real ambiguity in Durkheim's analysis now emerges in relation to the meaning of 'the sacred', a term which points simultaneously in two directions. The sacred is both the social (as opposed to the natural) and the collective (as opposed to the individual). In the simplest society these categories merge and Durkheim uses the sacred/profane distinction to refer to both structural and functional relations, to both the logical presuppositions and the empirical consequences of religion.

In the former sense (that the sacred asserts the social over the natural in human existence) the distinction quickly breaks down. There is nothing in the simplest society which does not partake of the social. All actions are conventional rather than natural, so all activities are qualified as sacred.[40] The whole force of the original illustration, and of his definition of religion, seems to dissolve. To maintain an empirical reference to the distinction between sacred and profane Durkheim must move to the second meaning of the sacred: that is, the symbolic representation of the sum total of functional relations. It becomes a kind of shorthand for the totality of human society in relation to individual consciousness. But, again, in primitive society this distinction hardly exists.[41] Everything in simple societies is collective; the whole society is immediately present and does not require the mnemonic trick of religious symbolism to recall its actuality.

Durkheim appears to have contradicted his own argument. Rather than being a tautology *The Elementary Forms* seems to end in unavoidable contradiction. It seems as if Durkheim can never quite make up his mind whether to describe, or try to describe, an absolutely ideal but non-existent society as a protean, undivided unity from which all differences emerge; or to confine himself to a (similarly ideal) fragmented and complex modern society. In the end he does neither, and, in trying to reconstruct primitive society, introduces logical elements which belong properly to neither abstract type. The unity of the primitive is an undifferentiated condition of oneness and belongs to the ideal world of 'nascent society'.[42] Such a society is without distinction. All its conventions are of the same order. It is wholly sacred, but, knowing nothing of the profane remains paradoxically unconscious of its ideal totality.

It is in fact more reasonable, in spite of its being formulated in relation to primitive society, to view the distinction between the sacred and profane as characteristic of *modern* society. It is modern society, after all, which, as a consequence of its own inner complexity, provides a social foundation for individual consciousness. And it is only in the separation of individual and collective consciousness that the distinction between sacred and profane can be sustained. There society exists as a recombined totality, and therefore can become present to its individual members only through some kind of symbolic representation. The position is complicated by the fact that, in modern, highly differentiated societies, the totemic object is nothing other than the individual himself or herself. Individualism, indeed, has become one of the most important *institutions* of modern society. In withdrawing into an interior world of private and personal existence each individual is, in fact, expressing the peculiar (but still collective) nature of the modern *conscience collective*. The individual, in other words, as a modern social institution and a modern cultural form, has become a sacred object. In celebrating our own unique experience we are engaging in a modern religious ritual. And the urge we feel to reconstruct the world from the point of view of our own ego is still the force of society within us.[43]

These two meanings of the sacred – the social as opposed to the natural, and the collective as opposed to the individual – can be associated with two phenomenological models of transcendence. The first is connected with the loss of identity in the 'oceanic' experience, and the revelation to the self of its own noumenal essence. The second refers to the awe and despair of separation, the sense of being crushed by the presence of something outside and beyond our own existence.[44] Again in the special case of modern society, as the individual is its most characteristic totem, this separation is internalized and becomes a sense of inward alienation and strangeness, a feeling of self-oppression.

Happiness, as a relation of transcendence, thus has, in Durkheimian terms at least, two fundamental forms. It exists as the experience of either *oneness* or *otherness*, as the dissolution of all difference, or as the apprehension of, and unconditional surrender to, absolute difference. It may be conceived as a relation to an unformed, infinitely generative subject, or to a perfectly formed and complete object. These are the sublime antitheses immanent in the distinction between mechanical and organic solidarity.

KARL MARX: THE SOCIAL MEANING OF SPIRIT

In a phrase made famous by its critics, Marx apostrophized religion as 'the *opium* of the people'.[45] The sentence immediately preceding this celebrated declaration is altogether more interesting; it reads 'Religion is the sigh of the oppressed creature, the heart of a heartless world and the soul of soulless conditions'. Although the phrase 'sigh of the oppressed creature' did not originate with Marx, the conception of modern religion expressed in this sentence was uniquely his own.[46]

Marx, in fact, wrote very little explicitly on religion. The whole formation of his thought, however, and the development of his particular conception of capitalism, was heavily indebted to his reflections, during the early 1840s, on the problem of religion. And the few pages devoted to an outline of a theory of religion are among the most condensed he ever wrote.

The immediate context of Marx's interpretation of religion was the critical reaction to official Hegelian philosophy among a group of radical 'Young' or 'Left' Hegelians in Germany.[47] More in sympathy with Hegel's own early theological writings, they viewed his mature philosophy as a sort of rationalized version, rather than a critical history, of Christianity. Hegel's system had absorbed a century of scientific rationalism and fierce denunciations of the errors of the religious world-view. Cleansed of the less acceptable elements of theism, Christianity re-emerged in his philosophy as a metaphysics of *Spirit*. The notion that all reality might be grasped, intellectually, in the form of a de-personalized principle – self-subsistent, self-generative and immanent with its own rational development – dominated philosophical discussion among the new enlightened intellectuals of western Europe. Paradoxically, for it had been framed as the apotheosis of impersonal secular rationalism, this view was conceived as offering a new, and seemingly more realistic, salvation hope.

Orthodox Hegelianism had quickly degenerated into a reactionary defence of the *status quo*, which was sanctified as the realization of Reason, the culmination of human history in the present. The progressive unfolding of the Rational Principle was held to be expressed in existing social arrangements, and particularly in existing, centralized political authority. Hegel's dictum that 'the Rational is real' and 'the Real is rational' was taken to refer uncritically to the contemporary world.[48] What was *actual* was taken to be Real and, consequently, the embodiment of Reason. It was this perversion of Hegelian ideas that was attacked by a group of younger philosophers, particularly in Berlin, among whom Marx was a prominent member.

A proper understanding of Hegel, claimed the Young Hegelians, depended upon viewing Reason as a potentiality within, rather than the actuality of, the contemporary world. Reason, projecting itself ahead of actuality, should be regarded as the authentic, and realizable, goal of history. It was real in the profound sense of fully comprehending and expressing the entire wealth of human abilities and attributes, and, as such, was not yet identical with our immediate, and limiting, experience of the empirical world. Reason furnished more than an intellectual means of describing and adapting to the particular conditions of existence. *Spirit*, immanent in but unfolding in advance of actuality, was, rather, the critical standard in relation to which the empirical world ought to be judged.[49]

Though Hegel expressed himself exclusively in the outmoded language of *Spirit*, the new generation of radical philosophers believed that he had detected the deepest tendencies of the contemporary age. In order to bring these tendencies fully to light, however, his expressive language had to be transformed. Hegel's attachment to an older metaphysical prejudice had inverted subject and predicate. Man, thus, was the instrument and creature of a wholly abstract Spirit whose inner drive towards Absolute Reason worked itself out through the deception of immediate experience. But this was to invert the true relationship between Man and Spirit. The *real* subject of history could only be man, as a generic being, as a species quite different from any other. From this more 'natural' and modern viewpoint the whole history of Spirit was seen as the progressive development of an illusion. The real nature of man had somehow been conceived in an obscure and abstract fashion, and projected into an unreal and purely ideal world of mere *concepts*.[50] Hegel's work was seen as the culmination of a purely philosophical development, and therefore 'as a hidden and self-deceiving mode of human self-understanding'.[51]

Hegelianism and Christianity were at one in being the 'esoteric expression of human consciousness and self-consciousness',[52] but this *critique*, originally formulated in relation to the former, received its definitive expression as an interpretation of the latter. And it was, consequently, Feuerbach's *Essence of Christianity*, published in 1841, which, provoking the most intense controversy, provided Marx with the immediate context for his own critical assault upon Hegel.

Feuerbach's view of religion was primarily *anthropological*; religion was nothing other than the historical expression of 'human nature'. Religion in general *expresses* the uniqueness of the human species; it has 'its genesis in the *essential differences* between man and animal'.[53] Following Hegel he assumes that self-consciousness is the distinctive character of the human species, that only man is capable of an internal dialogue with himself and therefore of projecting himself beyond the confines of the present. Indeed, he has an unlimited capacity for imagining himself to be other than he is. 'Religion is the consciousness of the infinite', therefore, just because man's 'own essential nature' is an 'infinite nature'.[54] And 'what man calls Absolute Being, his God, is his own being'.[55] The transcending power of the Absolute is, then, nothing other than the purely human consciousness of man's own internal, unlimited nature as a species.

The peculiarity of religion is that it transposes human self-consciousness into something strange. 'His own being becomes the object of his thought first as another being'.[56] This is a rather complex relation. God is conceived to be an absolutely objective and necessary being because man cannot doubt the substantiality of his own being. And in making his own being Absolute and unconditional man objectifies himself; he represents himself as a being *other* than himself. But it is only as a *species being* that man can become conscious of himself as an infinite subject, and thus, aware also of the limiting conditions of his own individuality, he subordinates himself to the projected image of his own nature. Feuerbach claims that 'Man — and this is the secret of religion — objectifies his being, and then again makes himself the object of this objectified being, transformed into a subject, a person. He thinks of himself as an object, but as an object of an object, as an object of another being'.[57]

Feuerbach was enough of an Hegelian to look forward in some sense to the end, not certainly of religion (which is grounded in the necessary disjunction between man's species being and the particularity of actual existence), but of theology. Certainly he anticipated its transformation into a new demystified philosophy. If religion expressed what was hidden in human nature, then a radical 'philosophy of the future' should offer the prospect of open self-knowledge and, beyond that, the possibility of genuine self-realization. Philosophy could become a kind of intermediary between man's estranged nature, in religion, and the free expression of his authentic nature in his own activity.

Feuerbach's argument provides genuine insight into the necessity of religion. The self-consciousness of man's species being, if indeed it is infinite, must be symbolic in nature. A limited individual nature cannot grasp the infinite, but, as part of an infinite species being, human beings remain intuitively but obscurely aware of themselves as unbounded subjectivity. This relation can only be expressed in the irrationality of a symbol.[58]

Marx seized upon Feuerbach's transformative method and used it to demystify Hegel's conception of the modern world. The Feuerbachian method, however, had not in Marx's view gone far enough. He had replaced an abstract, timeless concept of Spirit with an equally abstract and timeless *concept* of man. Feuerbach's much vaunted 'sensuous philosophy' was as empty as Hegel's, and in his work human nature appeared every bit as ideal as Absolute Spirit. In one of his celebrated *Theses on Feuerbach* Marx acutely remarks that Feuerbach, 'not satisfied with *abstract thinking*, appeals to *sensuous contemplation*'.[59] A real understanding of the Hegelian philosophy, and of religion, then, depended upon grasping the human subject as an *historical* reality. 'But *man* is no abstract being squatting outside the world', Marx insists: 'The human essence is no abstraction inherent in each individual. In its reality it is the ensemble of the social relations.'[60]

It is not an irreconcilable estrangement between man's essence, aware of its unbounded potentiality as a species being, and the practical constraint of his real existence in the present, which is responsible for the illusions of religious consciousness. It is, rather, specific contradictions in the secular world which are expressed by this splitting off of certain aspects of human activity and their subsequent projection into a spiritual realm.

Marx does not develop his critique of religion to the point where these contradictions are fully revealed. He chose, instead, to demonstrate the manner in which he had progressed beyond Feuerbach through a detailed examination of Hegel's theory of the state. In this he cleverly argued that turning Hegel 'back on his feet' involved, at the same time, a radical critique of modern society. The orthodox Hegelian view, developing especially from French social thought of the eighteenth century, accepted a distinction between civil society and the state. The former was the realm of private individuals, each with their own particular interests, passions and motives. Within civil society there was no inherent tendency to order; it was, in principle, a pure Hobbesian condition of 'the war of all against all'. The state was conceived, on the other hand, as a higher expression of human rationality, the embodiment of orderliness, restraint, mutuality and co-operation. Marx argued that this distinction was misconceived. The state was viewed by Hegel as an alienated form of political life. It had been split off or detached from the rest of human activity and presented in a new, mysterious and higher form of life. But the truth was otherwise. Civil society was possessed of its own internal tendency to order; it was differentiated into classes according to collective interests which were rationally pursued. The state was only an extension of the superiority of the ruling class within civil society into the political sphere. Within this new sphere, however, it claimed an absolute existence, an unopposed and universal voice to express the interests of society 'as a whole'.[61]

Might we take Marx's critique of the state to be a paradigm for his incompletely developed critique of religion? This is a tempting but not really convincing possibility. Religion is a phenomenon of much greater diversity and historical tenacity than the state. The contradictions in the 'real' world which religion takes up and expresses must be of a very general, if not actually universal, form. Nor should we be taken in by Marx's off-hand comment that, for Germany at least, 'the *criticism of religion* has been essentially completed'.[62] It has only been completed in the sense that criticism has, so to speak, moved on to confront directly the reality from which religion has sprung. And Marx viewed that reality, in his early writings, in terms of immediate oppression and exploitation. Religion was then conceived as the illusory consolation of those in fact denied the possibility of real justice or Happiness. Thus, 'the abolition of religion as the *illusory* happiness of the people is the demand for their *real* happiness. To call on them to give up their illusions about their condition is to *call on them to give up a condition that requires illusions*. The criticism of religion is therefore in *embryo* the *criticism of that vale of tears* of which religion is the *halo*.'[63]

16

This passage calls, of course, for the realization rather than for the abolition of religion. In this it is at one with Feuerbach. It is the longing for the real Happiness (rather than genuine Enlightenment or scientific knowledge) which is the authentic *critique* of religion. The secret of religion, its hidden truthfulness, is this demand for real Happiness. It is just because of the uncompromising generality of the real foundation of religion that it should not be regarded simply as an ideology. Marx, though not developing the argument at this point, does not really accept Feuerbach's close association of Christianity and speculative philosophy. The latter, as Marx makes abundantly clear, can be understood in much the same way as he understands the modern state. It provides an abstract and universal language in which to express the truth of society from the viewpoint of its privileged class.[64] Philosophy cannot itself overcome (*Aufhebung*) the distinctions proper to civil society, and it is the deception of supposing that it can which is the common root of ideological thought. Religion, on the other hand, does express a general, and not a partial, truth. The demand for real Happiness cannot be identified with one class of society only, nor should it be confused with popular movements in pursuit of political liberation or fairer standards of distributive justice.

Marx did not pursue the significance of the demand for 'true happiness'. It is, nonetheless, his clear understanding of the uncompromising character of such a claim that distinguishes his revolutionary ambitions from other meliorative forms of nineteenth-century socialism.[65] He therefore defines the proletariat as a *universal* class. 'A class must be formed which has *radical chains*, a class in civil society which is not a class of civil society, a class which is the dissolution of all classes, a sphere of society which has a universal character because its sufferings are universal, and which does not claim a *particular redress* because the wrong which is done to it is not a *particular wrong* but *wrong in general*.'[66] Genuinely proletarian politics, in other words, is the historic transformation of the religious dream of the west, its translation into non-symbolic language.

The metamorphosis of religious longing into political struggle was not, however, the result of some purely intellectual process of demystification. It was, rather, part of a general social development which had as its general cultural accompaniment a process of secularization. Marx, therefore, turned his attention directly to the 'real' nature of this transformation. The human urge towards Happiness, he supposed, had found itself in the demand for unalienated labour. Marx, now relying more directly on Hegel than on Hegel's critics, viewed 'real happiness' as the 'free expression of human nature'. The unique human attribute, and man's advantage over all other species, was not self-consciousness directly, but the capacity to labour and the necessity of it. The satisfaction of any of his needs, that is to say, called forth a creative, rather than a purely instinctive, response. There was nothing fixed or natural in human activities. Labour was simply that general process in which human beings interacted with nature in order to procure the means of their own continued existence.[67] Society, culture and history were drawn out, so to speak, from this interaction. And it was in this process that human beings both made and expressed themselves.

It is this absolutely general characteristic of human activity which Marx fixes upon as the key to overcoming the illusions of both religious consciousness itself, and the philosophical vision with which the Young Hegelians had sought to replace it. Where Hegel and Feuerbach had viewed alienation as a division of consciousness against itself, Marx, by anchoring all its forms in the history of labour, was able to reconnect the history of 'estrangement' with the 'real' history of human society.[68] Towards this end he drew an important distinction, hitherto elided in the general notion of alienation, between 'objectification' and 'estrangement'. Objectification (*Vergegenstandlichung*) is the process through which human beings express themselves in objects. The process of labour issues in a new object world – a range of artifacts, tools, products, and an entire material culture quite distinct from nature, which forms the immediate environment of human existence. This object-world 'mediates' between man and nature and, in its various developments and major historical forms, expresses a particular moment in the history of human nature. Estrangement (*Entfremdung*), more specifically, refers to the particular circumstances in which this object-world, or part of it, appears to take on a mysterious power of its own and confronts human subjectivity with an inhuman, alien objectivity. This is not a logically or historically necessary feature of objectification. Marx conceives of the possibility of a social world within which human beings do not feel estranged; in which they recognize their immediate environment as a product of their own and others' creative efforts and which serves them as a tool and a means to a freely expressive life.[69]

The peculiar character of modern society, of capitalist society, is that the very process of labour, which is the primordial human activity, has been assimilated to the general process of production and circulation of *commodities*. Human expressive and productive activity, consequently, has been constrained, perverted and corrupted. The human essence has become disguised as a demonic force. Labour, subject to the law of capital accumulation, is now just another commodity. And in being forced to sell it, the worker 'alienates' rather than 'expresses' himself or herself. Every productive act enhances the objective and alien power of the world of commodities, a world whose internal relations have become regarded as the 'natural', and therefore immutable, parameters of the social world.[70]

The overwhelming otherness of the social world, 'its entire system of estrangement'[71] with its seemingly irresistible power and awe-inspiring objectivity, is more than the source of a distinctively modern religious consciousness. In many ways it *is* the distinctive form of modern religiosity. All Feuerbach's insights have been preserved and reappear in Marx's critique of political economy. In moving from religion to labour Marx has preserved the spirit of Feuerbachian anthropology. Religion is the expression of human nature, and human nature is essentially infinite. The modern commodity world, like the sphere of religion, confronts the human subject as a detached and objective realm responding to its own inner necessity and shaped by its own laws. Yet, like religious consciousness, the commodity world is only the product of human 'self-activity'. Capitalism has, therefore, for the first time in history, supplanted religious consciousness directly with the world of objects. This is, from one point of view, the secularization of religion, but from another viewpoint it might be seen as a consecration of labour. Capitalism, in this sense, is the 'infinitizing' of the object world. For the first time the world of objects, the potentially endless variety of which expresses the human essence, has actually outgrown the human power of surveillance and recognition, of keeping track of its own origin in the process of labour. This is because all objects have become commodities, 'use-values' produced only to enter and perpetuate the general process of exchange, and in being exchanged they have taken on a 'mystical character'. The moment the object 'emerges as a commodity, it changes into a thing which transcends sensuousness'.[72] And as the process of exchange is, in principle, endless, the human subject 'loses himself' in contemplation of his own work. In passing so quickly from the *critique* of religion to the *critique* of political economy Marx is not actually changing the subject matter of his investigation; he is still pursuing the *same*, human, social reality.[73]

'A commodity appears at first sight', Marx reassures us, 'an extremely obvious, trivial thing. But its analysis brings out that it is a

19

very strange thing, abounding in metaphysical subtleties and theological niceties.'[74] The 'religious halo' that an earlier generation had
thought easy to dismiss has penetrated to the core of modern reality,
to the commodity, rendering all appearances a 'veil of illusion'. The
'real' world has absorbed (or re-absorbed) into itself those very
qualities of mystery, superiority and strangeness which had marked
the religious as peculiarly its own. Religion has not, after all, been
abolished. The estrangement which is the real root of religious
consciousness has, in fact, become even more pronounced. But in
doing so it has become more appropriately located within the process
of labour itself. The commodity 'transcends sensuousness', not by
being reflected upon philosophically, but by entering into exchange
relations which have liberated themselves from the use-value of the
commodity. Each commodity carries within it, as it were, a 'religious
consciousness' of its own, its alienable value, which it expresses in the
process of exchange.

Marx's distinction between the universal necessity of objectification and the historical contingency of estrangement gives the
impression, at first sight, that he will propose a purely historical
account of religion. That, as religion is a form of estrangement, it is
reasonable to expect it to 'wither away' in a freely created society. It
becomes clear, however, that his conception of such a future society
retains much that is central to the religious conception of Happiness.
The humanization of the social world, its recognition as the product
of labour, and the overcoming of the strangeness and distance which
alienated labour has imposed upon the world of objects is its central
theme.

There are two related, socially meaningful conceptions of transcendence that can be derived from Marx's work. Both are quite
distinct from the ideas of transcendence found in the writings of
Durkheim.

The first is related to the process of exchange. It is the circulation
of commodities that gains a 'life of its own'. The commodity, and
particularly in the form of money, becomes charged with supernal
qualities. These qualities, therefore, are best described philosophically. Exchange is a form of *abstraction*, and not just the application of
an abstract idea. It is the process of exchange which the philosopher
reflects upon and uses as a tool of pure discourse. Because all exchange
suppresses incommensurable qualitative differences and, from its
particular point of view, treats all goods as identical, the 'space'
created by the process of exchange offers a social model for a timeless

realm of ideas.[75] Exchange negates all the qualitative characteristics of objects and considers them simply as carriers of an identical, quantifiable value. Of course, nothing would be exchanged if the items involved really were identical. It is only because they are different that there is any point in exchanging them. The equivalence of exchange is really a piece of practical metaphysics. There is, therefore, in the west a close association between the forms of exchange, and the philosophical and scientific theories through which the nature of the world has been described.[76]

There is in Marx's work, however, another conception of transcendence. It is as a consequence of the alienation of labour that religious *consciousness* reappears in the commodity form. Authentic labour, therefore, will abolish its oppressive estrangement from human qualities. In freely creating objects for their own use human beings will still express themselves in an objective form, and this activity will still give rise to a world divorced from the immediate subjectivity of being. The urge to close the gap, to overcome the distance between subject and object, and, in a single movement, both to express and satisfy human needs will remain as the distinctive and irreducible realm of spirit. It is this realm of feeling which Feuerbach had isolated as the 'organ' of religion. And Marx, as much as Feuerbach, looks forward to its liberation rather than its abolition. Authentic spirit is remote from the pure abstraction of Hegelian Reason; it is the 'heart of a heartless world'.

The object-world which is the product of labour is transformed into commodities by exchange. In capitalism labour is subordinated to the entire process of rational exchange, and profit is derived from the fact that labour itself enters into this process as just one other commodity. But this whole system of moving objects, when viewed from the point of view of use-value, has its spirituality restored. Authentic spirit is the sphere of 'absolute' use-value, a reality which, divested once more of all quantitative attributes, has restored to it the inner freedom of an infinity of possible qualities.[77]

MAX WEBER: THE RELIGIOUS MEANING OF RATIONALIZATION

Among the classical authors of sociological theory, Max Weber devoted far more time and energy than any other to the study of religion. Yet religion rarely appears in his works as a problematic phenomenon. He appears to be interested almost exclusively in the consequences of particular religious doctrines and practices for the organization and subsequent likely development of major civilizations. Unlike Durkheim he is not concerned to reveal the social foundation of religious belief in general, nor, like Marx, is he concerned with the critical unveiling of modern religiosity. In much of Weber's work religious ideas and activities take their place unexceptionally alongside other social phenomena. He opens his general study of the sociology of religion, indeed, by remarking that 'The essence of religion is not even our concern, as we make it our task to study the conditions and effects of a particular type of behaviour'.[78]

This caution, however, together with Weber's well-known disclaimer to being 'religiously unmusical', should not blind us to Weber's real purpose. Since, he argues, 'the external course' of religious behaviour is so diverse 'an understanding of this behaviour can only be achieved from the viewpoint of the subjective experiences, ideas, and purposes of the individuals concerned – in short from the viewpoint of the religious behaviour's "meaning" (*Sinn*)'.[79] Religious activities must be understood on the same basis as any other form of social behaviour, that is, in terms of meaning. But the peculiarly transcendental character of (especially western) religion is revealed in its affinity with the entire province of meaning. Religion *is* the process of ascribing meaning to behaviour. This is its essence, and it is as religious systems of meaning that, most generally, the ultimate values which impart significance to social behaviour enter into the course of history. For a sociology founded upon the elucidation of meaning, religion, therefore, must play a central role. The differentiation of large-scale societies into different social groups, the critical distinctions among the great world civilizations, and the fundamental changes in the mechanisms which create and maintain social order are all, for Weber, aspects of religion.

Meaning is not inherent in behaviour; it is not a naturally occurring form. Nor can it be predicated upon any invariant logical or scientific procedure. It is, in the last analysis, an expression of (irrational) human wilfulness. No behaviour can escape the irresistible human propensity to interpretation, or avoid the ceaseless urge towards valuation. We are fascinated by the motives and reasons, rather than the causes of behaviour. This is no idle curiosity on our part, but springs from a deeper source in our constitutional need for society. It is, in fact, from just such conventional understandings that the givenness of the world, which is the very substance of society, is constructed.[80]

Meaning is, in the last analysis, the outcome of an arbitrary valuation, but, and partly because of this, it is subject to a process of progressive rationalization. No amount of scientific investigation or logical analysis can lead to the establishment of the superiority of some particular ultimate value over any other. The dispute over values is irreconcilable.[81] However, the system of meaning generated from the primitive assumptions of one, rather than another, ultimate value comes gradually under the sway of purely formal criteria of consistency, lucidity and coherence. And social behaviour consequently, though only in part, comes to conform more rigorously to systems of meaning which exist primarily to interpret the world.

Not all ultimate values are apparently religious in nature, but Weber, by refusing to define the essence of religion at the outset, gives the impression at least of believing that all the more complex and developed of such systems are. They constitute, indeed, a rather limited range of humanly possible religious systems. The specific character of western Christianity, in particular its conception of a monotheistic and transcendental God, makes it peculiarly the 'carrier' of the process of rationalization. Christianity, more than any other world religion, has been subject to this formal development: a powerful movement towards consistency and abstraction which, while similarly at work in all other religions, is nowhere else able to shape and form meaning into doctrine to quite the same extent.

Even in the west, however, rationalization is a process that can be brought into focus only in terms of a very long time-scale. In its earliest stages it is far from obvious that Christianity would become the supreme example of a fully rationalized religion. Weber begins in fact with the differentiation of a rather diffuse religious sphere from the magical orientation to the world which he assumes preceded it. In any event, he asserts, the 'most elementary forms of behaviour motivated by religious or magical factors are oriented to *this* world'.[82] Weber accepts the evolutionary perspective, common in the latter part of the nineteenth century, which saw animistic, mythological and magical thought as antecedent to religion proper. Primitive, archaic mentality is overwhelmed by the pressure of everyday needs, and both religion and magic are the, largely ineffective, social tools first developed to organize the purely practical tasks of the mundane world.[83]

The potential for rationalization within magic remains strictly limited. It is always constrained by the practical and unpredictable demands of everyday life. Though tending towards a type of abstraction the magical conception of the world remains an essentially *ad hoc* set of recipes designed to coerce a 'spirit' or 'god' held responsible for some, usually undesirable, state of affairs. The characteristically religious techniques of prayer and sacrifice both have their origin in magical coercion, and retain, in all popular religions, a good deal of this original meaning. But the spirit world outgrows the limited and purely practical demands which first called it into existence. Weber, expressing himself in characteristically paradoxical fashion, notes that 'primitive rationalism' recedes and 'the significance of distinctively religious behaviour is sought less and less in the purely external advantages of everyday economic success. Thus, the goal of religious behaviour is successively "irrationalised" until finally otherworldly non-economic goals come to represent what is distinctive in religious behaviour'.[84]

Associated with the distinction between religion and magic is the development of a priesthood of religious functionaries which is part of a 'regularly organized and permanent enterprise concerned with influencing the gods'.[85] The priest, unlike the magician, is never 'self-employed' but acts in the interests of the members of a religious organization. Additionally the priest is characterized by 'his professional equipment of special knowledge, fixed doctrine, and vocational qualifications'.[86] And it is with a priesthood that doctrine becomes a central part of the religious life, 'the development of a rational system of religious concepts' and the development of 'a systematic and distinctively religious ethic'.[87]

Weber then tries to establish a series of categorical oppositions, one side of which, at each stage, proves to be the 'correct' choice leading progressively to further rationalization and the emergence of new religious distinctions. He produces, in fact, a sophisticated algorithm of the developing identity of western Christianity in the context of the world religions. Christianity, he believes, has proved to be the most rational of all religions, so its underlying structural features must be an essential part of, or at least exceptionally favourable to, the general process of rationalization. Monotheism, it is thus claimed, has a greater potential for rationalization than polytheism. A prophetic religion, particularly the 'exemplary prophecy' of Ancient Judaism, carries the possibilities of codification and systematization yet further. As compared to all traditionally orientated religions the prophet announces the possibility of radical change in doctrine and organization, and thus counters the historically most powerful single factor mitigating against the process of rationalization.[88] More than that, it was in a distinctively personal and inward vision that the prophet broke from traditional teaching and practice. And it is to the prophets that religious developments owed 'a unified view of the world derived from a consciously integrated and meaningful attitude toward life'.[89] Here, there emerged for the first time a self-conscious demand for meaning, for an ordered inner life. The historic link between the cosmic and the personal god was forged in the lives of the prophets, and it was on their charismatic example that, particularly in the west, subsequent religious developments were to turn.

The ethical inwardness of religion is charged with historic significance: 'The conflict between empirical reality and this conception of the world as a meaningful totality, which is based on a religious postulate, produces the strongest tensions in man's inner life as well as in his external relationship to the world.'[90]

Simultaneously with the appearance of prophecy, an organized priesthood and the intellectualization of doctrine came the formation of a congregation whose persistent everyday interests and demands were to some extent opposed to these developments. Increasingly, however, the congregation forged its unity and identity in explicit affirmation of officially formulated dogmatic truths. The priesthood assumed a more intimate pastoral role which, in ministering to individuals, reinforced the personal aspects of doctrine and made their own positions of religious leadership the more secure.[91]

The inwardness of personal, ethical religion is deepened through its moral and intellectual confrontation with the actual world. This is conceptualized as a contradiction between God's perfect goodness and the existence of evil, a contradiction which is resolved through the development of specific religious beliefs. Once again Weber's central interest is in determining which of the possible resolutions promising personal salvation carries with it the greatest potential for the further rationalization of both religious and, more importantly still, all other forms of social action.

The religious solutions to the world's imperfection, Weber suggests, are strictly limited. The first, and perhaps most popular, is ethical dualism, as exemplified in Zoroastrianism, in a variety of gnostic sects contemporary with the early development of Christianity and, most significantly of all, in the spectacular development of Manichaeism.[92] In these systems evil exists as an autonomous spiritual force in continuous conflict with the good. In most versions of dualism, however, the ultimate victory is held, in principle, to rest with the good, so that the entire history of the world is reduced to a process of spiritual purification.[93]

The 'most complete formal solution to the problem of theodicy', however, 'is the special achievement of the Indian doctrine of *karma*'.[94] This doctrine is the logical antithesis of all forms of dualism; in it 'the world is viewed as a completely connected and self-contained cosmos of ethical retribution'.[95] Each individual is held absolutely accountable and each 'forges his own destiny'. Strictly speaking the ethical category of sin does not even exist, for there are in reality only 'offenses against one's own clear interest in escaping from this endless wheel'.[96] The consequences of such a belief tend, of course, towards extreme ritualism and traditionalism. It is a major obstacle, indeed, to the breakthrough of rationalization to non-religious spheres. Weber's theory, therefore, must become more complex at this point. He distinguishes two fundamentally different types of salvation: 'other-worldly' and 'this-worldly'. The rationalization of the former reaches its purest version in *karma*, in a wholly self-sufficient religious world. The personal relation expressed in such beliefs is one of utter submission to God. The aim of religious asceticism here, apart from the sustaining interest in gaining promotion beyond the recurrent cycle of existence, is to become a 'vessel' filled with the divine presence.

It is in terms of his second conception of personal salvation, to act in the world as God's 'instrument', that the third logically consistent, and characteristically western, theodicy has been developed. This view depends upon eliminating all intermediaries between man and God. It is the recognition of the uncompromising transcendence of God which is the distinctive feature of such a view. From a personal, human viewpoint salvation depends, absolutely, on the will of God. Any possibility of exercising some influence, let alone of coercing the divine will, would be to contradict this absolutely clear and logical requirement. It is inconceivable that He would either not know the ultimate fate of any particular individual, or that the individual's behaviour might in some way colour his or her state of grace. Omniscience, taken seriously, leads to a theodicy of predestination; this logical implication was clearly recognized by Augustine, but obscured in the medieval development of Christianity, before being revived in its most forthright version by Calvin.

There is a close association between the religious solution to the problem of evil and the development of particular types of salvation religion and their techniques. Systematic eastern religiosity conceives of salvation in terms of a mystical union with God, whether in terms of a flight from the world or, more rarely, in purely inward, personal, contemplative terms. The western type of religiosity with its stress on the *otherness* of God has an affinity with ascetic religious practices of a rather different sort.[97] These are incompatible, and mutually incomprehensible religious tendencies.

> From the standpoint of the contemplative mystic, the ascetic appears, by virtue of his transcendental self-laceration and struggles, and especially by virtue of his ascetically rationalised conduct within the world, to be forever involved in all the burdens of created things, confronting insoluble tensions between violence and generosity, between empirical reality and love. The ascetic is therefore regarded as permanently alienated from unity with god, and as forced into contradictions and compromises that are alien to salvation. But from the converse standpoint of the ascetic, the contemplative mystic appears not to be thinking of god, the enhancement of his kingdom and glory, or the fulfilment of his will, but rather to be thinking exclusively about himself.[98]

Weber, again joking with the concept of rationalization, points out that 'to practice inner-worldly asceticism (the ascetic) must become afflicted with a sort of happy stupidity regarding any question about the meaning of the world'.[99] God is beyond all possibility of explanation. Weber is aware, of course, that asceticism cannot be deduced as a moral imperative from such a rigorous theology. As he makes clear in a famous essay, asceticism is in fact a practical compromise between rigorous transcendentalism and the persistent demands of everyday life. Rational self-control, dedication to a vocation and the avoidance of all spontaneous enjoyment of the world are primarily techniques to create and sustain that inner certainty the believer interprets as faith. And the believer cannot resist the further pseudological deduction that as faith cannot be proved by empirical demonstration or logical argument it must be a gift from God and, therefore (!), a sign of election.[100]

The various critical decisions which lead towards the rationalization of religious and secular life are not simply the product of an immanent logic of religious development. They are consistent with the primitive beliefs of the various world religions, but their subsequent development is part of a general process of social change, no aspect of which should be treated in isolation. Weber, therefore, also represents these distinctive religious forms in terms of the character-istics of the secular social groups which become their 'bearers'. Quite unlike Durkheim, and more clearly than Marx, Weber regards reli-gious practices as one, if not the most important, of the mechanisms of social differentiation. Religious ideas do not represent society to itself, but, rather, define a specific social group in relation to others. And, if that group is successful in the struggle for social power, their religious ideas come to represent that group to the rest of society.

The long-term rationalization of western religion, therefore, is also progressively the history of the bourgeoisie. A rational ethical religion, Weber claims, has little appeal to the peasantry. The religiosity of peasant groups is never far removed from magical practices. Control of natural forces, upon which their livelihood is intimately and manifestly dependent, remains their paramount religious interest.[101] Similarly the life experiences of a warrior nobility, or of feudal powers generally, are inimical to an ethical religion. 'The life pattern of a warrior has very little affinity with the notion of a beneficent provi-dence, or with the systematic ethical demands of a transcendental god.'[102] Indeed the very notion of sin, salvation and religious humility 'appeared reprehensible to its sense of honour'.[103] A bureaucratic leadership, particularly as exemplified by the Chinese mandarins, is similarly, but for quite different reasons, utterly opposed to salvation religion. The elimination of all emotional elements, and the cultivation of pure conventionality is its hallmark. Equally, large-scale traders and financiers, who have always tended towards religious scepticism or indifference, cannot become the carriers of a rationalized salvation hope.

Weber argues that the specifically rational development of Christianity was from its beginnings 'characteristically a religion of artisans'.[104] Its saviour was a semi-rural artisan, its first missionaries were wandering apprentices, and its earliest communities were over-whelmingly urban. The decline in the significance of kinship within the ancient city, as well as the distinctive character of economic life among the middle classes, 'inclines in the direction of a rational ethical religion'.[105] Their life was typically less closely tied to nature, and was once more obviously influenced by conditions which could, in principle, be brought under rational control.

The primary function of religion emerges as the legitimation of each group's own life pattern and aspirations. Amongst privileged groups, therefore, salvation religions do not develop. Thus Weber connects his general sociology of religion with his political sociology.

The creation of a legitimate social order is not the task only of religion, nor does it depend, even when religion does play a central role, upon the 'false consciousness' of the underprivileged or subjected groups. Weber views society as an arena of competing groups founded upon shared interests which can never be wholly reconciled, and religion, as expression of these group interests, cannot transcend such differences. The only question is which group will succeed in its quest for domination, a quest in which religion often plays a leading role as legitimating the questing group's privileges *to itself*.[106]

The peculiar character of western rationalization has profound implications for both the problem of legitimation and the fate of its religiosity. Where, in the other world religions, the process of religious rationalization comes up against obstacles generated from deep within their own systems of meaning, in the west no such obstacles stand in the way of the ultimate consummation of formal standards of consistency, coherence and unity. The whole process of rationalization, set in motion by primitive religious convictions, and nurtured through the development of the west as an urban civilization, outgrows its religious meaning. In Weber's view the inherent tendencies of western Christianity reach their logical conclusion in Calvin's doctrinal purity. This theological position, which is absolutely consistent with the assumptions of a transcendental world creator and personal god, are humanly intolerable. The subsequent development of a new social ethic has the consequence of triggering the process of rationalization in all other non-religious, and particularly economic, spheres of life. Rational capitalism, therefore, within two generations of its birth had freed itself from any religious presuppositions. 'The Puritan wanted to work in a calling', Weber remarks ironically; 'we are forced to do so'.[107]

The sense in which all ultimate values might be considered as forms of religion becomes more evident in Weber's description of modern capitalism as a disenchanted world. Having overcome any dependence upon religious meaning, modern society is bereft of *all* (irrational) significance. Society becomes perfected as a rational mechanism which can accomplish nothing but the reproduction of its own instrumental efficiency. The triumph of formal rationality reduces judgement of any social action to a matter of efficiency, to the linking of means to ends according to the strictest scientific standards of suitability. No discussion of the ends of social action, invoking, as they necessarily must, a freely chosen value which does not itself fall

29

within the scope of scientific analysis, can be permitted. The result is that modern society remains ethically frozen at the period when its last religious conflagration set it upon its present course. Its values are anachronistic and, ceasing to have any personal relevance, are embedded in purely external and objective social relations, in the 'iron cage' of modern bureaucratic institutions.[108]

Western religiosity, in this sense, has destroyed itself; or, rather, the rationalizing process that was so long harboured by Christianity, has finally overwhelmed its host. We are estranged from the modern world just because we *do* recognize it to be a wholly human product. It is *only* a mechanism, merely a tool; it is its instrumentality, rather than its hallucinatory perversity that oppresses us. Society has become transparent, cleansed of all its illusory (and humanizing) dreams of salvation. Weber's developmental history of religion might, then, be viewed as an ironic comment on the Enlightenment. Rationalism, which is really the consummation of the west's religious history, is itself most fully realized, paradoxically, as the empty freedom of life devoid of meaning.[109]

A considerable literature has developed in response to one particular aspect of Weber's sociology of religion.[110] Yet Weber's contribution only makes sense in the much broader context of his avowed aim of defining the uniqueness of the west. This question could never, for him, be resolved by an argument over the origin of capitalism. It is also from this broader perspective that certain peculiarities of Weber's approach become more evident. His thesis is both paradoxical and *prima facie* unconvincing. In defining the west in terms of progressive rationalization it certainly seems perverse to then seek the origin of this movement in religion, the supremely irrational of social phenomena. This, of course, is deliberate, intended provocatively, and quickly emerges as the real strength of Weber's argument.[111] There nonetheless appears to be a persistent contradictoriness running through his argument. Rather than trace the rationalizing spirit of western Christianity to its interaction with Greek culture and especially Greek philosophy, Weber insists on discovering its root in the less credible soil of the prophetic tradition within Ancient Judaism.[112] At the same time (perhaps an aspect of his personal religious background) he denies to the magical tradition any inherent tendency to a rationalization of its own. The culmination of the western tradition is found, therefore, in the Reformation, with its powerful anti-magical and also anti-classical overtones, rather than in the Renaissance, which, superficially at least, appears the more likely source of modern pagan rationality.[113]

THE SOCIAL CATEGORIES OF CHRISTIAN RELIGIOSITY

Marx, Weber and Durkheim were not the only sociologists to have written extensively, or insightfully, on the nature of religion. Their writings, however, in placing religion in such a prominent position in the formation of sociological theory in general, have an unusual range and generality. It would be pointless, however, to attempt to extract some bland common ground from among these three writers and claim the result as a dubiously vindicated theory of western religion. It is neither religion 'as such', nor western religion in its entirety, but the strictly limited range of forms in which its western variant has manifested itself as Happiness that is central to what follows.

By focusing specifically on the theme of personal salvation (rather than on religious cosmologies), the social character of religiosity is put into a somewhat different perspective. The relevance of society to preoccupations about Happiness may seem obvious, too obvious perhaps to be worth labouring, but, in fact, it has been little explored. The problem is not merely that of reconstructing the social context of specific religious beliefs and practices (as if such beliefs and practices were somehow other than social relations), but of defining the particular forms in which salvation hopes have been successively embodied and expressed.

We cannot help but interpret such hopes in terms of categories that are valid for our own society. In terms of the primary interests of the classical tradition in sociological theory these are drawn, almost exclusively, from the social processes of production and exchange. Marx, thus, interprets modern religious consciousness as a phase in the history of self-alienation, which, linked to a particular form of human labour, is an eccentric representation of the process of production. Weber, and Durkheim in a somewhat different way, prefer to view religion through the category of exchange. The development of the sphere of circulation in western society provides, for Weber, an interpretive model of the process of rationalization which he believes to be internal to Christianity. And for Durkheim, the same development, viewed as the growth of organic solidarity, is made possible only on the assumption of its religious counter-image.

31

Strangely absent from the classical traditions in sociology, however, is any systematic attempt to understand western religion in terms of the social process of consumption. Yet it is to the 'synthetic' form of consumption, rather than the 'analytic' process of circulation, or the 'creative' activity of production, that we should turn, if we wish their original insights to be preserved and extended.

A deeply rooted prejudice in sociological analysis against the autonomous explanatory potential of consumption must be overcome. Consumption, apparently, stands at the end rather than at the beginning of the social process and everything associated with and stemming from it is too easily regarded as inessential and superficial. The consequential restraint upon sociological theory – to draw its categories exclusively from the most 'profound' and the most 'real' of social processes – is a needless variety of asceticism.

In (partially) associating the transformation of salvation ideas within western Christianity with the history of consumption some of what follows can be misread in either of two ways. It might be viewed (by those who hold consumption to be an insignificant social process) as an attempt to claim that religion is not really 'fundamental' to the development of western society. Alternatively (for those who already 'know' that religion is central to the history of the west), it could be seen as an effort to establish the theoretical autonomy of the category of consumption in historical sociology. The intention, however, is to avoid either dogmatic position. *Both* religiosity *and* social relations are conceivable only in terms of the same shifting categories which, dissolving and then reforming in a different pattern, constitute the complex morphology of western society. Happiness might be viewed, thus, as the most general expression for the concept of *value* in western society. In consuming things we seek to appropriate their value, to make their incommensurable qualities part of ourselves, and thereby reconnect ourselves with their human origin and our own source of being. The mystery of value lies less in the recalcitrant otherness of the forms in which it is embodied than in the apparently effortless redemption of subjectivity which their consumption allows.

In the west the redemptive power of use-value is conceivable as spirit. All consumption connects the inner and impenetrable world of the private soul to a common modality. And each use-value draws the subject into a direct relation to *being*. In seeking to appropriate the value embedded in things we long for value 'in itself' , for a renewal of being within us – in a word, for Happiness. This experience transcends the limitations placed upon us by the rational categories of production and exchange. In what follows it will be argued that the particular character of western society is best viewed in terms of the sequence of forms in which this transcendence has been expressed. That is to say, the 'social' categories of the history of consumption, and the 'religious' categories of the development of salvation doctrines come together in a typological progression from *Faith* to *Belief* to *Morality* and then to *Passion* before emerging in their distinctive modern dress as *Sensuousness*.

To describe each in turn is not to offer a history of Christianity or of its doctrines, nor is it simply to recapitulate from a perverse viewpoint the better known litany of transitions: ancient society, feudalism, capitalism, modernity. Each arbitrarily bound period of the west in fact contains a heterogeneity of modes of consumption. The above distinctions will be used only in a general and provisional sense to convey the significant innovations or the predominant forms which have, at a later date, been used to characterize the separateness and identity of a particular epoch.

No single classical sociologist can be adopted as an exclusive guide in such an enterprise. Their writings act as sources of inspiration rather than of systematic analyses. Marx's work (somewhat unexpectedly), for example, appears more relevant to the understanding of early Christianity than does that of Durkheim, and Weber's approach seems to cast as much light on the Christianizing of barbarian society as it does on the Reformation. This eclectic approach will further be exaggerated by borrowing heavily from religious writers themselves, and from philosophical, psychological or literary works which offer additional insights which, too frequently, have been ignored or dismissed by contemporary sociologists.

2

FAITH: HAPPINESS PROCLAIMED

Ernst Troeltsch introduces his influential study, *The Social Teachings of the Christian Churches*, by insisting that Christianity cannot be reduced to just one other 'sociological factor' or 'force of association'.[1] The unity and history of Christianity is, he insists, an essentially *religious* phenomenon. The foundation of Christianity cannot be understood, therefore, as 'in any sense due to the impulse of a social movement'.[2] In a strikingly bold statement he goes on to claim that:

> Christianity was not the product of a class struggle of any kind; it was not shaped, when it did arise, in order to fit into any such situation; indeed, at no point was it directly concerned with the social upheavals of the ancient world.[3]

Troeltsch, from the outset of his work, sweeps aside all reductive sociological accounts of Christianity. This is, for him, a methodological principle. To capture the distinctive character of Christianity it would be foolish to describe it as a disguised version of something other than itself.

Troeltsch had in mind, perhaps, Kautsky's celebrated explanation of Christianity as a form of proto-communism, the essence of which lay in an appeal to social justice.[4] But those 'who imagine that all religion is merely the reflection of social conditions in transcendental terms' fail to grasp the simple fact that the rise of Christianity 'is a religious and not a social phenomenon';[5] and that, as such, it has 'its own inner dialectic'.[6]

This, of course, is not to deny the possibility of a genuine sociological account of religion, nor should it encourage indifference to the social context within which Christianity was formed. Troeltsch himself draws attention to the destruction of the *polis* and the collapse of a secular ideal of freedom and unity as 'fertile ground' for the

34

adoption of novel religious values. It does serve to highlight, however, the more urgent, and more difficult, task of describing the uniqueness of Christianity in such a way as to preserve its inner *quality* of religiosity. To this end we must accept as uncontroversial the basic ethnography of early Christianity: that its adherents claimed the life of Jesus to be an act of Divine Revelation.

The first task, therefore, is to establish upon what grounds Christianity itself distinguished the nature of its religious claims and demands from those of other religious, and secular, groups within the same environment. This is, in fact, a more complex task than might be imagined, and no more than a sketch can be offered here. The claims of Christianity took a considerable period of time to mature into a coherent form. Orthodoxy was the achievement of at least two centuries of fiercely contested debate, repression, and innovation.[7] And with every subsequent 'dialectical transformation' of its fundamental assumptions, religious revolutionaries, by seeking to discover the roots of their own doctrines in the authentic faith of the primitive church, have further obscured its original demands. Modern scholarship has done a good deal to correct the excesses of earlier polemical histories, but it would be misleading to suppose that it has arrived, even where there is a broad measure of agreement, at a wholly objective account. We have, in fact, no option but to reconstruct the past from some particular viewpoint. Paradoxically it is just from the perspective of modern secular scholarship that the distinctively *religious* character of the Christian revolution becomes most apparent.

The emergence of Christianity, and its particular promise of Happiness, should be seen in the context not only of a number of other specifically religious movements, but, more generally, against the background of philosophical and spiritual upheaval characteristic of the Hellenic world.

MYTHOS

There was no national or official religion in the ancient Greek world. In classic Greek, indeed, there is no word which might be accurately translated by our term 'religion'. *Eusebia* means only 'regular performance of due worship', while *hosiotes* refers to ritual purity.[8] Prior to the time of Alexander the Great the Greek cults were associated with specific cities, and this was a pattern which persisted well into the Christian era. Such cults, which were regarded simply as one of the territorial attributes of a people, 'neither were nor could

35

be missionary'.[9] Their aims were severely practical and limited. Their gods, who were not immortal, were little more than human beings endowed with special skills, strength or talent. For all that, they remain strangely remote figures; disdaining to 'hold the world in a close maternal embrace', they neither expect nor require obedience. In Greek religious consciousness, 'there is no divine court which sits in judgement over men'.[10]

In such a mundane religious atmosphere, 'piety lay in a calm performance of traditional rites and in a faithful observance of traditional standards'.[11] These rites (libation, sacrifice, first fruit offerings), were, nonetheless, the ritual acts through which a sacred sphere was defined.[12] Polytheistic and locally variable it was a religion in which 'there is no priestly caste with a fixed tradition, no Veda and no Pyramid texts; nor is there any authoritative revelation in the form of a sacred book'.[13]

Cultic religion was organized, generally, as an association among free men. And as 'the patrons and givers were also the leaders', brotherhoods became important primarily in secular, political terms as a means of mobilizing factions within the urban élite.[14]

In Rome the cult became a public, state religion modelled on Egyptian example. Suppression of private religious practices, however, was incomplete, largely because religion was rarely seen as a matter that touched public life. When novel cults were introduced, therefore, they were able to co-exist with established practices for quite some time. Mithraism became popular just because, in remaining a cult that was observed in a purely domestic setting, it was not conceived as posing a competitive claim upon the public loyalty of the subject. Private cults, in fact, made few ethical or spiritual demands upon their observers. Initiation, followed by the observance of correct ritual procedures, guaranteed specific secular benefits that fell far short of what was to become the conventional western notion of Happiness.

The impulse to personal spirituality remained fundamentally separate from Hellenic culture and its continuation in the Roman world. It was just because 'there never was a religion so cold and prosaic as the Roman' that Hellenic culture became progressively influenced by Asiatic 'mystery cults'.[15] It was from eastern spirituality that the sober Romans learned 'how to reach that blissful state in which the soul was freed from the tyranny of the body and of suffering, and lost itself in raptures'.[16]

The novelty of Christianity lay, similarly, in 'eastern' rather than 'western' modes of thought and sensibility. 'The Gospels presented purely Syriac, not Hellenic, ideas, even though they are written in Greek, and for a Greek and Gentile public'.[17] And the real genius of the Christian church lay in its preservation (in spite of everything!) of this unassimilated and alien message. Indeed, in the context of Syriac culture, Christianity initially appears unexceptional; in a sense it is its subsequent world–historical significance which differentiates it, in retrospect, from other religious movements of Theism. Judaism, Mithraism, Zoroastrianism and numerous smaller movements were all developments within the 'axial age' of Syriac spirituality; and 'we find in them all a recognizably similar doctrine of God as Spirit, personal, transcendent, the Creator and Providence of the world, righteous and holy in Himself and the ground of morality in men'.[18] In Syriac thinking the ultimate reality upon which human life rests lies beyond anything in immediate experience, and beyond any purely human conception of nature or society.

LOGOS

A good case can be made for viewing the classical Greek philosophical schools as part of the general and progressive spiritualization of Hellenic culture. Philosophy, more than cultic practices, was the genuine Greek religion. The common bond between a master and his students was the foundation of a community of scholars which demanded renunciation of a previous way of life and the adoption of new ethical standards, as well as new practical arrangements, for daily life.[19] Particularly after the exemplary death of Socrates the philosophical mission to find and live in wisdom bore the character of an authentically spiritual quest. It amounted to nothing less than a 'turning around of the soul'.[20]

The appeal of the philosophical prophet is primarily a belief in his intellectual personality. There is something more in it than a passive surrender to a specific and connected sequence of reasons which carries its own inner necessity. It is, rather, upon the non-specific charisma of its leaders that the various philosophical schools are founded. The progressive tendency towards abstraction within the philosophical movement initially lacked any radical notion of salvation. The realization of a philosophical ideal of a life (*wisdom*) 'made man at home in the universe',[21] whereas the (eastern) religious inspiration was, intentionally or otherwise, to estrange him from the world. And, quite separately from the tradition of philosophy, it was a consequence of the rise of salvation religions to 'destroy the dream-harmony of Man, Universe and God, to isolate man from the other elements of the dream stage of his mythical and primitive consciousness'.[22] Religious developments, in opposition to significant elements in contemporaneous and earlier philosophic movements, involved a shift in human awareness away from natural and towards autonomous moral (though not necessarily ethical) phenomena.

For Plato, thus, wisdom is not simply the satisfaction of idle curiosity, but the 'turning of the soul towards what is good'.[23] And for him the gods have become moral *because* they value only the good. The gods, that is to say, are not themselves the source of value; their superiority over men lies only in their unfailing recognition of value which is generated independently of them. As humans we acquire value through knowledge of the Forms. In them Goodness is found, so to speak, in greater concentration and in a more evident manner than it is in material things. But in both material things and the Forms to which they are related 'Goodness is what matters, and it can be superadded to persons just as it can to all kinds of other "items" in the world'.[24] The Good, therefore, is not itself a Form, but is a necessary condition for the existence of the Forms. The Good is the *ultimate* value whose existence is reflected in the goodness of every Form and particular thing.

Wisdom, therefore, is knowledge about, and the acquisition of, Goodness. And as in man, the soul, but not the body, resembles a Form, the soul is of greater intrinsic value than the body. Indeed, when the soul becomes fully preoccupied with Goodness, man, through knowledge of the Forms, becomes divine.[25]

The moral impulse to wisdom is thus personal rather than civic or familial. It involves the turning away from luxury, self-indulgence and superstition, in favour of self-discipline and scientific or mystical contemplation. This impulse is felt first as *eros*, as the desire for something distant, a blind reaching out for the Beautiful which, elevating the soul towards its true object, points beyond itself towards the Good. The attractiveness of things is a deception of the senses. What we really seek is the Good concealed within them; 'sensuous beauty is merely the starting-point of the ascending movement, which reaches its goal only in the world of Ideas'.[26] To the extent that goodness is acquired the desire for it becomes refined and rises above the distraction of bodily stimulation. We become more 'soul-like' and less 'body-like'. Plato, indeed, in effecting a radical disjunction between soul and body, established what was to become a tenacious philosophical prejudice in favour of the former. The immediate world of physical experience, by virtue of its materiality alone, is necessarily 'haunted by evil'. And the love of wisdom is, consequently, a longing to escape from the body and its sordid appetites.[27]

Plato's philosophy contains and expresses the hope of salvation. The wisdom he espouses is not an objective propositional knowledge of the world but a dialectic of engagement with the whole of existence; 'it is the task of philosophical Eros to set the soul free from the fetters of sense and raise it up to the supersensible, heavenly world'.[28] Thus, in opposition to cultic religions, Plato 'substituted righteous conduct for initiation as a qualification for happiness'.[29] Salvation is, for him, nothing other than the *recollection* of our true nature, a fragment of which (the soul) lies hidden within us. The task of philosophy, which is only an extension of *Eros*, is to bring this hidden nature into the light and to assist in the 'sublimation of physical passion that reaches out for the Good'.[30] Happiness is viewed as a return of the soul to its natural condition of disembodied freedom, and, although this ultimate release demands a supreme effort of virtue, it is a consummation the means to which lie within itself.

Whatever criticisms and misunderstandings Plato's writings excited amongst his followers and successors, they established a tradition of philosophical reflection which became a constant companion to the specifically religious doctrines of salvation which were to follow it. It was a tradition prodigal of both rational and mystical tendencies, which exalted the inherent power of the human soul and, in addition, offered consolation for its pitiful weakness. It was also a tradition which, as part of Hellenic culture, was able to absorb and re-express ideas and movements originating beyond its own thought world.

This syncretic quality in Platonism becomes very evident in the works of his followers contemporary with early Christianity. In Philo of Alexandria, for example, Judaic monotheism and Platonic transcendentalism are completely intertwined. He can be read, indeed, in the context of pagan philosophy, Jewish mysticism, or Christianity.[31]

Philo holds that the source of all value is the one God, who, remaining apart from the sensible world is 'known' only through the human intellect (*nous*), which is itself part of God's *Logos*. God creates the Forms upon which the sensible world depends; this is the action of the *Logos* through which 'God is continually ordering matter by his thought'.[32] God's thought 'furnishes to sensible things the principle of their existence', and though this endows them with value it is no more than a 'beginning of being'.[33] The human intellect, that is, cannot touch God directly. The Divine *Logos*, although it is an *image* of God, as well as the act of cosmological fabrication, is not itself the *being* of God.

Thus, although 'the human soul could never have conceived of God had he not *breathed* into it',[34] making of the human mind a 'fragment of the Divine *Logos*',[35] God's being is ineffable, and consequently inconceivable. Philo points out, in a remarkably modern formulation, that, while the human mind exists only through a network of formal relations, 'God is without every quality'.[36] Indeed, anticipating Feuerbach, he remarks that

> we are incapable of conceiving anything independently of ourselves, and have not the strength to sidestep our own defects. We crawl into our mortal envelope like snails and like hedgehogs wind ourselves into a ball, and entertain ideas about the blessed and the imperishable identical to those about ourselves.[37]

Our ignorance of God and our inability, therefore, to attain 'the limit of happiness', which is 'the presence of God',[38] consists simply in 'the flesh and our affinity for it'. The soul cannot wholly escape the confining body, and is unable 'thus weighed down and oppressed, to gaze upwards at the revolving heavens'.[39] Philo advises us, therefore, 'Escape, man, from the abominable prison, your body, and from the pleasures and lusts that act as its jailers'.[40] Bodily pleasure, he argues, bears a no more than adventitious relation to Happiness, and the wish for bodily pleasure can never become an authentic human motive. But we cannot wholly break free of its temptation. We may approach God in an ecstatic, unmediated apprehension of the Forms, His *Logos*, but carrying with us, even there, a kind of residue of the sensible world we draw back from complete mystical union with the Divine.

The philosophical longing to overcome the body – to purify the soul of sensuous appetite and liberate the mind from the illusion of empirical reality – became central to that tradition of neo-Platonism which was to play such a significant part in the development of Christian ideas about salvation.

Rather as Philo represents a world between Judaism and Christianity, we can find in the writings of Plotinus a version of Platonic philosophy that occupies, so to speak, the ground between Hellenic thought and Christianity. Here the distinction between soul and body, and their relative valuation is, if possible, even more sharply drawn. Porphyry, his ardent student and biographer, tells us that

'Plotinus, the philosopher our contemporary, seemed ashamed of being in the body'.[41] The empirical world is itself declared to be evil. 'Void in all share in Good', Plotinus asserts, 'this is the meaning of matter.'[42] And matter is not merely a 'neutral' obstacle to the freedom of the Intelligible; Forms lodged in matter 'are corrupted in the Matter, they have absorbed its nature'. Thus, 'what enters into Matter ceases to belong to itself'.[43] Happiness, therefore, belongs to the Soul alone. 'It would be absurd to think', he tells us directly, 'that happiness begins and ends with the living-body: happiness is the possession of the good of life: it is centred therefore in Soul, is an Act of the Soul.'[44]

In Plotinus a double movement, of creation (downwards from the One) and spiritual liberation (ascending from the sensible world), is complicated by a series of intermediate stages, each defined by its own formal characteristics. The attainment of value is, again, a movement away from a created and changeable existence towards its pre-existing and permanent archetype. Happiness is the cleansed soul, 'all Idea and Reason, wholly free of body'.[45]

The soul's liberation is conceived by Plotinus as an inner psychic release. It is by withdrawing into the self that the soul sheds its weight of corrupting flesh, and realizes its original nature 'emancipated from all that embodiment has thrust upon it, withdrawn, a solitary, to itself again'.[46] Salvation is, therefore, a discipline of inward vision. 'He that hath the strength, let him arise and withdraw into himself, foregoing all that is known by the eyes, turning away for ever from the material beauty that once made his joy.'[47] Of all objects of mere pleasure 'he must know them for copies, vestiges, shadows, and hasten towards That they tell of'.[48]

The Plotinian One, 'existing beyond and above Being', in performing the task of cosmic generation *and* in providing the hope of inner eternal bliss could be mistaken for the Christian God.[49] The difference, however, that the Christian God is identified as Being itself, proved crucial.

For the philosophical tradition, to be at home in the world was to become indifferent to the provocation of immediate experience. Its vision of Happiness lay in appropriating the *Logos*, and remaining careless of all but its abiding reality. Philosophical antagonism towards the world was, thus, principled but superficial. The world is without value, and it is just the illusion that it does contain genuine value which makes it evil. Salvation lies, therefore, in rising above, rather than in suppressing, the sensible.

NOMOS

The personal quest for wisdom in the Hellenic world lacked the spiritual radicalism of the Syriac longing for inward transformation, for salvation. Such a longing, with its fundamental trust in the possibilities of personal transcendence, was conceived in terms of an obligation to participate in the community formed as a Covenant with God. The entire life of the community was directed by such a Covenant, whereas in the Greek world the community was nothing more than an arbitrary constitution.[50]

The tradition of Judaism became historically the most important for the context of developing Christianity, and remains the most familiar version of Syriac religiosity. Here the Covenant was interpreted in terms of *Law*. Yahwe's continuing protection of, and the fulfilment of His ultimate promise of salvation for, His chosen people depended upon a collective observance of His law. Weber detected, in the strict monotheism and legalism of Ancient Judaism, the beginnings of a process of rationalization. At a later period this process was quickened and deepened through the appearance of prophets who were able to reinterpret the Law in a non-traditional and revolutionary fashion. They became the vehicle for the development of the first genuinely ethical religion.[51]

That a process which might be termed rationalization occurred does not seem to be in much doubt. But Weber's antipathy to the mystical elements in religious consciousness seems to have encouraged a somewhat one-sided view of the matter. More recently Gershom Scholem has argued that a specifically mystical tradition in Judaism underwent just the kind of development that Weber regarded as exclusively the province of legalism and prophecy. Discussing a later period, in which this underlying process is more clearly visible, he claims that 'The magic hand of mysticism opened up hidden sources of new life in the heart of many scholastic ideas and abstractions'.[52]

It is, indeed, to the mystical tradition of religious speculation in the ancient world that we must turn to find the most extensive initial rationalization of the cosmos. Judaic and gnostic mystical traditions contained a quite definite notion of personal salvation. It was, however, just because this salvation was viewed exclusively in terms of an eventual contact with the Divine, that the rational development of their thought turned upon cosmic speculation rather than upon personal ethics. The way to God was by contemplation, but the

Divine could not be seized and assimilated at once. An elaborate series of intermediaries provided a set of graded exercises through which the spirit could progressively mount towards its target. These intermediaries were, in fact, the various orders of creation; thus, 'the consensus of Kabbalistic opinion regards the mystical way to God as a reversal of the procession by which we have emanated from God'.[53] Creation, which was an outpouring of the *pleroma* or 'fullness' of the Divine nature, was, from the mystical viewpoint, nothing but an obstacle to the attainment of true knowledge of God. The mystic urge to know the world is really a desire to conquer and subdue, to overcome its resistance. Scholem, again characterizing a tradition that was to become influential within Christianity, points out that 'The Jewish mystic lives and acts in perpetual rebellion against a world with which he strives with all his zeal to be at peace'.[54]

The close relation between developments within Judaism and the formation of Christianity has been made evident in much recent scholarship. Not only the mystical tradition, with its hidden tendency to rationalization, but the apocalyptic and eschatological background to early Christianity was fundamentally Judaic. For a number of pre-Christian Jewish sects the Incarnation had already taken place as the descent of the *Word* through the angelic spheres; 'for the Jew the *Torah* is the true incarnation, as the Koran was to be for the Moslem'.[55] It was 'a book fallen from heaven'.[56] Daniélou, thus, feels justified in defining Jewish–Christianity as a distinct type of religious experience; it is 'a type of Christian *thought* expressing itself in forms borrowed from Judaism'.[57] Christianity, therefore, cannot any longer be viewed, as it was by Weber and Harnack, exclusively as an historical transformation of mainstream, legalistic Judaism syncretized with Hellenic modes of thought.

GNOSIS

It is not so much the major internal developments of official Judaism, therefore, as the proliferation of its fringe movements, which, since the discovery of the Dead Sea Scrolls, and the library at Nag Hammadi, are now seen as the vital ingredient in the complex religious situation of the Romanized near east.[58] That is to say, immediately prior to the mission of Jesus a considerable number of sects – gnostic, mystical and apocalyptic, some politically self-conscious, others not – sought personal salvation by new religious means.

Gnosis means 'knowledge', not public philosophical or historical knowledge but 'secret' and protected knowledge. Influenced particularly by neo-Platonism, gnostic sects, some of which came into existence prior to Christianity, flourished throughout its first two centuries. Recent discoveries have made it abundantly clear that they should not be viewed (as they had been since Ireneus and other church fathers had written against them) as heretical offshoots of the early Christian movement. Non-Christian, Jewish and Christian variants of gnosticism have been detected, each transforming its spiritual environment in a characteristic 'anti-cosmic' direction.[59]

It is here, indeed, that the primordial conception of Syriac religiosity (upon which Weber laid such stress) – the extramundane, wholly transcendent nature of God – is most consistently and rigorously interpreted. Gnostic speculation refused to compromise the fundamental principle of the absolute otherness, and therefore human unknowability, of God. Marcion calls Him 'the alien and good God'.[60]

The first and most radical implication to be drawn from this principle was that God could not Himself be responsible for the creation of the world. He could not exist other than as Himself. The presence of the world, including our own consciousness within it, offered incontestable proof of an unbridgeable dualism. Creation was the work, not of some Platonic demiurge, but of another, autonomous, evil, but ultimately less powerful, god. Human beings, though containing within themselves an authentic *pneuma*, felt themselves moved by the alien forces of creation, by passion and appetite from which they longed to free themselves. To release the *pneuma* was the work of *gnosis* or 'knowledge'. It was by coming to know God that the oppressive strangeness of creation could be overcome. And to know God we must first know the cosmos within which we are trapped. In complete opposition to the philosophical trust with which the Platonic tradition invested the psyche, gnosticism was founded upon the conviction that all spontaneous manifestations of feeling betrayed a profoundly alien spirituality. Gnostic dualism does not propose a distinction within existence, but between (evil) existence and non-existence. 'The world is *in* the soul' and, therefore, the Hellenic route to transcendence is illusory; 'a profound distrust, therefore, of one's own inwardness, the suspicion of demonic trickery, the fear of being betrayed into bondage inspire gnostic psychology'.[61]

There is no tendency here towards ethical rationality. Morality, for the gnostic, is part of the cosmic tyranny from which the spiritually gifted sought to liberate themselves. Most commonly gnostic sects adopted a rigorous asceticism in relation to the sensuous world. This inevitably resulted in the emergence of an elementary spiritual hierarchy. To cleanse the body of its alien appetites was a possibility open only to a small élite within the religious community. The spiritually 'perfect' adopted a strictly celibate life of austere renunciation supported by a larger group whose asceticism was compromised by the necessity of having to maintain the community.

Less frequently, and with more daring theoretical consistency, some gnostic groups achieved a deeper and more universal asceticism through radical antinomian action rather than in (an ultimately incomplete) withdrawal from the world. The contaminating and constraining effect of contact with an evil world could, for them, be overcome by rejecting the binding character of *any* human conventions through which such contact was regularly organized. All genuine spirituality thus became an act of rebellion against the world. Disorderly relations to the world of both nature and society were, therefore, a means of liberating the *pneuma* from the artificial constraint of law. Rigorously applied such ideas had dramatic results. The amoral libertinism of such groups had nothing to do with self-indulgent hedonism. It was, rather, a type of rebellious nihilism.[62] Value was not consecrated to creation; to consume genuine value, therefore, every created thing (including human law and convention) must be deliberately negated. Yet, while the *pneuma* was trapped within existence, there could be no complete escape from the contamination of contact with the work of the evil god. By refusing to live conventionally the gnostic effectively denied value to the 'unreal' world of creation and sought to protect the unknowable *pneuma* which lay hidden within it.[63] This, in its extreme form, seems to be a powerful counter-example to any Durkheimian theory of religion. In the gnostic identification of spirituality with the negation, rather than the positing, of conventions, however, a Durkheimian might well reply that it is this very act of negation which itself constitutes a conventionalization of the natural world. Society, like nature, whether or not it is evil, is certainly inescapable. The antinomian as well as the ascetic gnostic, therefore, is caught in a tragic contradiction.

Furthermore, in the context of Weber's sociology of religion, it might be argued that with a strict and logical application of underlying principles gnosticism developed an internally more highly rationalized world-view than that contained in the prophetic tradition of Ancient Judaism, in the Christian revelation, or in abstract pagan philosophy. Any initial impulse to mysticism (ignoring for the moment any rationalizing tendency inherent in mysticism itself) was firmly rejected in the clarity with which the fundamental assumption of God's utter alienness was accepted. The absolute difference between man and God could never be dissolved, therefore, in an act of contemplative union. Marcion, thus, worships a God who redeems 'to eternal life wretched mankind, who *yet are entire strangers to him*'.[64]

Gnosticism, like pagan philosophy, was inherently selective and exclusive. But where philosophical movements made the attainment of inner freedom rest upon intellectual qualities which could never be imparted to all, gnosticism reserved for an élite of spiritual 'perfects' the final act of pneumatic liberation. It was ideally, therefore, the religion of an isolated community of believers. Yet in its most highly developed form it proved to be one of the most popular of third-century religious movements.

RIGHTEOUSNESS

In the context of these varied salvation hopes primitive Christianity, while establishing its uniqueness through the person of Jesus, must be considered as typical of a more general spiritual movement. In this sense Christianity simply intensified a process that had been developing within Judaism for centuries.[65]

Not only are the earliest followers of Jesus linked, particularly through eschatological and apocalyptic expectations, with developments in Judaism and elsewhere, they differ significantly among themselves as to the manner in which the Christian mission should be proclaimed and organized, and about the ultimate significance of the sayings of their Lord. Christianity in its early development, therefore, was far from a coherent movement. There were no canonical works to which matters of dispute could be referred. Many practices and ideas which were central to the self-definition of new Christian communities were later declared heretical. Indeed, in its initial phases, forms which were to emerge as orthodoxy were in a minority.[66] The gospel literature, which shaped earlier oral and written records of the sayings of Jesus into the *kerygma* of Christ, must be viewed as a theologically creative tradition.

The earliest written sources for a life of Jesus, as well as the common material from the synoptic gospels from which an earlier written source 'Q' can be reconstructed, take the form of wisdom sayings. Similar collections define a characteristic genre within eschatological Judaism. The most primitive source material was itself part of a tradition 'formed according to certain patterns that can be recognized in other popular literature, both secular and religious'.[67] These narratives and collections of wise sayings seem free of the theological intention of the gospels, which were 'patterned after the kerygma of the cross and resurrection'.[68]

Jesus did not found a church, and the movements which sprang up after his death were bound to reconstruct his life in terms of a philosophical and spiritual language that would make sense of it in the context of particular, and diverse, communities. The literary pseudo-biography of the gospels is, therefore, an understandable consequence of the missionary activity of the early church.

In Hellenized Judaic, as well as in pagan Roman and oriental religious cultures, a general tendency towards philosophical abstraction, spiritual transcendentalism and organizational conservatism have been detected, all of which conditioned the composition of the gospels. These tendencies are noticeable also in the progressive emergence of Christological terms contemporary with, and following from, the composition of the gospels.

The earliest post-Easter sources speak of Jesus as an eschatological figure, as the Lord of the Future, Son of God and Son of Man. These terms identify Jesus as a *potential* salvation figure, and in being thus adopted by the church 'Jesus is transformed into a divine figure of the imminent future'.[69] In Hellenized areas, in conformity with the purely philosophical concept of the descent of divine power into a charismatic being, Jesus was commonly described as the Divine Man. Greek ideas were fused with traditional Judaism, however, in the characterization of Jesus as Wisdom, or Wisdom's Envoy. Here Jewish theological traditions merged with the *Logos* of middle Platonism. Again, in a more popular eastern variant Jesus was known as Raised from the Dead, in which resurrection is a mythological metaphor for God's victory. An impressive variety of fundamental terms and concepts, therefore, is found in the movements which were to emerge as Christianity. The original credal statements of the church were, thus, not wholly dependent on the words or deeds of Jesus who was adopted, retrospectively, as its founder.[70]

The success of Christianity is consequently made all the more difficult to understand. Weber himself senses the difficulty. Christianity's affinity with the process of rationalization, he thought, guaranteed its long-term future; its initial appeal, however, was the prime example of irrational charismatic leadership and its rapid routinization under the apostles. The social and political condition of Palestine, and in particular the complex relationships between, on the one hand, indigenous Jewish institutions and rule centred on the synagogue, and on the other the imperial governing power, was one of semi-permanent crisis. Especially in rural areas a rootless and impoverished section of the population espoused eschatological ideas as a more or less direct expression of secular resentment. It was from this section also that the first generation of Christian missionaries was drawn. Homeless, without family or possessions, and travelling without authorization or protection, they directed their proclamation of the kingdom to the poorest communities.[71] In the first instance, that is to say, the gospel was carried orally to the dispossessed of rural Palestine. And in this form it spread eastwards where it found the fertile and well prepared ground of Syriac religiosity. In these areas Christianity tended to develop rapidly towards a radical eschatology.

Better known, because it was borne by a written tradition, Christianity spread simultaneously west and north through the great trading cities of the eastern Mediterranean. It was this specifically urban, conservative and rationalizing development that so impressed Weber. In many details modern scholarship has amply documented Weber's insight into the affinity between early Christianity and the urban artisan.[72] And it is just this group, mobile and free from the traditionalism of village communities, that was best adapted to its rapid spread. It is this group also who, modestly educated and urbane in manners, sought to express the new salvation hope in Greek terms. When Celsus, the first pagan writer to take Christianity seriously, claimed that the new sect was attractive only to the 'foolish, dishonourable and stupid, and only slaves, women and little children',[73] he was clearly indulging in polemical excess, or had failed to distinguish properly between Christian and what were progressively to be defined as heretical sects leading a more withdrawn life as religious communities outside of the civilized urban world.

The unity of Christianity had to be constructed retrospectively and lay in proclaiming faith in Jesus as the prophesied Redeemer whose coming was the fulfilment of Jewish history. The new faith was instituted by the resurrection. This was not the automatic consequence of Jesus manifesting himself after the crucifixion. The appearance to the living of the recently dead was not held, at that time, to be impossible. And the closely associated view that Jesus, in his life, was the reappearance of John the Baptist, or another of the prophets, was not uncommon. The real significance of his resurrection lay less in the miraculous aspect of his return in some form from the dead, but that he did so in fulfilment of the sacred scripture.[74] It was the realization of a hope founded on scriptural authority that lent coherence to the primitive church. Thus, 'when Peter saw the first manifestation, his faith arose'.[75] This was the starting point of the new religion; it was a 'faith in the risen Christ, something quite different from his former trust in a living Master'.[76]

In declaring a new covenant and the imminence of the kingdom, the first Christians sought only to renew a faith they believed to be inherent to Judaism. But in expressing the content of this faith the spiritual originality of Jesus was made more apparent. When defined in terms of the sayings of Jesus, particularly in terms of the Sermon on the Mount, it was clear that 'faith in the kingdom was to make no change in the existing order of public affairs'.[77] The Commandments remained intact, but they were given a new inward significance. The lawfulness of the Pharisaic tradition was, for Jesus, an exterior and morally insignificant conformity. Its rules were observed out of respect for an exterior power. Righteousness, however, was right conduct which issued spontaneously from the deepest motives of the person. Inward obedience to the will of God, an obedience which was experienced as an effortless inclination to act correctly, character-ized the original Faith of the Christian. 'Think not that I come to destroy the law or the prophets; I come not to destroy, but to fulfil'.[78]

Outside of the group of immediate followers of Jesus, whose Faith was built upon personal contact and the sharing of charisma, sub-sequent believers had no direct experience of the kingdom promised by Faith. As early as Paul's conversion, then, a new theological element entered the primitive church. Paul, thus, was aware of a 'flash of light' as an inner illumination of his own soul rather than, as it was for the disciples, a direct external apprehension that the Jesus with whom they had met and spoken was the risen Christ. His particular contact with the Divine was modelled, in fact, on the Old Testament rabbinical tradition of 'seeing the light' of God and hearing His voice. It was the absence of personal contact that impelled Paul 'to justify his position by means of reason'.[79]

The *fact* of Faith, of trust in the reality of the Risen Christ as the Son of God, among those who had not been privileged to share in the actual life of Jesus, became additional 'evidence' of its truth, and implied in some sense 'the present possession of the kingdom of God'.[80] The Incarnation, that is to say, had ushered Spirit into the world, and 'It is this Spirit which lives in the hearts of believers'.[81]

The Spirit is the organ through which the Divine Will is sensed, so that 'the man who has this spirit thinks with the thoughts of God'.[82] The religious life, as the cultivation of the Spirit, could not therefore be one of mere outward conformity to Law.

Spirit was frequently conceived (except in the wholly exceptional case of Christ) in opposition to flesh. The inward and non-material was opposed by, and not merely distinct from, the sensuous. Paul talks, thus, of sin, in the singular abstract, as well as of sins of a more specific, ethical sort. Indeed the original Christian conception of sin as opposed to righteousness has very little to do with the development of specifically ethical concepts. There was even a hint of gnostic radicalism in thus identifying the simple existence of matter (particularly in the form of the human body) as an obstacle to salvation.[83] But it must not be forgotten that the authentic Christian view is founded in a faith on the risen *body* of Christ. Spirit, it was held, transforms, but does not negate, sensuous existence. And righteousness was not to be conceived as the subjection of the flesh to the revelation of Law, but as a genuine inward liberation from a rebellious and unruly *will*.[84]

The growth of the spirit in the life of human beings could only be the work of Spirit itself. And this could not be a process of development that was wholly internal to the individual, but was, rather, a relation of the individual to the new church which, as a community of the faithful, was itself the manifestation of Spirit.

Paul's anti-legalistic spirituality, it ought to be remembered, was worked out in relation to a mission to the Gentiles which sought to exploit powerful eschatological hopes. The doctrine of Spirit effectively established the independence of the Christian movement from its Judaic roots, and appealed directly to the metaphysical longing of the Hellenized pagan world. Conversion to the faith was, however, a matter of urgency. The final judgement was imminent, even in Hellenized regions. Thus:

> The earliest Christology was not expressed in the cool identification of Jesus with the Logos as the rational principle of the universe, but in the fervid vision of the Son of Man breaking the power of the demons and ushering in the new aeon with divine judgment and mercy.[85]

It was the Apocalyptic vision, that is to say, rather than any inherent tendency to rationalization, that was the immediate stimulus to dogma.

But even by the time of the Epistle of John a somewhat different,

50

ethical, framework to early Christianity was proposed. At one remove from the fervour of eschatological convictions John expressed the transition from sin to righteousness as a spatial rather than temporal metaphor – the 'above' and 'beyond' in contrast to the 'below'. Any movement from the one to the other is made possible, he claimed, only by the action of the eternal *Logos* of God. The Incarnation, indeed, is the completion of the *Logos*, which begins with the flicker of reason in which man himself recognizes the cosmic necessity of God. It was, in fact (and contrary to the expectation aroused by either Weber or Harnack) in a reworking of mystical themes that the *Logos* doctrine made its first appearance in Christianity. Its roots were sunk deep into the Jewish mystical tradition, wherein God was conceived as the *Word*. *Logos* is the power of rationality permitted to man, but it is self-expanding and capable of infinite extension, not so much as Greek science, as in an inner and unlimited freedom of Spirit. The spiritualization of the flesh could thus be viewed as a divine gift, as a gratuitous liberation from the constraints of sinful existence.

The *Word* as the living God is a form of spirituality irreducible, in principle, to philosophical concepts; although it is a form easily corrupted by such concepts. It is hardly surprising that it was as an already compromised philosophical *Logos* that Christian spirituality made its way in the pagan world.[86] And that it was in the image of Christ as the Divine *Logos* that a point of contact between Christianity and the Hellenic world was firmly established. The *Word* could be both 'spirit' and 'thought', so it was in these terms that the Greek world could 'think' Christianity; and thus inaugurate the long and difficult relationship between Christianity and Philosophy.

THEOLOGY

During the first three centuries of the Christian era the majority of educated people within the empire were wholly ignorant of the spiritual content of Christianity, and regarded the primitive church, if they regarded it at all, as an incoherent cult. Farther removed than Paul had been from the immediate context of revelation, talk of redemption made little sense in a Greek-speaking urban environment. And where there was an intuitive grasp of the meaning of salvation, the way of *gnosis* might well seem more attractive.[87]

To extend its mission to the Gentiles, and to make clearer to potential converts and to the existing faithful the fundamental differences between the Christian word and all others, the church rapidly developed its own theology. A highly specialized literature, associated particularly with the Church in Alexandria, served this double purpose. In practice, as doctrine was fashioned to meet the challenge of particular circumstances, it developed in a somewhat unsystematic fashion. The orthodoxy of one generation could be rapidly superseded by the next. Origen, for example, arguing powerfully against the pagan religions of the empire himself became the target of anti-heretical writings.[88]

The first and most persistent tactic of the apologists was to claim that philosophical wisdom had unwittingly 'anticipated' the Christian revelation. They argued not only that there was nothing in Christianity to contradict philosophical reason, but that reason, properly understood, strove to grasp just that spirituality which had become incarnate in Christ. The supreme object of philosophical speculation, claimed the apologists, was God. The intimate relation to God which the Incarnation had made possible was, in that sense, the personification of philosophical virtue.

Clement of Alexandria, for example, was willing to admit that 'by divine inspiration philosophers sometimes hit on the Truth'.[89] Even more generously he declared 'all sects of philosophy contain a germ of truth'. But this is only because 'truth is one' and the subordinate position of philosophy is soon confirmed by its failure 'directly to declare the Word'.[90] And Justin the Martyr, expressing a lower opinion of philosophers as 'those who hold doctrines of their own pleasure', nonetheless believed the inspiration of the poet testified to the universal truth of the Word which was 'the seed which is from God'. [91] What was true in philosophy and poetry was so by the same inspiration that had been granted, in greater measure, to the Christian revelation. And importantly, unlike either philosophy or the exclusive sects which promised initiation into a more perfect knowledge of God, Christianity 'democratized mystery' and made the Word, potentially, the possession of all. Thus, 'all who have abandoned the desires of the flesh are equal and spiritual before the Lord'.[92]

Prior to Christ philosophy was 'necessary to righteousness'.[93] Now, however, 'philosophy is the handmaid of theology'.[94] And although the understanding 'is unable of itself to behold God Himself as He is',[95] this must not become an excuse for failing to express the faith in a rationally comprehensible form. Retreating somewhat from his original 'intuitive' position Clement goes on to argue that 'righteousness', which is the manifestation of faith in daily life, 'is not constituted without discourse'.[96] And although 'a man can be a believer without learning, so also we assert that it is impossible for a man without learning to comprehend the things which are declared in the faith'.[97] This contradiction, a faith that could not be understood, and an understanding that was the most exalted object of faith, spoke directly of the difference between man and God.

The difficulty and ambiguity of the relation between philosophical knowledge and the world of Faith was summed up by Clement in the formula 'that we may believe in the Son, we must know the Father'.[98] This was a formula which, he felt, allowed a philosophically sophisticated discussion of the *concept* of God, as a cosmic principle, to proceed without unduly diluting the spiritual force of the Word. In the Alexandrian effort to render the *Word* both a living presence and a rational *Logos* it is easy, from this distance, to see a fatal compromise rather than an inspired synthesis. Yet, in its own terms, it proved remarkably successful. It was served by a group of brilliant writers, who, themselves converts to the faith, were not brought up within the Judaic tradition and whose cultural background and learning, therefore, was more accessible to the educated élite within the empire.

'Greek preparatory culture' turned out, they claimed, to be something more than a mere anticipation of Christianity. If 'faith is discovered, by us, to be the first movement towards salvation' rather than salvation itself, its subsequent development and growth could only be through the instrument of 'discourse'.[99] 'Every man should therefore give himself up to philosophy'[100] because, although it is only the 'knowledge of *that which is*', it has suddenly become rhetorical to ask 'how can you hope to comprehend any of the things which tend to happiness, unless you are first grounded in such studies?'[101]

Christianity's positive evaluation of the world in the physical realism of the Resurrection was assimilated to the premise of all philosophical thought. The world of appearances offered a means for the further elucidation of the spirit. Origen, declaring God to be 'an uncompounded intellectual nature, admitting within Himself no addition of any kind',[102] nonetheless valued the world as a route to positive knowledge of Divine things. The understanding 'knows the Father of the world from the beauty of His works and the comeliness of His creatures'.[103] This invitation to 'natural theology' was, in fact, slow to be taken up and more immediately appealing was a form of 'practical theology' which, in a similar fashion, endowed the world of morality with a positive value.

Cyprian, Bishop of Carthage, tirelessly exhorted to righteous deeds as well as to a virtuous soul. He counts himself, and most of his followers, 'philosophers, not in words, but in deeds'.[104] And more directly than many other early church leader he preached the necessity of almsgiving and good works. The 'saving labour of charity', however, had for him primarily an expository significance. Its practical benefits were viewed largely from the viewpoint of the almsgiver; it is 'an illustrious and divine thing . . . a great comfort of believers, a wholesome guard of our security, a protection of hope, a safeguard of faith, a remedy for sin . . . needful for the weak, glorious for the strong'.[105] For the majority of philosophically disinclined or inept, that is to say, practical charity filled out and expounded the hidden inwardness of Faith.

It is from this point of view also that Cyprian's exhortations to martyrdom can be understood.[106] Martyrdom bore the unambiguously mystical significance of sharing in Christ's fate. Such an exemplary death was a uniquely positive act of faith, the only form in which spiritual inwardness could be directly expressed and communicated. The martyr, in sharing Christ's earthly fate, made a symbol of his or her own life. He or she went fearlessly to torture and death. It was, religiously, the triumph of a wholly spiritualized will over natural fearfulness; but it is also easy to see it, philosophically, as a paradigmatic liberation of the embodied spirit. For the witness to such a fate, martyrdom could be viewed as an act of moral charity. The numbers who suffered were fewer than, for a long time, was generally thought, but their example had incomparable propaganda value.[107]

A gradation of spiritual perfection, in spite of the early Christian denunciation of gnostic élitism, was difficult to avoid. The martyr was the Christian's 'perfect soul'. And beneath that generally unattainable goal the ecclesiastical hierarchy, professing celibacy, self-denial, and disregard of comfort, was held to lead an inherently more righteous life than the ordinary Christian who, moved by a free inner conviction, adopted a regular and respectable life in conformity to law and custom. And as all conformity ought to spring spontaneously from righteous motives, the Christian had to guard against sinful thoughts and inclinations as well as wicked deeds.

Faith, conceived as apprehension of the Word, might be viewed as a form of knowledge. It was, however, knowledge of a special sort. Or, more properly, all knowledge was derivative of its unique privilege. Knowledge was an aspect of that inwardness whose perfection

was called Faith. Man, uniquely among God's creatures, was marked
by such a capacity. Clement of Alexandria expresses this privileged
position by saying that, while all other creatures 'He made by the
word of command alone', man 'He formed by Himself, by His own
hands, and breathed into him what was peculiar to Himself'.[108] And
all knowledge is a more or less faint residue of this breath.

Origen, the most sophisticated as well as the most controversial of
the ante-Nicene Hellenistic theologians, elaborates the nature of this
community between man and his creator. God is an absolutely simple
being. He lacks all internal difference; He exists as a perfect unity.
Now such a being cannot be thought of as like a natural substance of
any kind. All material beings are complex and differentiated. Only He
'has the privilege of existing apart from all material intermixture'.[109]
God, however, can be thought of as like the mind. The intellect is not
itself material and must, in fact, be that aspect of human nature which
most directly resembles the Divinity. But it is a tenuous likeness. This
is due partly to the distance between man, in his present condition,
and his Creator. But the new Christian theology, unable to resist
philosophical elaboration, regarded it also as a faintness due to its
essential, but unfortunate, embodiment; 'our mind is shut up within
bars of flesh and blood and rendered duller and feebler by reason of
its association with material substances'.[110]

Origen immediately deduces, from the formal resemblance relating
man and God, that Divinity is the natural object of human knowledge. He argued additionally, by analogy with knowledge derived
from the senses, that:

> Sight is connected with colour, shape and size; hearing with
> noise and sound . . . Does it not then appear absurd that these
> inferior senses should have substances connected with them, as
> objects towards which their activities are directed, whereas this
> faculty, the sense of mind, which is superior to them, should
> have no substance whatever connected with it?[111]

The mind, then, could be viewed as an internal sense planted in man
by God so that He might be sought as the end appropriate to such a
capacity. God is hypostasized mind; the being, that is, which makes
possible the activity we recognize as mental.

It was the mind turning inwards upon itself, rather than contemplating in the order of things a natural theology, which was the most
obvious and direct route to faith conceived as knowledge of God. In
a very real sense Origen could still claim, against both philosopher and

gnostic, that 'when we understand, we understand by faith'.[112] Yet, at the same time, he demanded that God be bound by the *Logos*. He must act in conformity with His own nature, that is in a way which, by virtue of the Word, He has allowed us to understand. The central difficulty of theology then becomes one of rendering a coherent account of what we know of His nature. From this perspective the Creation is deeply puzzling. If God's spiritual existence lay beyond all material entanglement, what reason (for Origen insists there be one) had He for creating the universe? Origen supposed creation is 'on account of Himself' and is, thus, what we know as His goodness. But interestingly he went on to argue that as he had 'no reason' to create one thing rather than another, or to arrange them in any particular way, the original creation must, like Himself, be without difference:

> As He Himself, then, was the cause of the existence of those things which were to be created, in whom there was neither any variation nor change, nor want of any power, He created all whom He made equal and alike, because there was in Himself no reason for producing variety and diversity.[113]

And only subsequently, because these creatures 'were endowed with the power of free will' leading 'either to progress by imitation of God, or . . . to failure through negligence', did difference arise.

Origen, more directly than the other Greek apologists, therefore, stressed the obligation to righteousness as a continuous struggle to exercise the will in an elevating direction. We are justified by faith; faith, however, is given to us, not in a finished form, but as the feeble remnant of the breath through which God imparted life to human creatures. It is only through spiritual exercise that, turning it towards and gathering strength from its transcending source, we can bring this guttering human soulfulness to perfection.

Origen's view of salvation as human Happiness was a central part of his elaborate Christian cosmology. The cosmological order, and the possibility of personal Happiness are directly linked in the Divine mechanism of Creation.

Even in its earliest forms, therefore, a distinctively Christian theology has to be seen as a moving synthesis of a number of characteristic beliefs which could not easily find expression in a unified or systematic manner. But within a very short period the endeavour to discover such systematic expressions for faith had become typical of its development.

ILLUMINATION

The most impressive and the most successful of such attempted syntheses is to be found in the writings of Augustine, Bishop of Hippo. Yet, in spite of his classical education and systematic ambitions, it would be misleading to regard him as exclusively, or even primarily, a theologian. His works cover every aspect of Christianity, doctrinal, pastoral and organizational; and among his contemporaries he was unsurpassed as a psychologist. It is, indeed, as a brilliant observer (particularly of himself) that he is most read today. His *Confessions* are rightly regarded as a literary and psychological masterpiece, and something of the tense self-exploration, which is there brought to unsurpassed intensity, pervades all his work. What is immediately obvious from his gifted self-analysis is the enormous difficulty he experienced in becoming and remaining a Christian. His love of pagan learning and classical culture is less disguised than we might expect of a convert. His admiration for the literature and values of his youth was supplanted but not totally destroyed in a transition to Christianity that was fraught with what were to become paradigmatic difficulties. Indeed, his is the first genuine spiritual autobiography just because his past has not really been renounced. At times he seems to regret this inability to tear himself away from his own youthful error, to be tied to memories which he proclaims (too loudly) to be inherently without value.

In his writings salvation emerges in a fresh perspective. It becomes a personal and individual development, a progressive deepening of self-awareness, experienced as a continuous struggle against both the world of the senses *and* the secular soul. Conversion to Christianity is no longer a once and for all event, but a lifetime's struggle. He need not, as Paul, adopt a new name and see the world, wholly and without exception, anew. In the quest for autobiographical coherence, faith is regarded as a qualification, rather than a precondition, of the soul. Augustinian Christianity, thus, is more intimately personal than was generally common among the earlier apologists. Although his language and demeanour are deeply affected by the eroticism of neo-Platonic thought, and by the ecstasy of a secret *gnosis*, he escapes the arrogance of either in portraying himself as a struggling individual.

In Augustine's humanized Christianity, faith/sin, rather than spirit/flesh or form/matter, is established as the definitive religious categories. Sin, as well as faith, becomes a quality of the soul. The Alexandrians, Clement in particular, and in the eastern Greek

Church, John of Chrysostom, had implied as much by stressing the significance of human freedom in the persistence of sin. The more established view, however, stated authoritatively by, for example, Tertullian and Cyprian in the third century, and Hilary of Poitiers in the fourth, had derived the entirety of human corruption from the notion of original sin. Augustine, in his writings against the Pelagian heresy (which amounted to a denial of the inheritance of original sin), made both viewpoints part of a general doctrine of sin as a species of inverted or perverse faith. Faith is the authentic inwardness of God in man; and sin, rather than being identified simply with all that is outward, material or sensuous, should be viewed as a falsification of this spirit. Sin is human perversity rather than inhuman ignorance.

The corruption of the flesh is only the superficial reflection of a purely spiritual conflict. Indeed, he argues that it is 'by reason of sin the human race has brought on itself not spiritual death merely, but the death of the body also'.[114] Original sin is an act of defiance from which flows the inevitable separation of man from God, and the necessity of redemption through the mediation of Christ. He declares that 'every man is separated from God, except those who are reconciled to Him through Christ the Mediator; and that no one can be separated from God except through the sins which cause separation'.[115] The distinction between spirit and flesh is, then, the necessary outcome of an original division of the spirit from itself, which is in turn the consequence of man's own inner rebellion against God. But for that rebellion man would not be confined within a corruptible and mortal body. This division, inherited from the prim-ordial rebellion, is experienced in the contemporary world as 'an unlawful inclination of our will' which has 'yielded assent to the lustful desires of the flesh'.[116] Sin and faith, flesh and the spirit, are opposed but do not constitute (as the gnostic speculation suggests) two equal, contrasting realities. The difference only arises as an aspect of human freedom, which is itself an aspect of Divine benevolence unconstrained by natural necessity.

The necessity of nature, which Augustine sees as directly experienced in the appetites and the mortality of the body, is not original to creation; 'the flesh which was originally created was not that sinful flesh in which man refused to maintain his holiness amidst the enticements of Paradise'.[117] Nature, in fact, is really a punishment inflicted upon man by God, 'whence God determined that sinful flesh should propagate itself after it had sinned, and have to struggle hard for the recovery of holiness'.[118]

Augustine, thus, insists upon *both* the unconditional nature of grace, and the necessity of human freedom, as essential to salvation. No 'righteous action' can earn grace; salvation is given 'freely by God's grace'.[119] This unconditional gift, endlessly available as God's unquenchable *agape*, can, however, be refused by an act of wilful disobedience. Grace is abundant, and because of this he insists that Faith 'is in our own power'.[120] All that is needed to acquire its profound and unlimited goodness is the initial act of renunciation in which the secular psyche is overthrown in favour of absolute obedience to the will of God. But this is only simple in the abstract; in reality it is this very condition which human beings find most difficult to fulfil. As the *Confessions* so beautifully document, such a renunciation is almost always half-hearted or insincere.

Augustine at times expresses the same idea in a more paradoxical and positive fashion as a 'will to faith': 'Since faith, then, is in our power, inasmuch as every one believes when he likes, and since, when he believes, he willingly believes'.[121] This is a formulation which accommodates the philosopher, or tries to, but obscures the sense in which Faith is felt as a *compulsion* to believe, once the perverse entanglement of the soul in secular existence has been cleared away.

Faith, as it were, automatically asserts itself when the human desire for particular, limited goods has been controlled and suppressed. Since 'The perfection of all good things and our perfect good is God' faith is, in reality, the opposite of self-denial.[122] And as man's greatest good is God, who is infinite good, the love of God is more authentically self-assertive than any, limiting and particular, passion. All good things should be sought, therefore, in virtue of their goodness – which is the absolutely general value embedded in them by virtue of God's perfect Goodness – rather than for any particular and limited qualities they might possess.

Augustine, thus, views the material world as filled with objects of genuine value. 'Nature', he admits, 'cannot be without some good.'[123] It is not, therefore, the actual existence of nature that estranges man from his own spirit, but the existence of evil, which is a wholly human creation. Philosophically, however, Augustine identifies the consequence of evil directly with non-existence. 'Corruption tends to non-existence', he says bluntly, in comparison to which God exists 'immediately and incorruptibly'.[124] Augustine's language shifts from the neo-Platonic Good to the Christian Being as part of his rational rejection of unorthodox opinion. The Good is a Platonic Form, a timeless abstraction of the *human* mind. Being is the authentically Christian category, God *is*. And creation is the super-abundance of His being; it is overflowing love.

It is in the context of its separation from both neo-Platonism and gnosticism that the Christian orthodoxy, established in the year 325 at Nicaea, is best understood. Augustine's most ambitious and systematic theological work *On the Trinity* expounds this orthodoxy, 'to guard against the sophistries of those who disdain to begin with faith, and are deceived by a crude and perverse love of reason'.[125] The doctrine of the Trinity is beyond reason, but it can, nonetheless, be the subject of theological clarification. It is not possible to know God but we can state that He has 'a nature incorporeal, and unchangeable, and consubstantial and co-eternal with itself', that Father, Son and Holy Spirit are but one God, yet also separate.[126] This relation of identity, Augustine admits, is difficult to conceive; indeed it cannot become an object of knowledge at all.

The soul, and not just that part of the soul we call the mind, should be oriented towards God. The elevation of the spirit through Christian love is therefore quite different to the self-deification promised by the pagan philosopher. Secular thought longs for what cannot be possessed. Paradoxically it is because philosophical categories are immanent in things themselves that reason can never reach its goal. Reflection leads into a world of ideas, linked endlessly and effortlessly to other ideas. Human beings can represent such a world to themselves but they cannot enter it directly. Reason, therefore, always apprehends itself as something profoundly alien. The Christian elevation is, through willed obedience, to love Being. Love, here, is not to be understood as desire. To love Being is not to long for that which is absent or distant from the self, but to *consume* that which is already possessed. And as God's love is only another name for the simplicity of His being, it is to consume Him. Man discovers faith, therefore, simply by allowing himself access to Divine *agape*.[127]

'Corruption tends towards non-existence', so that the human exercise of unredeemed will takes man away from his real existence; it leads him into nothing. To consume goods (material or otherwise) without regard to their spiritual content leads only to the recurrence of appetite and the aggravation of desire. It is for this reason that Augustine can claim that 'you love yourself when you love God better than yourself'.[128] Love of God is love only of that part of the self which exists in His likeness, the only part of the self that can truly be said to exist. The hidden identity of self-love and love of God is founded upon the doctrine of grace, upon the real presence of the divine in the human soul.

Through sin, human beings are 'exiled from the unchangeable joy' of true Being, but, through Christ's redeeming sacrifice in which the realm of authentic value is reestablished, they can once again find Happiness.

THE SOCIAL REALITY OF EARLY CHRISTIANITY

Early Christian theology, in both its cosmological and in its redemptive aspects, had to establish its uniqueness by opposing itself to two fundamentally different worlds of belief. Against pagan philosophy, and especially the neo-Platonism of Plotinus and his school, it had to assert the *personal* inwardness of God's Oneness. And in opposition to gnostic speculation it had to establish the absolute singularity and uniqueness of the supramundane Divinity. The response to both these challenges very quickly involved the elaboration of Trinitarian orthodoxy as a link between the cosmic God of the philosophical Greek and the personal God of Syriac culture. In the process Christian orthodoxy, and particularly its conception of salvation, was penetrated by *both* its opponents. Weber and, from a different point of view, Harnack have drawn attention to the progressive rationalization of early Christianity, but until more recently the persistence and even strengthening of Syriac elements has gone almost unnoticed.[129] Both tendencies, however, are central to the single most important Christian writer of the late imperial period, Augustine.

This entire development, from a rather diffuse spiritual awakening to the authoritative synthesis of Augustinian Christianity, took place against the background of the expansion and subsequent contraction of the Roman Empire.

It is, first of all, the expansion of the Roman Empire eastwards that precipitated the confrontation of Hellenic and Syriac modes of thought and feeling. The two came into contact on an unequal basis; yet the conqueror did not destroy, or assimilate, the central cultural values of its subjugated peoples. The survival of Syriac theism with its incalculable long-term consequences was due primarily to its inherent adaptability to the way of life of a subjected people. Its general social passivity, tendency to privacy and promotion of an interior spirituality all predisposed it favourably to an alien ruling power. There was little to be deemed dangerous in such religiosity, which for the most part did not appear to encourage acts of rebellion or lawlessness.[130] The uniformity of the Hellenistic world after Alexander was unprecedented:

In the form of the central government, in the system of administration, in the organization of the law courts, in taxation, there was very little difference between Seleucid Syria and the Anatolian monarchies, or between the Asiatic monarchies and Egypt.[131]

The eastern empire in particular had ceased to be an exotic and little known land. This tendency towards uniformity and integration, founded upon conquest and the imposition of an official language, was accelerated by the use of money as a medium of exchange. The Attic standard introduced by Alexander was common to the whole Mediterranean world. And in all the Hellenistic monarchies Greek bankers were available to transact business, including currency exchanges where necessary. Indeed, 'all parts of the Hellenistic world were connected with each other by active and almost uninterrupted trade relations'.[132] Thus, Greek travellers to the east found familiar institutions and a familiar way of life, similar forms of municipal administration, education and, of course, Greek temples and cults, as well as Greek forms of domestic life. Marriage contracts in Egypt during the Hellenistic period were substantially the same as Athenian practice.[133] Similar leisure activities were instituted and developed. Sporting festivals, dramatic and musical performances became a focus of civic culture.[134]

This was a unity of institutions that supported a ruling class possessed of a powerfully coherent cultural identity. Yet this identity hardly touched the lives and thoughts of the native population, who 'remained as diversified in its national, social, religious, economic, and cultural life as it had previously been'.[135] In Egypt and the eastern Hellenistic monarchies the division between Greek and native was gradually transformed into a class distinction. The real meaning of the Greek term *laoi* was 'labouring class' rather than 'native', in opposition to the 'foreign' bureaucracy, clergy, army and 'bourgeoisie'.[136] The *laoi* were, in practice, those who lived by manual labour. It was a group that comprised both free and bound labour: slaves, peasants, free artisans. Slavery was common and, although generally domestic in form, included a great deal of household production including cloth making and flour milling. Slaves were in various circumstances accorded rights to their own property and were frequently entitled to purchase their freedom if and when they could accumulate sufficient wealth.[137]

The eastern monarchies were regarded as lands of great material abundance. But from the second and first centuries BCE they suffered a marked and continuous decline (due in the main to excessive taxation and uncontrollable inflation), and it is against this background of steady decline that Christianity emerged.

The Roman intervention, on the pretext of restoring liberty to the Greek cities, replaced indigenous royal households with governors. Rostovtzeff, virtuously overgeneralizing from the worst cases, sums up what was doubtless the view of the vast majority of native populations:

> In place of the personal, paternal, benevolent rule of hereditary
> kings whose interests were identical with those of the country,
> a rule regarded as at least tolerable by the people, there was
> substituted a truly "colonial" regime, arrogant, selfish, corrupt,
> cruel, ruthless, and inefficient.[138]

And even where the governor might be enlightened he ruled as over an estate.

The colonial status of the eastern Mediterranean is relevant to the emergence of faith as a specific form of subjectivity. The very necessity of social conformity does not explain the nature of Christianity but it is consonant with its basic form. The secular ascendancy of the imperial ruler was taken for granted, by both sides. The authorities, therefore, tolerated, and even encouraged, the preservation of local customs and rites. The Jews, thus, were guaranteed freedom to worship in their own way, and, it followed, so must the Christians. This protection allowed Christianity to become established. And no doubt its promise of salvation was attractive to colonized people.

There is no need, however, to see the formation of Christianity exclusively in terms of *ressentiment*. Nietzsche's famous thesis is too general. It might apply to any cultural movement that sprang up among the subject people of the empire.[139] And as tolerance, not to say indifference, in cultural matters was, until its later phase, one of the most distinctive characteristics of the empire, there was really no objection to the maintenance of local Dionysiac cults of the kind which held for Nietzsche such a powerful fascination. There was no need, in other words, to conceal the 'real' meaning of the cult behind an elaborate growth of repressive symbols. And later, when Christians were persecuted, it does not appear to have been part of an organized campaign of political repression. Indeed, taking place at a time when Christianity was established but still politically insignificant, it seems even to have gained from such periodic attacks.[140] The example of martyrdom apparently suggested to many that the new religion must be worth taking seriously.

The empire had been constructed, politically and administratively, as a collection of cities, urban centres of various sizes that included within their administration the surrounding rural area with its villages. Cities were administered by councils, responsible for imperial tax gathering, which were made up of ex-magistrates or elected members, qualification for which depended upon substantial property rights, amounting in almost all cases to large-scale land ownership. During the developing phase of the empire civic pride and the pursuit of personal glorification encouraged local notables to seek office. But as civic display and entertainment became more lavish, this acted as a general disincentive, even among the wealthiest, to hold office. The consequent reluctance to become involved in political life coincided with a decline in the real power of the central institutions due to the substantial loss of tax revenues through accelerating inflation.[141]

At the time of Constantine's conversion Christians were a 'tiny minority and belonged predominantly to the urban lower classes. The senatorial aristocracy was pagan almost to a man and the vast majority of the educated classes were pagans'.[142] The success of Christianity owed a great deal, therefore, to the 'conversion' of the emperor Constantine. There seemed to many educated people to be no compelling philosophical arguments, in spite of the best efforts of its apologists, in favour of Christianity and the psychic comfort it offered appeared markedly less certain than that readily obtainable from traditional cults. Its distinctive spirituality was of little account, either to the powerful, or to the majority of the powerless slaves and peasants.

Christianity maintained its precarious foothold among the flux of religious movements which characterized the later Roman Empire largely through its support among urban artisans. Weber was surely correct in viewing the style of life of the urban artisan in the early centuries of the Christian era as having an affinity with the new faith. Quite apart from their 'distance' from nature (which was true of the ruling class including the large and complex bureaucracy that remained unaffected by Christianity), and their colonial status (which was true equally of the slave and free peasantry), they were unprotected from the insecurity of the market.

Their life, additionally, brought them more directly and intimately into contact with the new social reality of the *commodity*. The Christian conception of God was as a *maker* of the universe (rather than simply a declaimer of Law). He possessed, to an infinite degree, the artisan's genius for making 'from nothing', of creating *value* where none had previously existed. They were also the group who, rather than receiving goods in tribute, or by traditional right, or by purchase from an often honorific state salary, were most dependent for their subsistence upon the sale of their own products. It was only for the urban artisan that the consumption of commodities was a process transparently symmetrical with their production. In consuming their use-value they were able to recapture the value alienated in the process of exchange. The wish to consume was deeper, for them, than any simple bodily and natural appetite. It was a longing to be reunited spiritually with themselves, and to rediscover their lost inwardness in the object-world. In embryo their need for things was revealed as a universal participation in *agape* rather than a particular instance of *eros*. It was only orthodox Christianity (as opposed to pagan philosophy, mystery cults or gnostic speculation) that came to value the object-world in this way, as intermediary between self-consciousness and the spirit which is the carrier of the true Happiness from which we have been estranged. Christian orthodoxy, that is to say, decisively turned its back on the 'world-rejecting asceticism' of the philosopher or the radical gnostic community.

For other groups commodities appeared magically, as the direct product of nature or as the reward of conquest, and could not provide a model for the source of ultimate value.

Philosophical abstraction, thus, took the new reality of the commodity to be a phenomenon of *exchange* and erected upon it a timeless world of ideas. How a commodity came into existence was of no concern to members of a noble ruling class; their relation to the object-world was impersonal and disdainful. The world of objects was, after all, made by slaves and could hardly be endowed with value beyond that inherent in the natural properties of the materials from which they were made. Truth, for them, lay within the psyche, as a recollection of the sublime archetypes tenuously bodied forth in the phenomena of consciousness. Philosophical reflection, though it could not wholly transcend such appearances, strove to liberate thought into the realm of pure forms. It consequently became trapped within a process of endlessly circulating 'ideas', which were themselves representative of the interchange of actually worthless commodities.

The gnostic's uncompromising devaluation of the world dwells upon a productive image of inauthentic spirit. Developed within rural communities controlled by a foreign and alien power it describes the

65

hopelessly unattainable spirituality of undivided being.[143] The object-world is an alien realm, a domain of total estrangement, which man must overcome in order to attach himself to his original and authentic spiritual source.

The spread of Christianity beyond the social world of the Jesus movement, which culminated in Augustinian orthodoxy, absorbed elements of both rationalism and gnosticism. Its ultimate success, however fortuitous politically, rested upon the syncretism of an image of spirituality which was rooted in a world-confirming process of consumption. The infinitizing and subjectivizing of primitive Christianity, which was the theoretical precondition of its universal mission, transcended the particular and little known world of production. The object-world had been made, effortlessly, by God. For the faithful Christian philosopher creation was fabrication without labour; nature is the direct consequence of God's *thoughts*. Christianity is a religion of consumption; it 'potentiates' the unifying inwardness of consumption into a cosmic principle and a dream of salvation. It seeks to consume the infinite, to reunite the inner world of human value with the realm of objects it has created but which has been lost to it, to reunite man with God, and God with Himself.

Hence the significance of charity to early Christian writers, particularly to Augustine. Only love of God (charity) bestows authentic being, and, consequently, it is only in that love that true Happiness is humanly accessible: 'For that is to be called love which is true, otherwise it is desire.'[144] In relation to God, which is an inward relation, Faith, there is no 'distance' and no 'estrangement' between the longing subject and the object of longing. The soul is present *as* love, as the being of love, and not as love of something other than itself. The inward dialectic of faith, announces the Christian, reunites man with God and God with Himself. As opposed to the pessimism of the philosopher or the gnostic, the Christian proclaims the living presence to be the abundance of 'overflowing' love; a paradise of endlessly consumable value. This kingdom is already present as God's *agape*, in which, through a righteous will, we can share without limit. The constraining and negative aspect of consumption – exclusive possession, destruction of the object, temporary assuagement – are all overcome in Faith.[145]

Hence also the new significance of self-knowledge: 'The knowledge of things terrestrial and celestial is commonly thought much of by men. Yet those doubtless judge better who prefer to that knowledge, the knowledge of themselves.'[146] The interiorization of spirit as faith transforms the world of fixed objects into a transitory realm of mediation between man and God, and establishes, thus, a human link to the source of all value. By Faith love expands within the soul and bestows gifts greater than any secular good. It is the gift of Being itself. Christian charity is not a form of knowledge and is, in principle, open to all. Man's privilege in the order of creation is self-reflection, which, unlike philosophical knowledge, can only begin with the unconditional acknowledgement of God's *agape*.

SOCIOLOGICAL THEORY AND THE FORMATION OF CHRISTIANITY

Christianity defined itself, spiritually as well as intellectually and socially, in relation, on the one hand to the traditions of Platonic philosophy, and on the other to gnosticism. A good deal of the subsequent development of a distinctively western culture can be understood as a continuing series of collisions and accommodations among these three movements.[147] In this context classical sociological theories do not provide simply a variety of perspectives which allow us to analyse retrospectively the complex interactions through which each became conscious of possessing distinctive characteristics. Sociological theories, rather, can themselves be viewed as distant echoes of this original and fundamental differentiation of Spirit.

Weber, thus, in viewing the formation of Christianity as a process of immanent rationalization, exploits a basically philosophical view of religion. His point of departure, and his whole mode of argument, display unmistakably 'Alexandrian' tendencies. The defining characteristics of Christianity are manifest, for him, primarily in the gradual unfolding of all the logical implications hidden in the primitive assumption of an extramundane source of personal salvation. The actual history of western society is conditioned by the tension between this rational development and the tenacity of irrational and conservative forces which have their locus in the everyday psychological needs of people. From this perspective modern society becomes the final triumph of the purely philosophical element in religious life.

Marx, alternatively, in spite of his anti-metaphysical protestations, reconstructs the reality from which religious consciousness springs from the viewpoint of a world-rejecting gnosticism. His theoretical analysis of capitalist society provides a contemporary version, as well as a comprehensible explication, of the most popular of early heresies.

In interpreting the experience of contemporary society through an apocalyptic category of estrangement, he implicitly reclaims the continuing relevance of the gnostic vision. And in providing a *critique* (and not simply an intellectual criticism) of religion he restates the gnostic's radical rejection of Christian 'illusions'.

Durkheim, from a somewhat different point of view, invokes the undivided unity of 'pre-axial' religious consciousness. But, in tracing the roots of its solidarity to the ultimately arbitrary conventionality of 'collective representations' he, paradoxically, comes closer than either Weber or Marx to making the Christian category of groundless Faith central to a general theory of society.

Each theoretical perspective, as each of the spiritual movements it echoes, comes to terms with the social world primarily, though not exclusively, in terms of one rather than another of the fundamental processes into which the 'total social phenomena' of more primitive societies became differentiated. The abstraction of philosophy is, so to speak, the first consciousness of the generalized process of exchange, and Weber's sociology takes as its point of departure that same process. Marx, a modern gnostic, fixes upon the process of production as the secret of estrangement from an inauthentic creation. And, Durkheim, in viewing the critical problem of society as the creation and maintenance of symbols of value, hinted at, but did not develop, a sociological theory of consumption that was fundamentally Christian in inspiration.

3

BELIEF: HAPPINESS OBSCURED

The conversion of Constantine, though it did not immediately mean the adoption of Christianity as a state religion, had an incalculable effect on its future. A more secure legal status, exemption from some forms of taxation, and, not least, substantial gifts of money, gave it advantages over its competitor religious movements which it was not slow to exploit.[1] The less tangible gain in status it received through association with the emperor's household was equally significant in winning converts among the ruling class. The social relations from which the category of Christian spirituality had been derived, or for which it could have any immediate meaning, comprised a tiny minority of the empire. The more successful it became, therefore the more urgent was the need to translate the unfamiliar ethnography of Faith into a set of universally valid Beliefs. The transcending Happiness promised in Christianity became present in an orthodox creed conceived as an external and abbreviated form of its inner, omnipresent truth.

In becoming *de facto* head of the Christian church, Constantine exercised authority over councils and synods.[2] This politically most important conversion was, however, quite unlike Paul's moment of inner illumination, or Augustine's hard won spiritual maturity. Constantine, preparing for battle, glimpsed a cross against the sun. The victory won, he took this vision to have been a miraculous sign, and, much as he had in the past consulted oracles, subsequently believed in the Christian God as the most powerful and efficacious of divinities. There was, that is to say, a self-consciously practical motive for his conversion; to please the Christian God would protect the empire. Thus, although reversing the policy of his predecessors, who had occasionally persecuted Christians as heretics for their refusal to make obligatory sacrifices to the pagan gods (and thus endangering the empire), his protection flowed from a consciousness as far removed as his predecessors had been from the authentic Faith of the early church.[3]

THE END OF ANTIQUITY

The conversion of Constantine was a blow from which Christian spirituality almost failed to recover. Already compromised by the development of a hierarchically ordered and dogmatically inclined church, Constantine's insistence that Christian inwardness be rendered into a simple formula of words accessible to the whole empire propelled Christianity beyond the geographically and socially restricted world of Faith. The alternative, to preserve its esoteric origin in all its developing forms, would doubtless have been – along with Marcion's church, the school of Valentinus, and western Manichaeism – its gradual disappearance.

In 410 Alaric pillaged Rome. Saint Jerome, writing from Bethlehem, expressed himself 'astonished and stunned', and lamented 'in one city the whole world perished'.[4] But this event, dramatizing rather than creating the political forces of a new epoch, did not, in fact, end the Roman Empire. From 396 the empire had been formally divided, west and east, and in the west an irreversible process of political collapse had been going on for over a century. The eastern empire, withdrawn to Constantinople and progressively detaching itself from western influence, developed its own institutions and culture.

Barbarian society

Formally speaking the empire as a social and political unity continued, but it did so largely because it was willing to tolerate a continuous process of shrinkage from the west and north, and even more because it was willing to recognize and live with the barbarians who had forced this process of shrinkage upon them. From the mid-fifth century 'Romans' lived with the 'Germans' they allowed to settle on what had previously been their territory. Both the ecclesiastical and political centre of the empire shifted to Constantinople or, occasionally, Ravenna.

The compromise, brutally arranged to begin with, worked in both directions. Barbarian customs were more modified in the encounter than were imperial institutions. The settlement by German tribes left the Roman *latifundia* intact; and 'even among the Vandals the newcomers merely replaced the old proprietors of the soil'.[5] Internal trade persisted, and, in spite of the third century inflation, was still conducted by means of the imperial currency. Pirenne, exaggerating somewhat for effect, claims 'there could be no greater mistake than to suppose that the idea of the Empire disappeared after the dismemberment of the Western Provinces by the Barbarians'.[6] He claims, indeed, that almost no fundamental change was effected by these invasions: 'language, currency, writing, weights and measures, kinds of foodstuffs in common use, social classes, religion, art, law, administration, taxes and economic organisation' persisted in much the same forms as before.[7]

Many barbarian leaders, adopting the language and customs of the empire, became Christian; some, such as the Visigoth Ulfila, became bishops. And in one of the greatest of Christian strongholds, Ravenna, the Goths built a cathedral.[8] The survival of Christianity, which had been quite uncertain before the conversion of Constantine, became a force ideally uniting the new diverse elements of the empire.

The social reality of such a religion was, of course, even more removed from the conditions of the primitive church which had instigated the movement of Faith. If that movement had culminated in Augustine, it had done so already as an anachronism. The bewildering diversity of Christian beliefs, stemming from the deeply rooted contrast between western Hellenic and eastern Syriac forms of Christianity, had been temporarily resolved by the Council of Nicaea in 325, which was presided over and directed by Constantine himself. But the fundamental differences which had been expressed there persisted in a variety of forms.[9] The eastern bishops could never accept the secular philosophical language in which the western (and particularly north African) church expressed its Faith.

A further century of barbarian incursions deepened the divide for other reasons, and brought an irrevocable split in the development of Christianity between west and east. The sophistication of the Africans (who, Augustine excepted, could read Greek texts) was soon forgotten. After Jerome, in the west, most ecclesiastics were ignorant of Greek and had little inkling of the theological subtlety of the early church. The eastern church, however, integrated and subordinated to the Byzantine state, maintained its own scholarly tradition.[10]

In the west, Christianity was propagated in terms of a body of Beliefs held to constitute the fundamental doctrines of the Faith.

71

There was no question here of a quasi-philosophical exposition of the Faith; it was, rather, a matter of establishing a minimal credal statement acceded to by all Christians. The inwardness of Faith became a distant goal rather than a present reality, and in the mean time the church felt obliged to provide a dogmatic statement of religious truth. Even Augustine had admitted the necessity of such a statement.[11] Such 'symbols' or unexplicated shorthand versions of orthodoxy, were modelled on earlier sources and particularly followed the unsatisfactory example of the Nicaean creed.[12]

Religious Beliefs, in other words, were uprooted from their place of origin and imposed, with only partial success, as a superficially unifying orthodoxy. Eastern heresies persisted in various guises until finally denounced at the Council of Chalcedon in 451.[13] And it was from this point that the western church established its own orthodoxy and systematically expunged the influence of Syriac spirituality from its early development. The Coptic church, so influential in the formation of monasticism – which was later to be revived and extended in the west – was anathematized as Monophysite and its most significant writer Shenate was sufficiently carefully ignored as to make him a genuine discovery of modern scholarship.[14]

It was, thus, in a cruder and more elementary form, that Christianity survived and became important in the developing kingdoms of the west. In late antiquity Christianity had furnished the empire with an official religion. It was a state religion in the sense that it was the beneficiary of authoritative protection and privilege. The state encouraged and in some circumstances required its exclusive services. There was no sense, however, in which the church had a significant political role of its own. Of course, with the growth of its landholdings, and the richness of its buildings and endowments, the ecclesiastical hierarchy naturally exercized secular political functions. Yet the church was not itself institutionally part of the state. Hence the continuous efforts it made to wrest from the state those immunities and privileges which would secure its secular survival.

The adoption of Christianity by barbarian leaders, on the other hand, brought Christianity directly into the political domain. They were able to exploit credal orthodoxy in their attempts to establish and maintain political authority. The church, as a result, quickly came to adopt an openly political role, in part legitimating secular rule, and, more importantly – itself becoming one of the most significant concentrations of political power – directly co-ordinating and ordering secular relations.

The Gallo-Roman church was, that is to say, self-consciously political. Its bishops were men like Hilary 'eager to exercise authority outside his own ecclesiastical province'.[15] The bishops provided, in fact, a continuous link with the administrative and political procedures which had been previously established. The Franks could hardly avoid using the church as an instrument of rule; they needed it 'for its moral witness, its spiritual protection, and its reassuring semblance of continuity with Roman ideals'.[16]

Clovis, like Constantine, was converted by a practical demonstration of the efficacy of Christian belief. Placing his trust in a new God before battle, he also was rewarded with victory. The Franks, of course, had religious ideas and practices of their own; theirs was a religion centred on, and protective of, the communities which gave territorial expression to kinship relations.[17] Their gods were, from a Christian standpoint, pagan superstitions, but the fact that they could be relatively easily supplanted by Christian Beliefs is more a measure of the decay of Christian spirituality than it is of the spread of the Faith.[18] In fact it was not the Frankish people who were converted, but their political leaders; 'the upper crust, or part of it, had accepted a new, perhaps an additional, war god, on approval'.[19] This brought advantages quite separate from the promise of a more powerful protector. It gained the more active co-operation of the existing ecclesiastical organization, with all their administrative functions, and, at the same time, provided the means of controlling them.

The risk to barbarian leaders of losing the support of their own people was real but worth taking. The pagan notion of *fortuna* could be assimilated to a nominally Christian conception of *sanctitas* (gained through ritual baptism). The cult of local saints and holy relics allowed a communal and clan element to worship, and, above all, the new religion could (more markedly than with Constantine) be promoted as a more powerful magic than that which they had inherited from their ancestors. To his followers Clovis presented Christianity as 'a religion essentially aimed at the same objects as the paganism they were asked to abjure'.[20] It was a church established by the direct propaganda of miracles, relics, and magical wonders, merely the 'substitution of one kind of folk-magic for another'.[21] In terms of daily life Christianity had reverted to the form of a 'pre-rational' religion, if not that of a pre-religious cult.

And in terms of political life it became aggressively Mosaic. A tradition of divine kingship already existed in many barbarian societies and Gregory of Tours adapted the notion to link the Frankish church with early Christianity. Through the succession of divine kings the Franks became a new elect, the chosen people, whose historic destiny had been providentially established. The Frankish kings used the church to secure their successful rule, an enterprise in which, as they were orthodox rather than (as were Goths) Arian, they were supported from Rome and Constantinople. The Carolingians, when they finally surpassed them by force of arms, took their own success to be a sign that God intended them to be kings. The accession of Pippin was consecrated by the bishops, probably including Boniface, at Soissons in 751. The new dynasty was thus declared to be the real continuation of God's will, and Pippin to be the embodiment of a divine ordinance. This type of ceremony was also known in Visigothic Spain and in Ireland, and culminated in Charlemagne's coronation on Christmas Day, 800. By accepting Christianity and using it as an instrument of rule 'they had shifted its social emphasis towards warfare'.[22]

In the west, however, the complete identification of church and state – since the former had become a distinct institutional order circumscribed by its own body of beliefs – could not be effected. Pope Gelasius I, formalizing the ideas of Leo the Great, proposed a papacy that would transcend the empire. This was simply an institutional recognition of the distinction of two powers, 'the sacred authority of the pontiffs, and the royal (imperial) power'.[23] It was a view which, although the emperor might regard himself as the superior power, was not resisted by either side.

In Carolingian society, indeed, the mutual benefit to church and state of the theory of 'two powers', particularly as expounded by Alcuin, was evident to both parties. Pippin had been called 'Great' by Pope Constantine I, and Hadrian I glorified Charles as 'Great' so frequently that it became part of his name.[24] At the same time, however, Hadrian argued that, as the king's authority derived ultimately from God, he had a particular responsibility to defend the church. Charlemagne, *anointed* emperor, designated himself a 'most devoted son of the church', and never took it upon himself to direct its activities.[25] The king was head of the church 'in order that they may be well governed by worthy priests', and claimed only to stand 'beside the church, rather than at its head'.[26] Charlemagne therefore, unlike the Byzantine emperors, did not claim divinity. He insists that 'the honours due to a king are not paid him as such, but as the holder of an office that has been entrusted to him by God. He does not share in either God's divinity or in His holiness'.[27] The two powers, mutually supportive and institutionally intertwined, pursued separate, parallel aims: the peace of souls, and social tranquillity.

The possibility of Happiness (defined as security from warfare) depended upon the success of both church and state; and both could be objectified in a set of Beliefs which amounted to a simple catechism of obedience.

This 'de-spiritualizing' of Christianity affected the monastic tradition as well as the episcopate. The new monastic foundations, 'professional communities of prayer', and guardians of holy relics, were essentially private institutions devoted to the salvation of locally significant individuals and their families, rather than to the redemption of the community as a whole. The bishops should be concerned with the welfare of all, but in relation to monastic observance 'it was the founder and his or her kin and other benefactors who reaped the reward of intercession'.[28] Many large landowners, therefore, established monasteries. In addition to the ultimate benefit of salvation this was encouraged by the prospect of more immediately practical advantages. Religious institutions jealously guarded their legal privileges and immunities, and a local landowner could share in these secular benefits by 'giving' property to 'his' monastery. Various legal devices ensured that the family did not really lose control of its property, and that difficulties over inheritance could be avoided. This tendency became firmly established so that by the eighth century the *Eigenkloster*, or personal monastery, was common.

Byzantium

The division between eastern and western Christianity, which quickly became associated with a different pattern of social and political development, had its roots in the pre-Christian clash between Hellenic rationality and Syriac spirituality. The eastern churches never wholly absorbed Hellenic theological language, and throughout the fourth and fifth centuries this resulted in a series of complex Christological disputes.

The central issues concerned the *unity* in Christ of both a divine and a human nature. Where, in the west (which followed a path of developing separate ecclesiastical and secular hierarchies), the distinctness of these two natures was insisted upon, the eastern churches (which were always more closely integrated with secular powers) adopted a variety of trinitarian formulae expressive of the mystical union, in Christ, of logically incompatible substances.[29] The disputes were officially settled at the Council of Chalcedon which defined Christ's nature as existing 'unconfusedly, unchangeably, indivisibly, inseparably', but this dogma did little to conceal differences which were increasingly viewed as the foundation of separate traditions.

Byzantine Christianity continued to conceive of salvation in terms of an irrational deification (*theosis*) of the human personality, rather than of a growing knowledge of the absolute; 'God became human in order that man might become divine'.[30] Theology became, for them, a practical and liturgical pursuit of mystical grace, rather than an intellectual way to God; and more profoundly it was 'not a science of divine ontology but of divine revelation'.[31] God was known only in ignorance; He was beyond conceptualization and communicated, not Himself, but His love to us in the form of images which in some sense contained this perfection.

The mystical theology of, among others, Denys the Aeropagite (which was to be of considerable importance to the later monastic tradition in the west) encouraged liturgical practices which were viewed by western observers as the blasphemous worship of icons.[32] And although sophisticated defences of iconoclasm were frequently made – particularly in extending the double analogy of Christ's being the '*image* of God', and man being made in His '*image* and likeness' – it was its popularity as a cult which guaranteed its survival in the face of orthodox western criticisms.

It was, thus, 'in their role as intercessors between man and God that the icons commanded particular devotion'.[33] Infertility and diseases were regularly treated by prayers directed to icons, occasionally, indeed, to icons of the patriarch or some other living saint, rather than to images of the Holy Family alone. Icons could be possessed by individuals or families and became the focus of private, non-congregational worship. Most significantly of all, public icons were held to be responsible for the safety of the community, particularly in confronting the threat from Islam. When this threat proved stronger than the supposed defence against it, as in the early decades of the eighth century, the icons were blamed and despised.[34] It was at this point that 'the iconoclasts saw how faith in icons was thus reduced to a mystic belief in supernatural aid and condemned it'.[35] Henceforth responsibility for the defence of the Christian realm ought to belong to the emperor. This was a point of view that proved difficult to impose whenever minor military successes (sought after by the state, of course) seemed to provide counter-evidence of the efficacy of icons.

The icon was held to be a non-arbitrary symbol, an object into which is poured the real potency of transcendental Being. Every aspect of liturgy is controlled by this bodying forth of fundamental Beliefs. The Byzantine world of Belief (in contrast to developments in the west) translated Faith into a directly imaged structure of worship, iconology, ecclesiastical architecture and design. Eastern and western orthodoxy in fact came to view each other from oddly symmetrical perspectives. Each regarded the other as introducing an inessential and distracting system of mediation between the human reality of the world and the transcending reality of God. On the one hand, a dogmatic creed was viewed as a veil obscuring the direct apprehension of a divine presence; and on the other the hypostatic image seemed irreligiously magical.

'The most obvious characteristic of the Byzantine polity was the overwhelming power of the central government', and, as a theocratic state, the church was rigorously subordinated under the secular authority.[36] The church could thus use secular authority to establish its own orthodoxy and propagate its creed. In the west the pope more often than not envied the patriarch this weakness in relation to the state. In the west the state used the church as much as the church used the state, and there was no legitimate secular figure to which the pope could point as *imprimateur* of his own decisions. The growing absolutism of the papacy, indeed, was to become the focus of intense conflicts which the eastern patriarch largely avoided.

In the west, however, religious art could be utilized for propaganda purposes without running into the theologically troubled waters of iconoclasm. There the superstitious longings of the masses had been channelled into the cult of the saints and holy relics, neither of which roused the doctrinal difficulties associated with the worship of images.

The Synod of Frankfurt (794) brought the nominal unity of the Christian church to an end. Charlemagne assumed responsibility for the correct observance of the Faith in his Christian empire, and Constantinople insisted on maintaining its own traditions. Neither, in fact, could claim to uphold an original vision, and their religious divergences mirrored their separate and very different political and social development.

Islam

Pirenne has argued that it was the establishment of the Carolingian dynastic empire which marked the real end of antiquity and pushed beyond any hope of reconciliation the split between the eastern Mediterranean world and the west. This movement west and north was matched by an equally decisive movement to the south of the Mediterranean. The explosive expansion of Islam in the mid-eighth century destroyed whatever illusion might remain of a Mediterranean civilization: 'With the Carolingians Europe finally assumed a new orientation. Until their advent Europe had continued to live the life of antiquity. But all the traditional conditions were overthrown by Islam.'[37]

Pirenne's famous thesis has not been without its critics.[38] Since its publication, however, it has not been possible to talk of the development of either the west or of western Christianity from this period other than in relation to the development of Islam.[39] Yet, as Islam can itself be viewed as a late and spiritually exhausted version of Syriac monotheism, this confrontation is in some ways only a further encounter between the polar tendencies within western religious life.[40]

In the rise of Islam, as in the western ascendancy of Barbarian society, and in the growth of Byzantine culture, we see the same corruption of primitive faith into an ideologically potent body of beliefs. As much as Christianity for the Franks, Islam was a type of syncretism responsive to the demands of warfare: 'Muhammad's career and the doctrine of Islam revolutionized both the ideological bases and the political structures of Arabian society, giving rise for the first time to a state capable of organizing and executing an expansionist movement.'[41] Thus, just as all versions of early Christianity tended towards inward spirituality, so all forms of Christianity and its associated heretical movements tended, during the collapse of antiquity, to degenerate into a politically effective set of Beliefs.

It was to face the challenge of the Islamic expansion that both Byzantium and western Europe transformed, indeed created, themselves. The Muslim expansion was uninterrupted in north Africa and reached northward through Spain until it was halted by the Frankish unions. It was this confrontation which, more than anything, made explicit the end of the Mediterranean civilization of the Roman empire, and marked the real end of the Hellenic world. 'Europe' was formed by this process – a non-slave, rural and village-based society united by the common bonds of orthodox Christianity.

The manner in which religiosity was integrated with a developing state was, in the case of Islam, rather different to that of the northern barbarians. Immediately prior to the Islamic revolution Arabia was essentially a tribal society, with a settled population and a form of centralized authority in the north, and in the central and southern regions semi-nomadic groups. Mecca had for centuries been a typical *haram*: a combination of pilgrimage centre and marketplace. It was a characteristically non-agricultural trading town but developed a unique concentration of long-range commercial activities and financial institutions. Muhammad was a merchant before he became a prophet.[42]

His teachings were, from the beginning, *both* religious and political. The implications of strict monotheism for the 'community of believers' was fully developed in the notion of *umma* and it was in these terms that Islam had a revolutionary impact on Arabian society. Religious ties defined a new, centralized, and obligatory community. The fundamental religious truth, the *one* God, united all under His absolute power. What, more particularly, was new in this idea was the self-expanding character of *umma*, to include, ultimately, the entire pagan world. It was not one community among others, but the embryonic form of an all-inclusive society. The individual could not, therefore, break with the *umma* and join some other, alternative, community. This was, additionally, an exclusive community and meant, in principle, the rejection of all relations with non-Muslims; with those, in other words, not yet included in its world.

This new emphasis on extra-tribal loyalties provided the basis for a novel form of centralized, and absolute, authority, from which singularity sprang a new divine empire. The centralized authority was not simply a 'state' in the barbarian sense of an ability to command followers in warfare and impose (to some extent) an administrative and taxation system, but provided a source of direction for every aspect of daily life. Prior to Muhammad, and throughout barbarian society, legal and juridical rules were little developed. In the Salic Law, as in the pre-Islamic Arabian *lex talionis*, formal recognition of feud and vengeance were accepted as guiding legal principles. They were codes laying down forms of compensation in recognition of dishonourable attacks; neither was predicated on any abstract or general conception of justice or authority.[43] But in the Prophet, as the *only* channel of communication between God and the people, was vested a new form of authority.

This was a much more potent force than the western church's anointing of the secular political leader. There was a genuine fusion, in Islam, of political and religious life, and, consequently, a completely unified demand for obedience. There was established as a result, and very quickly in the Arab world, the dominance of the

Muslim over the non-Muslim, of an essentially *Hijaz* ruling élite over other tribal groups, and the hegemony of a sophisticated sedentary élite and their state institutions over nomadic groups.[44]

Once the crisis of succession had been resolved by the election of Abu Bakhr as caliph (*khalifa*, successor), and the process of political concentration had been completed by suppression of the *ridda* rebellions, Islam's explosive growth began.

Barbarian society, Byzantine culture and the Islamic revolution each developed a different relation between political authority and religious belief. Barbarian society used religious beliefs as a means of acquiring control over the ecclesiastical organization and the social relations implicated in it. Often, of course, this worked in the other direction as well. Bishops became, through their personal wealth and position, important secular political leaders and, at the very least, they tended to be identified with the local magnates. Synodal efforts to control their misappropriation of church revenues and endowments, to constrain their exploitation of the church's slaves, and to regulate their misconduct in relation at least to the nobility (commoners did not matter) were too frequent for many of them to have been in the least successful.[45] In contrast to such developments, Byzantium rigorously subordinated religious institutions and activities to an existing, legitimate state, while Islam created a new state through the fusion of religious belief and political action. In spite of these variations, however, all conceived of religion in terms of a few central and easily communicable Beliefs.

This was the case not only in terms of ecclesiastical organization. A monastic tradition, which existed within each, also lost its spontaneous inwardness and developed a number of orthodox *Rules* in obedience to which a *community* of monks could seek salvation. The spiritual leaders of such communities travelled to establish sister houses, to spread by example the practical demonstration of belief. John Cassian, thus, established a community at Marseilles after close inspection of the desert eremitics with the avowed intent of softening their unrelenting asceticism. Benedict, likewise, formulated his famous manual as 'a little rule for beginners', rather than as a book of instruction for the 'spiritual athlete'.[46]

The transition from Faith to Belief as the defining criterion and central purpose of the religious life coincided with its becoming, or attempting to become, a popular cultural form. To an uneducated audience theological disputes over the meaning of the Trinity were thought to be of little significance. What was held to be essential was the provision of a clear, easily memorized and authoritative formula of Christian truth.

Pagan worship continued after the barbarian invasions. The Franks captured the church but not a religious people. In Visigothic Spain, for example, pagan and Christian ceremonies seemed to run into one another. And the canons prohibiting Christians from sacrificing at the temple, or Christian matrons from lending their best dresses to adorn pagan processions, were, like most canons, easily ignored.[47] The value of the creed, however, was recognized by church and political leaders alike. 'Let your memory be your codex', advises Isidore of Seville, and in recalling the creed he claims the believer has 'enough for salvation'.[48]

The interior vision which suffused all versions of early Christianity was rationalized, not into a sophisticated Hellenic theology, but, more bluntly, into a practical accommodation with the state, on one hand, and the persistently magical demands of the populace, on the other. Theology after Nicaea, adapting to new forms of ritualism and cultic worship which rapidly developed in the face of the political realities of post-Roman society, became increasingly irrelevant to the organization of religious life. Or, where such tendencies reached their most developed forms – in the iconoclasm of the Byzantine church – it was overtaken by mysticism. Icons were not symbols, in Augustine's sense of credal statements which corresponded to the inwardness of Faith, but contained within themselves a semi-magical power.

Christianity was not, of course, reduced to a series of naïve beliefs. A scholarly and philosophically sophisticated tradition persisted, particularly in the monastic institutions. But this tradition became less visible, and was itself subject to the same transformation that was taking place in other aspects of Christianity. The monasteries had ceased to be fortuitous collections of ascetic athletes and became genuine communities, organized under a rule and supported by the community in the interests of its collective salvation. The scholarly work they undertook was largely unoriginal. It was not philosophical curiosity, but a veneration for their own origins which prompted the continuation of the manuscript tradition. But in investing a large part of their resources in this activity they sensibly added to the conception of religion as an organized body of Beliefs. It was Belief, rather than Faith, that could be written down, read aloud, committed to memory and taught to others. And monks became as infected as others with the need to render their religious life into the objectivity of written documents and public statements.

In the west Happiness was increasingly identified with the secular benefits deriving from the excellence of kingship inspired by, and in devotion to, the one true God. The people were, in a phrase of Charlemagne's, 'faithful followers of God and the king'.[49]

The religious transition was connected with the slow but decisive shift away from kinship as the fundamental ordering principle within barbarian societies. Initially founded upon the sacredness of familial relations and marriage alliances, the growth in scale and subsequent centralization of political authority through successful (aggressive and defensive) warfare required and encouraged the formation of extra-familial bonds of loyalty. As advantageous to all concerned as such bonds might be, however, they could be established and developed only against a background of Beliefs held in common. The solidarity upon the basis of which a nobility might conduct their relations with each other provided, often enough no doubt, an insecure foundation to social life. Nonetheless such a society could not have existed at all in the absence of the elementary trust that increasingly became focused in the ruling class's self-identification with Christendom.

Durkheim, in quite a different context, makes a similar point. But it applies with equal, if not greater, force to the emergence in western Europe of non-kinship-based social authority. And it is in this process that the role of Christianity appears to be highly significant. A common body of Beliefs, particularly in the absence of a complicated administrative or state structure, was the mechanism through which that degree of social co-operation necessary to pacify social life was generated. Religion did not play a direct role here (for example, by claiming personal salvation was attainable exclusively through peaceful social relations), nor even ideologically (by legitimating an authoritative centralized power whose primary interest was the maintenance of order), but indirectly in providing a framework within which the 'solidary' bonds of a nobility could develop. It was within the ruling élite, that is to say, that religious Beliefs became important in defining a common interest and a shared culture. These Beliefs became central, therefore, in the transformation from barbarian society to feudalism which was consequential upon the emergence of just such a noble class.

FEUDAL SOCIETY

The continuous pacification of barbarian societies was not, as it was in Islam or Byzantium, primarily a process of state-formation. In the west political authority was dispersed and remained so, and the rudimentary administrative apparatus, being essentially ecclesiastical, was never wholly under the control of the political leaders. The king claimed the legitimacy of divine selection, but the authenticity of this claim had to be demonstrated by success in warfare. The 'civilizing' pressures which, over a prolonged period, tended to pacify barbarian society thus had the somewhat paradoxical effect of making the king less secure.[50] The authority initially established in invasion and settlement was weakened and diffused when not regularly reinforced by the same means. Local magnates claimed their own territorial rights, while ecclesiastical bodies retained and added to their privileges.

The interests of the king, of the powerful lords, and of the lesser members of the small group who comprised legally free and independent individuals were mutually served through the formation of relations of vassalage. The singular character of such feudal relations was its voluntarism. Vassalage was a freely entered relation of mutual assistance. In becoming a vassal, the promise of service, particularly armed service, and loyalty, was made in return for enhanced honour and, usually, the means of providing the services required (*fief*). It was a relation of near equals which had the effect of rendering them, in a sense, less equal. It might be initiated by either the superior or the inferior, but, once entered into, was ideally binding. The formation of such relations could be continued downwards or upwards, terminating at the lower end at the boundary of the free population and at the upper end in the person of the monarch. In practice one lord could have several vassals, and one individual could be vassal to more than one lord. The resulting network of relations was highly complex, and in practice rarely corresponded to the continuous structural model of which it was held to be a copy.[51] Its general effect, however, in creating a complex network of personal loyalties, was to enhance the solidarity of the ruling group.[52]

From the point of view of the monarch, encouraging his greatest nobles to form feudal relations made sound 'economic' sense. It was a means of retaining, without immediate expense, an army of trained and equipped fighting men, while simultaneously establishing a complex structure of personal dependence and loyalty.[53] And from the subordinate's viewpoint vassalage brought with it the enormous material and cultural benefits of landownership. To be the 'man of another man' was to be assimilated to his status, to share in his honour, to be part of his very being.

The reproduction of the one basic relation in varying circumstances generated a hierarchy, a structure formed from acts of personal, rather than principled, subordination. The ideal of a linked chain of personal subordination provided more than a practical scheme of social organization. The hierarchy terminated, in a secular sense, in the person of the king; but from a somewhat different perspective the monarch was only another, if crucial, link which led upwards through the chain of being to God. The king, the greatest of feudal lords, was only a man, but in acknowledging a purely personal dependence upon him, or upon someone dependent upon him, every vassal partook in some measure of the divine aura that clung to his being.[54]

Feudalism can be regarded as a stabilization of this decentralized polity. The social relations among the nobility were formalized as vassalage; and the resulting hierarchy of such personal relations, ideally at least, drew the entire nobility into a single structure of rule. The Beliefs which characterized this structure were not, in themselves, responsible for the social relations they described. Those relations, however, cannot be adequately conceptualized in their absence, nor, equally, can these Beliefs be understood in isolation from the feudal structure to which they were so closely tied. Both were, in fact, symbols of a transcending reality which held, in its unassailable objectivity, the continuing promise of human Happiness.

The development of feudalism thus stimulated fresh theological reflection and, in comparison to the search for a minimal statement of credal orthodoxy typical of the religious development of barbarian society, the elaboration of Belief associated with feudalism was formidably complex and sophisticated. Two fundamental tendencies within this development, each proposing its own vision of Happiness, can be readily distinguished. Scholasticism, representing the feudal hierarchy as an image of creation, sought in an intellectual ascent of the chain of being to know God. And in the monastic movement Belief, objectified as a *Rule* of life, was the precondition for the love of God through which He became known.

Knowledge

Those intermediaries between man and God which had played such a significant part in the gnostic cosmology, and in Jewish mysticism, became secularized within an orthodox Christian framework. And the mysticism which remained, even in its most scholastic form, a fundamental part of western as well as eastern medieval Christianity, was expressed as a quasi-naturalistic cosmology. The higher beings, angels, the archangels, seraphim and so on, were embodied in the cosmic divisions of the spheres of the sun, moon, planets and fixed stars.[55] Each sphere moving outward from the fixed and degenerate core of the universe defined a place more perfect than the one beneath its lower limit, while being itself less perfect than the one which, closer to God (who was 'outside' every such 'place'), it touched at its outermost limit. Beyond the sphere of the moon, where all matter was quintessentially perfect, this became a hierarchy of loftier distinctions.

To arrive at God by an intellectual ascent of the chain of being (that chain of which the feudal hierarchy was a partial, earthly replica) was ultimately to transcend all difference and distinction. It was to overcome, in other words, the material world with its constraints. And as one descended from God, through the created spheres of the cosmos to the pitiful creature at its centre, one fell farther and farther from His direct command. Each sphere, consistent with the feudal vision of the social order, was wholly dependent for its existence upon its superior, and existed, in fact, only as an aspect of its own nature. But it was only an aspect, not the whole reality, so that in descending the chain of being, God's presence was, so to speak, diluted. Each descending order within the chain of being had less of His nature in it, and since He was simply Being itself, each was possessed in a sense of less reality.[56]

The medieval theologians were wary of the gnostic heresy and never suggested that the material world was, in itself, other than a corrupted version of perfection, a world decayed as a consequence of man's original sin. The material principle was not in opposition to the Divine nature; if it were it would not be redeemable, and its (which included our own) redemption was at the very heart of the Christian promise. God's transcendence was approachable, intellectually at least, by considering Him to be the fullest potentiation of the hierarchy of being, the material segment of which was man's spoiled world.

In another and more particular sense, the intellect could also be seen as the route upon which the Divinity might be approached. By virtue of its own non-material nature man's intellect was that part of him which most closely resembled the Creator. His 'image and likeness' was reproduced in man's inner nature, and in particular in his contemplative and reflective capacities. These capacities were self-expanding; one thought could lead to another (higher) thought in a seemingly endless progression. The self-expanding mind was, in fact, a genuine progression through the chain of being idealized within the mind, and not simply a random succession of images. It was a progression defined by the *telos* of the human intellect. Simply on the basis of its own inner dynamism, then, the intellectual soul as the 'image and likeness' of God would spontaneously tend towards the contemplation of Being itself.[57] The intellect, when allowed its proper freedom within the universe of Belief, will manifest the natural tendency of man's whole nature, once it is redeemed from the dead weight of fleshly existence, to ascend to God. The intellect can, thus, anticipate a more general salvation and gain a foretaste of Happiness.

There was much in this picture of reality that was drawn from the neo-Platonists. But the medieval, Christianized version of neo-Platonism, unlike its pagan original, is understandable only in the context of feudal relations. The cosmos according to Plotinus is without personal significance. And even in Eriugena the hierarchy of being remains a philosophical theology. But in the medieval world the chain of being is also, and more importantly, an immediately apprehended reality, a deduction from, and a symbol of, God's uniquely necessary existence.

Without Him, that is without Being, nothing else could exist. The real theological difficulty is to explain, rationally, the necessity of creation.[58] God cannot be conceived as 'needing' anything beyond Himself, anything other than Himself. He is wholly self-subsistent Being. Theologians were forced to resort to a notion of inexplicable Divine benevolence, an aspect (indeed a rediscovery) of the original Christian, non-Platonic notion of Divine *caritas*. God's 'overflowing love' was responsible for creation. And because of it he had created a cosmos and placed within it a creature whose soul, containing the likeness of His own nature, could, by developing in freedom, 'return' to its maker. Man's unique privilege, therefore, was also his greatest burden. Freedom created only the possibility of redemption, not its necessity.

These ideas, when systematized in the developing scholastic movement centred on the expanding cathedral schools and universities, were elaborated into a compelling image of the rationality of feudal society. The development of a rational theology in feudal society was concerned primarily with the nature of God and man's relation to Him, rather than with the Christological imagery common to the early church.[59] It was pre-eminently a cosmological theology, in which personal salvation depended upon a correct understanding of the structure of the world. The celebrated proofs of God's existence adduced by medieval thinkers were not, therefore, tests of God's existence, or scientific demonstrations of His attributes; they were, rather, reason's way of illuminating what was already given and known by tradition and Faith. Yet, in being re-expressed as a rational system of Belief, this Faith became an objective reality.

The five 'ways to God' that Aquinas offers the discerning reader can be viewed, then, as versions of the symbolic hierarchy of feudalism. They hinge on the rational requirement of terminating an otherwise infinite regress, a problem which lies at the heart of the feudal order.

The demonstration from movement, for example, argues that every change is a movement from 'potency' to 'act'. Any subsequent change, similarly, is a transition from 'potency' to 'act'. Now, since only something already in act can bring about such a change, the passivity of existence is, in this sense, continuously receptive to a transcending power of act. Reversing the process the mind is led to posit, behind the act immediately responsible ·for an observable bodying forth of potency, a preceding act responsible for the transformation of some earlier state of potency. The process of continuous activation is apparently extendable at will. But such a regress cannot, in fact, be infinite. It must have begun at some specific point otherwise it could never have arrived at the present, which clearly is such a definite point. There must, in other words, have been an initial act of creation from which the whole process flows. And a condition of pure and changeless actuality must have preceded, and in a sense have contained, the potentiality of all contingent being. This pure actuality must itself remain unchanged through all subsequent movement. It is this changeless Being that we call God.[60]

It is the social logic, rather than the philosophical difficulty of the argument, which is, from the present perspective, the important issue. The transition from potency to act, though Aristotelian in formal language, takes on a new significance within the symbolic universe of feudal social relations. The sequence of activation gains a new personal context through the notion of 'dependence' which is central to both the theological argument and to social reality. Each successive change depends upon a previous state; this is not just a matter of mechanical causality. Any existing thing depends upon the overflowing activity of a being that stood above and before it in the chain of being. This is, in fact, a perfectly reasonable description of social action in feudal terms.

The argument from causes is formally similar. Each effect is linked to a cause which itself becomes the effect of a previous cause and so on. Again the regress cannot be infinite or the present, as the sum of such effects, could never have become actual. The fact of existence, therefore, can be used to outwit the imaginary regression to infinity. If we begin from an infinitely remote point we cannot arrive at anything actual. The 'uncaused cause' which stands before all effects, therefore, is a 'necessary' concept, which we know by the name God.[61] This, once again, is a peculiarly feudal conception of causality. Both cause and change are subsumed under a general notion of dependent being which has an obviously social reference to, and point of termination in, the feudal king as the source of all authority.[62]

God is held to be the essential reality symbolized in the contingency of existence, a contingency which is inconceivable other than by virtue of an original, and absolutely free, act of creation. The so-called 'ontological argument' is not, therefore, fundamentally different to the 'cosmological argument'. Anselm's unsurpassed formulation – God is 'than which none greater can be thought' – is often treated as a purely logical argument compared to the quasi-empirical demonstration of the cosmological argument.[63] Both, however, take their point of departure from assumptions integral to a hierarchical order. For both it is an order of graded dependence, in which the links are those of a personal kind, in which the 'nature' of the superior as it were 'spills over' into the inferior and guides his actions. Such an order must terminate socially in a ruler, and cosmologically in necessary Being. Existence depends upon it. Without the king no 'person', in a legal or political sense, could exist. And similarly in the creation 'nature' could exist only in relation to God's transcending actuality.

Anselm's argument makes explicit use of a 'feudal' mode of thought. Judgements of 'relative greatness' are fundamental to his approach. The evident fact that things are thus graded leads him inescapably to the conception of a being 'that than which a greater cannot be thought'. Anselm ingeniously concludes from this the necessity of God's existence, rather than merely the necessity of the concept of God. As it is 'greater' to exist in two ways rather than one way only, to exist 'in reality' as well as 'in thought' is greater than to exist in thought alone. For God to be a merely conceptual presence would be 'less great' a thought than that of God existing as absolute being. We are led, he concludes, to conceive of the real necessity of God, rather than merely the logical necessity of the concept of God.

In Anselm's mind concept and reality are indissoluble. The concept 'God' is a 'natural symbol' of His own existence. The human mind, which is simply the 'image and likeness' of God, is, therefore, that part of the created world in which God's presence is directly felt. This is an altogether different form of symbolism to that analysed by Augustine. It is not an abbreviated creed or statement, but that part of a greater reality which has, temporarily, become actual. Thought continually leads back from potency to act. Its movement is symmetrical with, but opposite in direction to, the act of creation. Belief, therefore, is a statement of the intellect's naturally ascending path towards God. It is the natural symbol of the Divine reality. Reason, the natural tendency of belief towards self-consistency and inner coherence, is not primarily a means by which we *reflect* upon reality; it is rather the purest form in which reality can become present to us, and that part of our direct experience, therefore, which most nearly resembles the Divine nature.[64]

The innovations in theology in the medieval world were primarily adaptations to the new social logic of feudalism. They adapted traditional doctrine and neo-Platonic thought to the contingencies of feudal social relations. It was through feudal imagery that Christian speculation merged its major thematic preoccupations: cosmological structure and personal existence. The links in the chain of being were conceived as primarily personal, the flowing of benevolence, will and intention from above to below. Existence was only a small segment, therefore, of a more inclusive reality of which it formed a part.

Spirituality, thus, flowed into and was expressed through the fixed hierarchical structure of creation, and this structure could be symbolically replicated as a rational structure of Belief. And it was in the ascent towards Being implicit in such a structure that Happiness resided. Religious Belief, thus, traced the reverse movement to that of creation.

Contemplation

It would be misleading, however, to regard the medieval world as wholly consistent and monolithic in its Belief.[65] The great period of heresies, formed into divergent national traditions, it is true, had withered or been reconstituted as the radical heterodoxy of belief beyond the boundaries of Christendom. Orthodoxy, for the time being at least, had been established. But the Church itself was a complex institution, and its various traditions could be interpreted in rather different ways.

The most obvious distinction, and one which was as evident at that period as it is in retrospect, was established through the continuity and reform of the monastic movement. The monastic tradition had its roots in early Christianity, and had been just as subject to internal transformation as had other ecclesiastical institutions. Indeed, it is the very attempt to 'withdraw' from secular social involvement and devote all aspects of human existence to a single religious end that, paradoxically, has rendered monasticism a kind of barometer of social and cultural metamorphoses.

The monastic movement in the ancient world grew directly from ascetic devotional acts.[66] In the barbarian age monasticism took on a new role as propagator of the word; a missionary zeal that was quite new, and in principle alien to its original purpose, pervaded, particularly, the monastic foundations of the Celtic fringes of Europe.[67] The relative pacification of western society that was the achievement of feudalism encouraged a further development of the monastic movement.

Beginning with Cluny, in 909, a number of major reforms of existing monastic institutions were carried out, and, even more significantly, entirely fresh orders were created.[68] Each sought to embody in its own *Rule* and daily practice the spiritual genius of Benedict. Each claimed, in smuggling in some particular innovation, no more than a return to the simplicity and purity of his example. The first essential for all reform, and new foundations, was to gain independence from lay *and* ecclesiastical control. This is why their various *Rules* were so important; they represented attempts, rare in medieval times, to establish an institution outside the direct control of a feudal superior, and regulate its practices with minute care and attention to detail. Rather than being controlled, as were many, by the secular authority of a local lord, or (what amounted to the same thing) being directly responsible to the bishop, monasteries were able to establish charters and found Rules the observance of which was the responsibility of the abbot alone.[69]

This is not to say that reformers were seeking to isolate monastic life from the rest of society.[70] There had been since the third and fourth centuries an ideal of spiritual purity served by such isolation, and, particularly in the east, the ideal of eremitic piety was frequently revived. But in the west this separation from the secular world was viewed as an ideal state in the inner life of the individual monk, and was almost always sought within the disciplined life of a community.[71] The closed community (which was never, in fact, wholly closed)

90

provided protection from the distraction of secular life, but to sustain a community of monks, the collectivity acted within feudal society as any other of its lords. Even the Cistercians who made a policy of accepting gifts only of worthless land, and sought the most isolated of locations, could not avoid becoming implicated in the feudal order at an institutional level.[72] And the Franciscans, at a later date, setting out to embrace collective, as well as personal, poverty, could not resist the powerful rationalizing forces regulating their communities, and succumbed to the ordered life of a *Rule*.

The fundamental reason for the expansion of the new orders was the political and economic success of feudalism. The pacification of society, its demographic expansion, and economic growth allowed far greater resources to be invested in religious ends. It is only in terms of the Belief that this investment makes sense. The monastery ceased to be a collection of ascetic perfectionists and became instead a central institution of the feudal world. Salvation for the entire society (or those members within it who enjoyed legal and political freedom) was most readily achieved by concentrating the religious resources of the society in a particular way.[73] The monastery was, in this sense, a rational institution. It gathered together a group of people whose specific task was the spiritual welfare of the whole community. Their closed way of life protected them from at least some of the more serious sins (particularly killing in warfare) that were the inevitable accompaniment of a secular life. The worship and prayers of those who were originally more pure (by virtue of their sheltered upbringing as child oblates, or from spiritual inclination and conversion) were held to be more effective than those of individuals tainted by action in the corrupted world.

At Cluny, for example, internal rationalization was evident in the development of an efficient 'shift' system of worship. Almost no hour of the day or night was free of liturgical rite.[74] And though successive orders rejected the excessive ritualism of such practices in favour of a more balanced devotional life which comprised study and manual labour (almost always domestic rather than field labour), in addition to regular forms of worship, this was the better to serve the ultimate purpose of spiritual salvation which they all took for granted.

The purpose of the *Rule*, and the necessity behind the independence from secular and ecclesiastical authorities which it represented, was less to prescribe a specific recipe of daily life which, pleasing to God, would commend the entire community in His sight, than to train the monk in humility. Obedience was the first and essential task of the monk's life. It was only through obedience that humility could be achieved, and humility was the virtue of the monk. Perpetual worship, as might also be the case in the extreme and isolated asceticism of the hermits, could conceal and even encourage a certain kind of pride inimical to the spiritual quest of the coenobitic life. The illusion of sanctity, as well as the more evident temptations of pride and concupiscence, were to be avoided. Bernard of Clairveaux, thus, warns of the difficulties of the monastic vocation. The more nearly it approaches its ideal the more difficult it becomes to recognize and reject the spiritual perversities which render it worthless.[75] Genuine humility is hard to achieve, and comes only gradually through willing subordination to a *Rule*.

By surrendering to another the care of the trivial details of everyday life the monk was not only freed to contemplate the greater reality of which his life was the symbol; it gradually removed the hard, resistant core of personal pride which was the greatest obstacle to Happiness. The monk's aim was to create within himself a condition of 'selflessness' in which he could receive, undiluted as it were, God's abundant love. To gain Happiness he need only surrender himself, unconditionally and completely, to be filled with this love.[76] The ordered cloister seems close, indeed, to Durkheim's vision of mechanical solidarity. The religious Belief of the community was expressed in a ritualization of daily life in which every highly conventionalized detail, in fact, became sacred. This process begins with insisting upon unconditional obedience to the *Rule* as such; obedience is the precondition of selflessness, a foretaste of Divine love, and no detail of practical life is therefore too trivial to be neglected or allowed to fall outside of its regulation.

The monk's 'way' to God is through love, rather than by way of rational thought. Rather than concentrate upon an actual and conceptual ladder connecting his own life to God, the monk gives way before the immensity of God and brings to the forefront of his own experience the love which leaps over this inconceivable abyss. The monk conceives of his soul as a mirror, which, turning inward, reflects within itself an image of the Divine nature. The steps in humility lead, more surely, and certainly more directly, than the dialectical movement of reason, towards God, towards a personal Being, who will be seen 'face to face'.[77] Love, indeed, is a faculty not dissimilar to any of the sensory faculties. To see or hear depends upon a certain conformity between the object perceived and the perceiving organ. The soul, thus, is the organ of love – the 'image and likeness' of God – which has been specially designed to perceive Him. The practice of love improves this likeness.[78] The soul expands in love until it is filled with the authentic object of its perception. This is less a strenuous process of intellectual self-expansion, than a willed passivity, an openness to Being which is profoundly antithetical to the demands of secular life.[79]

Devotion

In terms of feudal society's own vision of itself, the religious end of life was an unquestionable assumption. It was in terms of ultimate religious goals that the functional division of society into 'those who fight', 'those who pray' and 'those who work' was justified. These distinctions, by the time they were clearly enunciated, it is true, were already inaccurate and something of an anachronism.[80] But it would be misleading to regard this theory of feudal society as a mere ideology. It was, in a limited area of north-west Europe for a restricted period of time, a reasonably accurate description of the fundamental divisions of society. And, more significantly, it expressed in a general way and with relevance to a greater diversity of societies an ideal image of the social order. Religious motives played a fundamental part in the organization and inner meaning of such a social order. Considering only the crudest of material measures, the investment in ecclesiastical building, in servicing the large religious, 'nonproductive' population, and, most important of all, in waging war against the non-Christian invaders of Europe was staggering.[81]

Churches and monasteries were established and maintained almost exclusively through gifts, normally gifts of land, which became embedded in a complex pattern of feudal landholding. There is little point in attempting to 'explain' such generosity in terms of some other, exclusively secular, interest. True, there were often financial and social benefits in such transactions, but this was typical of a society in which no aspect of exchange was uniquely 'economic' in nature. All social transactions in feudal societies tended to be 'of a piece'. Each was coloured to a more or less significant degree by the personal relations which conditioned all activities. From the perspective of a more highly differentiated society, then, the religious life of feudalism appears no more exclusively 'religious' than the practice of warfare can be grasped as only and wholly a 'military' preoccupation. Kinship relations, property rights, political alliances and secular ambition might all be relevant to understanding the endowment of a new

93

monastery by a local notable. But it is equally clear that the religious motive which also formed part of this action cannot be reduced to any other element within such a relational complex.

The practical impact of a purely religious interest in salvation was manifest, for example, in the consequences of a widespread and ardent desire to die within the precincts of a monastery, preferably having been admitted to holy orders. This was, in fact, the most potent of all devotional techniques, and was considered an absolute guarantee of salvation.[82] The religious orders were able, consequently, to bargain in advance of granting the privilege of simoniacal entry to their ranks.[83] During their lifetime the rich gave generously so that, immediately prior to their death, they might be admitted to the security of the cloister. These death-bed conversions were frequently nicely timed, and the cause, subsequently, of considerable litigation as relatives attempted to retrieve some of the gifts which had secured it. It is, of course, easy from the perspective of the present to laugh (we are too distant from it in time to be outraged) at what seems such blatant hypocrisy. But this would be to misrepresent the sense in which, in the context of feudal society, such calculative acts of piety were integrated with an objective and obligatory structure of Belief. It was not the inner-motive of the individual action but the entire (social and cosmological) structure in which the act was embedded that authenticated its religious meaning and guaranteed its efficacy.

The pursuit of salvation through gift-giving was, therefore, far more than a calculative insurance policy taken out in favour of the afterlife. Again it is easy to be misled by modern cynical interpretations. The pursuit of salvation (in warfare as well as through generosity) also brought secular honour and not infrequently personal glory, all of which was enjoyed as part of the legitimate social rewards of a privileged position. But as all social activities were 'polyvalent' the religious rewards attached to such activities, though inseparable from them, were just as genuine, and just as real, as were their purely secular advantages. What, similarly, might appear to us as the feudal nobility's unrestrained pursuit of personal interest and a life of pleasure (as naked exploitation, or as a secular reward for the risk of warfare), in fact makes no more sense, eudemonistically, than does the asceticism of the monastery. Both serve, in their different ways, to codify and express the inescapable reality of Belief.

It was Belief, indeed, which alone could claim the privilege of being real. This is just the significance of Aquinas's discussion of Happiness. Happiness he reserves for the satisfactions of uniquely human values. Animals cannot know Happiness, and this is because they cannot know God. The ultimate end and first cause of all human satisfaction is the knowledge of God. Happiness is 'joy in the Truth', and it sets in train all the particular desires and pleasures which preoccupy our secular lives.[84] The 'final end with respect to rousing desire is like the first mover with respect to other notions', whereas 'secondary objects of desire do not attract except as subordinate to the supreme good, which is the final end'.[85] This was a point of view endorsed by the knightly, as much as by the spiritual, vocation. Knighthood, and the notion of vassalage, became progressively Christianized until they were inseparably part of the institutional network of Belief through which feudalism was constructed as a social reality.[86] For the knight, as for the monk or the bishop, 'manifestly man is destined to an end beyond himself, for he himself is not the supreme good'.[87]

Aquinas points out that, strictly speaking, Happiness, as the possession of ultimate value, appears to be an unattainable earthly ideal. We should only speak, in terms of a secular psychology, of a tendency towards such a state. Only God is essentially Happy, that is, only He is wholly complete and independent of anything beyond Himself. In that sense, therefore, 'it seems that Happiness is beyond us'. The urge to Happiness in human beings is, nonetheless, fundamental to their nature. It is an inherent tendency to perfect our own nature by joining it, or rejoining it, to His essential and necessary Being. Since man's origin lies beyond himself it appears that his Happiness can only be a despairing and unfulfilled longing. But in the expansion of his intellectual faculties beyond the constraints of material existence a more perfect Happiness can be secured. It is 'an act of mind that forms the essence of Happiness'.[88] And such an act should be identified with an architectonics of Belief, rather than with an evanescent inner state of the individual mind.

Release

The view of the feudal world as religiously uniform in the face of its powerful external enemies is a misleading simplification. The development of orthodox Christianity, the centralization of the Church under papal authority, the elimination of heresy and the formation of scholastic theology is only one side of a process of rationalization of Belief. The monastic tradition was, equally, a rationalization of the mystical route to salvation, and remained central to Christian orthodoxy. And beyond that the popular religion of the masses embraced a magical world-view which was, in its turn, a part of the Renaissance revival of Platonism, also to undergo a process of radical rationalization. However diverse the traditions, a transition from Faith to Belief becomes increasingly evident.

Throughout the medieval period Christianity, as Belief, remained primarily a religion of the élite. The spiritual life of the masses has been less fully documented, and can really only be guessed at. It is, nonetheless, fairly clear that orthodox Christian beliefs played a relatively small part in their religious observance. It is tempting to think that fear of Hell rather than the hope of salvation was the key to their religiosity.[89] Fear, certainly, rather than pride, and especially fear of death, was the human sentiment against which religious devotion was most generally pitted. Disease was omnipresent, death was pervasive and unedifying.[90] In a variety of ways an eclectic popular religion offered some relief from the intolerable burden of everyday life, and perhaps even the possibility of a more complete release from its constraint.

Popular religion was primarily ritualistic in form. Its orthodoxy centred upon the magical properties of holy relics, and the holy places, often monasteries, in which they were housed. Relics were commonplace. Parts of the 'real' cross, the nails used in the crucifixion, items of saintly apparel, and bodily parts of heroically deceased saints abounded.[91] We might well expect the masses to have been sceptical of official Christian theology. Such beliefs were held and transmitted, after all, by their oppressors. The multiplication of relics, then, which was driven by popular demands and tolerated rather than sanctioned by the church, testifies to the readiness among the masses, as among their rulers, for a symbolic interpretation of reality. The reality of their world was the same feudal reality as that of their lords, albeit seen from a different angle. And as that reality was essentially a symbolic hierarchy, even the uneducated and relatively unsophisticated were perfectly adept at construing objects as bodying forth meanings which those (educated and otherwise) of a later society would find fantastic. Relics with their shrines became the object of pilgrimage, and proximity to them was miraculously healing. To act upon such convictions, rooted as they were in the structure of feudal society, displayed neither gullibility nor 'false consciousness'. Popular religiosity, then, even where, in perpetuating a magical tradition, it appeared to depart most strikingly from the orthodoxy of an élite culture, was oriented to the same fundamental reality.

There was no clear dividing line, however, between these officially tolerated practices and the pagan magical techniques to which all routinely resorted in times of stress, insecurity and suffering. To be acceptable to the masses, in other words, religion had to become 'magical', but in doing so it lost any hope of retaining an identifiable character. The ritualism of the church, unlike that claimed by Durkheim in relation to primitive societies, seemed to have had little binding effect. The solidarity expressed in such ritual was the coherence of a single class, or of a particular monastic community, rather than of society as a totality.

Even more striking, the inclusive community rituals of the feudal period, where they did exist (and they were common), were explicitly pagan. The rediscovery of medieval popular culture as the carnival tradition has been a major theme in recent cultural and literary history. The carnival, rather than any explicitly Christian ceremony, appears to be the ritual expression of solidarity which Durkheim claimed to be both the logical precondition and the functional outcome of elementary religious Belief. Yet, far from expressing the transcending totality of society, such rituals are more readily seen as the dissolution of all social bonds and conventions.

Bakhtin has characterized the carnival as *grotesque*. It was a symbolic inversion of society as an ordered set of conventions. The feudal hierarchy was overturned and mercilessly parodied. Everything fixed and secure was undermined. The carnival did not simply invert the *order* of society and mock the authority of king and priest; rather it reconstituted the absolute spiritual freedom from which social life was constructed.[92] It regained a kind of paradisaical innocence. The world before the fall, with its sinless freedom and uninhibited sensuousness, was allowed, for a time, to exist again.

The carnival was a celebration of pure sensuous actuality, the destruction of every fixed category of the feudal cosmos and its replacement with open, organic and fluid transitions. It was a reality authenticated, in opposition to all hidden and symbolic being, by immediate experience. It was not just the inversion of feudalism, but the negation of any society, a momentary utopia within which anything became possible.

This release from the constraint of feudal hierarchy is logically complete. Yet in the very radicalism of this rejection there is preserved, in a transposed form, the most fundamental of feudalism's religious categories. It was the body, rather than the spirit, of the people that became possessed in a new way of the transcending

Happiness of Divine Being. And in the carnival pure Being could be lived rather than conceived, and directly felt rather than merely longed for. Just as in God all distinctions embodied in the hierarchy of actual existence were, abstractly, dissolved, so in the carnival a pure state of undifferentiated Being came actually into existence. The carnival, paradoxically, brought to life in the most degraded forms within feudal society (the continuous flux of sensuousness) the authentic value of changeless Being and allowed it to be touched.[93]

Again, it is important to realize that this is not just a matter of turning feudalism upside down. The carnival was not simply material where Christian orthodoxy was spiritual, or egalitarian where feudalism was hierarchical, or pagan where feudalism was Christian. Its opposition to any principle of social order as such was uncompromising. Its material principle *was* its spirituality. The carnival did not express *any* belief; it was bereft of theology. It held merely to an irrational Faith in its own illogical possibility. In it one image of the actual world was not so much counterpoised to another, alternative, image, as that a direct experience of the spirit was opposed to the indirect idea of God.

To transcend all the constraints of immediate existence was the explicit goal of life in feudal society. The actual world, therefore, was reduced to being a symbol of the more inclusive reality into which the spirit sought to release itself. The carnival offered, through the medium of unrestrained sensuousness, another and equally complete release. In its recreation of a primal world, prior to any of the abstract, conceptual distinction in which it had been prematurely brought to rest, the spirit recaptured the absolute inner freedom of infinite changeability. Sensuousness, it should be noted, does not have a fixed meaning, any more than does asceticism. Some radical gnostic sects, thus, share with the carnival a powerful antinomian tendency. But while the former is founded upon a rejection of the world and seeks to outwit the insidious grip of pleasure, the latter revels in sensuousness as Happiness itself.

The experience of carnival was coloured by the claims of Christianity to be a universal truth. The relatively fixed and rational structure of society furnished each with a platform, so to speak, from which they could launch their fantastic projects. In both Christian Belief and in carnival sensuousness, the power of the actual empirical world to circumscribe or exhaust human experience was radically denied. Both insisted that the social world was only a small portion of the reality which stood beyond or beneath it. The changeless perfection of God was indifferent, abstracted and infinitely above our experience of the immediate, actual world; while the perpetually mobile and transformative power of play in the carnival, which was His mirror-image, was located just as far beneath it. Both were, however, for the popular imagination, reachable in a collective ritual.

The consuming spirit

Medieval society, as Southern reminds us, placed on each person the obligation of Christian Belief. It was a religious society in the sense that its most fundamental institutions were either directly ecclesiastical in nature, or derived their meaning and purpose from self-evident Christian truths. Belief, therefore, was part of the institutional framework of society, and was possessed of a palpable reality. Belief, that is to say, became part of the objective structure of social life. The Beliefs through which society was ordered and experienced were, simultaneously, the categories through which both cosmos (macrocosm) and psyche (microcosm) were structured.

In suggesting that Christianity can be viewed sociologically in relation to consumption (spirit), as well as in relation to circulation (reason), or production (labour), it is not intended to render the transformative character of history into a fixed category. Happiness cannot be defined trans-historically. Its meaning, however, does not alter in terms of a shift in its sphere of reference in the social world (from consumption to circulation or production), so much as it continually responds to the changing social reality of consumption itself. Its variety of forms is an indicator of the transitions which the process of consumption (along with production and exchange) underwent throughout the development of western society.

Within the Roman Empire orthodox Christianity announced the primacy of Faith as subjectivite syncretism of various patterns of consumption. It united the incommensurable differences from which society was constructed in the promise of consuming an ultimate value. It was a value that evidently conditioned the consumption of all lesser 'goods' (including love, friendship, etc.). It was what made such goods valuable, and what ultimately gave meaning to the exercise of constraint in consuming them in an appropriate (lawful, conventional and socially harmonious) fashion. All satisfactions in consumption were linked to Happiness, and found in Christ the means through which this ultimate value could be appropriated without the necessity, as it were, of consuming God's entire creation.

Christ is a mediator between man and God; as cosmic principle he represents everything that God has created, and as Redeemer he represents everything that man can consume. Christ sums up, so to speak, the entire world of the commodity, and makes available to each individual consumer the entire (infinite) world of human creativity.

The slow destruction of the empire, and the rise of territorially more limited and politically less centralized societies within which there was no general market and exchange of goods of any sort, was limited and organized through kin and personal relationships, and formed the context within which Christianity became identified as a systematic body of Belief. It was through Belief that a synthetic unity could be achieved and a society be made to emerge from the complex and, in fact, incoherent mesh of personal relations. Christianity or, better, Christendom represented a society which did not actually exist; but without the fiction that it was actual, what did exist could not have functioned.[94]

The particular, limited, and determinate states which conditioned everyday life (for the rich) were extended symbolically to gain universal significance. All the divisions of the social world were organized into a hierarchical order which could be used, conceptually, as a device to pass beyond its limitations. Abstracted as the necessary steps of a rational argument, or miniaturized and concentrated as the daily practice of humility which became the progenitor of love, they drew out the Divine likeness and bestowed upon corrupted human being a redemptive selflessness.

In its own particularity human subjectivity was constrained by embodied flesh, and the circumstances of social life. The interior life unmediated by higher categories could not unite humanity, far less transcend its creaturely form. It was as Belief, the objective and authoritative structure derived from the 'image and likeness' which all experienced in their own fashion, that human being was drawn beyond itself and reconnected with its Divine origin. Beliefs constituted the universal value of feudal society, its connecting spirit which, in being consumed, delivered humanity to its universal *telos*. Belief was the privileged good of feudalism, that part of the object-world the possession of which promised Happiness.

The transition from Faith to Belief is a social transformation. Firstly, and simply, it is a consequence of the growing distance in time and space from the presence of Christ. This space had to be filled with an uninterrupted flow of Beliefs, a plenitude of spiritual substance that

100

connected each believer to the body of Christ and united all believers in a single community. Secondly, it is a result of the fading of the original eschatological and messianic idea of early Christianity. The variety of Christian peoples could not, so readily, be conceived as the uniquely chosen historic instrument of salvation. The immediate link between God and man was broken and dissipated in a complex variety of customs and cultures. The universality and objectivity of Belief, therefore, replaced the inner certainty of having been exclusively chosen.

Greek culture had achieved a certain universal value, a universality amplified by the political power of the Roman empire. The political élite of such a society, in adopting Christianity, began its transformation from the primitive Faith of the early Christian (consuming ultimate value without the intermediary of commodities) to a worldly compromise (Augustinian orthodoxy – consuming ultimate value through the intermediary of the church, as the expanded 'body' of Christ). The formation of barbarian and feudal societies forced the religious life into new channels of universality. The commodity was hidden in these societies. The particularity of 'everyday' consumption could be overcome only through acts of ungrounded domination. The religious life, therefore, partook of ultimate value through consuming commands. Obedience was its greatest religious virtue. Rule, founded only upon the evident command of the means of violence, was the general currency of such societies (its mode of internal ordering). The general pacification of such societies was primarily the substitution of Belief for naked power, and Christianity, in a degraded, non-philosophical form, provided a ready-made stock of such Belief.

The reality of Belief lay in an objective and visible order, represented in the imposing physical symbols of cathedrals, monasteries and churches. Beliefs gained more than a sacramental authority by this objectification. They were woven into the texture of legislation, into every political act, and into each new link in the chain of command forged by the ceremonial of vassalage. The rationality of Belief was self-evident. Its world lay directly before one's eyes. The theologian added nothing to human knowledge; his task was merely to make more self-conscious the truth which, inscribed in our soul, formed the external world of nature and society into an order and symbol of its ultimate value.

4

MORALITY: HAPPINESS POSTPONED

Morality, in the sense of rules appropriate to personal behaviour, was always present in Christianity. Indeed, as Weber suggests, its initial stress on inward conformity to the Law made Christianity, far more than had been the case with Ancient Judaism, an ethical religion. Yet, for all that, in both primitive Christianity and for the age of Belief morality was an adjunct to, rather than the core of, religious life. Value in these societies lay, by definition, outside of and beyond the self. Happiness, it is true, was held to be a personal relation to transcendent value, but it was inconceivable that this value could itself reside within, far less be identified with, the person. Morality, therefore, remained less important than either Faith or Belief. The fundamental character of religious life, and the specific uniqueness of Christianity, lay first of all in its groundless Faith and subsequently in the objectivity of its Belief. And in neither instance was the transcendent relationship sought in terms of the personal appropriation of its inner meaning as an end.

THE MORAL ECONOMY OF THE NEW COSMOS

The decline of feudalism, which was in part at least a consequence of the decadent cultivation of Belief and its symbols, was felt as a profoundly religious shock. The entire cosmological structure, which was the essential embodiment of the principle of hierarchy, was thrown into chaos, or what seemed to be chaos.[1] Another, and more powerful, ordering principle was, in fact, emerging through this decline, but, invisible for a long time, the transition from feudalism to capitalism had about it the air of catastrophe. And it was this very absence of a self-evident social logic that shaped the transformation of Christianity into a religion of personal Morality.

102

The social mechanism could no longer be conceived to be an objective and external necessity. The creation of civil society outside the bonds of the old traditions, or of direct control by new centralized powers, redefined the sphere of religion as a public institution whose prime task was the control of private feeling. And as the institutional order had lost its essential coherence and sense of totality, the creation and maintenance of order had to depend upon inculcating in each individual just those precepts which would lead him or her to act spontaneously in a socially appropriate manner. Society, that is to say, came to depend upon the efficacy of conscience; and religion, therefore, was to become supremely the educator and prompter of Morality. Its task was to suffuse social relations with a correct sense of duty and obligation.

The atomization of society was hardly apparent at the close of the Middle Ages. And in spite of a number of suggestions to the contrary, individualism in anything resembling its modern form remained alien to the culture of late feudalism.[2] Anticipating this social transformation, however, Nicholas of Cusa outlined some of the most vital cosmological and theological implications of the collapse of hierarchical principles.[3]

Of Learned Ignorance, in profound opposition to the hierocratic order, replaced the cosmic ladder or chain of being with the new and bewildering perspective of infinite space. The inherent unknowability of God, the consequence of His absolute transcendence, meant that no natural progression of being, however many steps or stages might be differentiated within it, could ever terminate in the Divine Nature. It was just because of this, in fact, that, as we have seen, Aquinas had insisted upon creation *ex nihilo* at some particular moment in time. The cosmological argument was, however (like any deep theological speculation), easily perverted. The chain of being, rather than a model of creation, had become a symbolic ladder upon which the mind could break free of every limiting condition of fleshly existence and ascend to God.

Nicholas of Cusa, grasping the original logic of the argument, revived its original rigour and turned it against the very idea of hierarchy. All judgements of a relative kind (that is, all human judgements) were justified in relation to an absolute standard which, in fact, could never become an object of the senses, nor an indisputable qualification of the intellect. God's absolute simplicity must remain a mystery; 'the infinite as infinite is unknown', Cusanus bluntly points out.[4] Not only were the common versions of the cosmological argument faulty, the possibility of any rational natural theology was denied. 'We are also unable to understand', he pursues the argument, 'how God can manifest Himself to us through visible creation . . . Who can understand how all things, whilst differing from one another by reason of their finite nature, are an image of that unique infinite form'.[5] By removing the Absolute to an unexaminably distant, indeed to an infinitely remote, point it could no longer (from a human viewpoint) furnish a fixed perspective from which to order our impressions of the natural world.

Cusanus was concerned primarily with the theological or, better, religious implications of this shift in cosmological perspective. It justified, in his view, a more wholehearted mysticism.[6]

The consequences for a rational view of creation were worked out over the succeeding two hundred years.[7] Rather than occupying a miserable, fixed, and central position within the cosmos, the earth, like any other heavenly body, was endowed with a motion of its own. Cusanus was unable to furnish the mathematical demonstration, which his admirer and fellow humanist Copernicus was to do, to support such a view, but nonetheless he felt confident on theological grounds, in his bold assertions. The relation of man to God was something more intimate than the depressing vision bequeathed in the chain of being. Man, created in the 'image and likeness' could claim – in spite, indeed because, of his having fallen from grace – a privileged cosmological position. This was no longer a matter of his occupying a special and humiliating place. God was no more remote from him than from any other point in the cosmos. This followed reasonably from the contention that God must be, in a realistic sense, no farther removed from the earth than from any other material point in the cosmos. Each point must be equally close and equally distant from its origin, and, 'Therefore the centre and the circumference are identical'.[8] The privilege of human being was manifest, rather, in the inner moral sense which, free of any natural constraint, God had planted in man.

The intellectual problem was to account for the apparent coherence of the universe in the absence of a natural structure of being. If there was no hierarchical order in which, like a nested set of Russian dolls, graduated substance was eternally distributed according to Divine necessity, then what kind of order could exist? And how was God's necessary being revealed in the absence of such an order?

Cusanus set the problem without providing a solution. The *mechanism* through which a capitalist social order was to emerge suggested itself as a generative model of the universe to some scholars almost two centuries after Cusanus had written, but at the time the solution to the difficulty could only be given in religious terms. To Cusanus it was not yet obvious that a principle of order must inhere in the nature of things themselves. But, once the hierarchical principle was abandoned, the assumption that the universe was *isotropic* – that it might be viewed, arbitrarily, from any point and appear to be the same – was an almost inevitable outcome of a process of rationalization. Some such relativizing principle was, in fact, a prerequisite to the formulation of a new conception of cosmic order as the expression of universal laws of nature. The cosmos, in principle, had as many centres as there were self-adhering quantities of matter.[9] The religious, as distinct from the scientific, implications of the new cosmology, however, were more quickly and unambiguously discerned. The dissolution of feudal orders and communities, and the subsequent differentiation of society into individuals was seen, long before the process was actually completed, as requiring everyone to become their own religious functionary. The task of redemption could not be left to the religious expert, and the prayers of monks could not save the community as a whole. A common obligation to follow the active devotion of a virtuous life was placed on everyone.

The task of the church, therefore, was to recreate within the individual soul the order which had been given as Belief and which still shone (however ambiguously) in the night sky. Its task was to interiorize Belief as a new moral imperative. To transform each individual into a self-adhering body whose spontaneous actions would generate a just society.

It is in the context of this intellectual revolution that the notion of secularization has gained its greatest credibility. Whether the modern world-view is understood as a transformed version of an older Christian cosmology (a pantheism founded upon a rational understanding of the actual infinity of the universe), or whether it is seen as a radically new departure within the history of ideas, creation could never again be construed as bodying forth a fixed structure of Belief. Yet it was just this development of a purely secular cosmology which encouraged a profound *religious* transformation in the pursuit of Happiness.

VIRTUE

The first significant shift in the moral assumptions of religiosity in fact became visible among humanist rather than ecclesiastical or academic writers. Erasmus, thus, writes an *Exhortation to Virtue*[10] as an attack on traditional scholastic ethics, a preoccupation which is also clearly expressed in his remarks on the education of a prince, and colours, indeed, his entire *œuvre*. Morality is no longer seen as the realization within society of an order symbolic of a transcending reality. Obligation, rather, becomes a personal effort to conform to those standards of rightness, fairness and virtue which alone are the foundations of an orderly society. Erasmus, thus, holds it to be inconceivable that a good prince could be other than a morally good person. 'There can be no good prince who is not also a good man', he roundly declares.[11] This is a principle, indeed, which applies quite generally, irrespective of rank or responsibility, so that, in his view, 'nothing is really "good" unless associated with moral integrity'.[12]

Erasmus does not, however, any more than any other humanist writer, view moral goodness in isolation from Christianity. It is just because the obligation of leadership is a *moral* duty that he urges upon the prince the necessity of a specifically Christian education; 'before all else the story of Christ must be firmly rooted in the mind of the prince'.[13] And there is no need to become a monk or a bishop to express, fully and directly, the virtue of Christianity. The prince should be the first to have 'followed the rule of Christ himself'.[14] To be a prince he must first be a philosopher, not in the Platonic sense of mastering dialectic, but in a new sense of adherence to a Christian way of life; 'to be a philosopher and to be a Christian is synonymous'.[15] However, just as there is, for an earlier period, a profound difference between Faith and Belief, so for the humanist Christian there is no simple identity between the old Belief and the new Morality.

In the post-feudal world, where qualitatively distinct orders of men had given way, or were in the process of giving way, to an atomized cosmos of individuated humanity, moral precepts must become absolutely general, and carry with them the force of a rational demonstration. The common context of such a demonstration should be constituted by a 'philosophy of Christianity' which was utterly remote from the scholastic theology whose 'thorny and cumbrous inextricable subtle imaginations of instances, of formalities, of quiddities, of relation' had made of Christian Belief the effective monopoly of a peculiarly educated élite.[16] A new Christian philosophy should be less a set of dogmatic propositions, or catalogue of abstract distinctions, than a practical example of the 'craft of virtuous living'.[17] Throughout the *Enchiridion Militis Christiani*, therefore,

Erasmus tirelessly couples the term 'Christian' with the notion of 'Virtue' or one of its synonyms.[18]

Educational reform, therefore, became the central preoccupation and unifying theme of northern humanism just because 'virtue' embraced a circle of meanings which overlapped, but never quite coincided, with that of 'Christianity'. Virtue demanded a continuous effort, diligent application and perpetual watchfulness. It was always associated with, but never reducible to, the careless rapture of inward grace. The 'philosophy of Christianity', that is to say, is not Christianity itself, but the ethical domain predicated upon it.

It was not sufficient, therefore, to teach Christian Belief. The prince must set the example in being guided solely by virtue; he 'should take special care not to sin, because he makes so many followers in his wrongdoings, but rather to devote himself to being virtuous so that so many good men may result'.[19] And since 'a country owes everything to a good prince' it owes most 'to the man who made him such by his *moral principles*'.[20] The distinction between essential 'Christianity' and 'secular' virtue remained unclear. The prince's tasks in life are secular, but can be achieved only if his will is educated in 'Christian' duty. At times, in fact, Erasmus seems very close to avowing the semi-Pelagian heresy. Eternal Happiness must rest with God, but personal human virtue remains a prerequisite for its accomplishment; thus 'the kingdom of heaven is not gotten of negligent and reckless persons'.[21] This conclusion, however, flows from the Erasmian identification of virtue as an authentic religious category. Indeed, Erasmus felt the religious significance of virtue to be sufficiently fundamental for him to make the notion of 'free-will' central to any adequate theology, thereby attracting the criticism of Luther.[22]

Yet, in the final, revealing, and beautifully composed pages of the *Encomium Moriae*, Erasmus reasserts, not the dependence of virtue upon a philosophy of Christianity, but the absolute independence of grace. It is not the rationalization of everyday life in relation to the absolute value of personal salvation, but the continuity of personal Happiness with every species of 'Folly', that inspires Erasmus to one of the finest and most accessible expressions of Christian Platonism.[23] And rather than regarding personal morality as a deduction drawn from principled Christianity, the social necessity and onerous obligation of virtue is viewed finally as no more than the secular precursor of Happiness, a state of bliss which, in fact, has little to do with moral exaltation. 'The happiness which Christians seek with so many labours', he assures his reader, 'is nothing other than a certain kind of madness and folly'.[24] It is not just the practical naïvety of Christians which makes them, from a secular viewpoint, strikingly foolish, it is 'as if their spirit dwelt elsewhere than in their body'.[25]

To be virtuous is to assume the responsibility of selfhood. It is significant that the model of Erasmian virtue was the 'good prince', which he held up as a new democratic ideal. Each person can and ought to become as complete a 'personality' as the prince. Yet to be happy is to perfect the personality beyond this secular ideal of independent self-control. Erasmus links this directly to the 'transcending' power of love. 'For anyone who loves intensely lives not in himself but in the object of his love, and the further he can move out of himself into his love, the happier he is.'[26] And, therefore, to consume God's absolute love is to become wholly 'outside' the self; 'and so when the whole man will be outside himself, and be happy for no reason except that he is so outside himself, he will enjoy some ineffable share in the supreme good which draws everything into itself'.[27]

Christian virtue, then, seems remote not only from Divine folly, but from the mundane forms of madness which constitute, more certainly than theological subtlety or credal orthodoxy, a foretaste of heaven. The underlying social logic of virtue, nevertheless, can be detected in the revival of mystical and evangelical Christianity. To be 'outside' the self was, from the perspective of a later period, a completion rather than a negation of the movement which begins with virtue. It is the extremity of a process of individuation rather than, as had been more generally the case within the feudal world, the annihilation of the ego.[28] The possibility of Happiness lies in the establishment of a universal inner selfhood unconstrained by time, or place, or circumstance, a possibility which is no longer seen to depend upon the humiliation of a particular ego. And it is from this perspective that the continuity between secular madness (ecstasy) and divine happiness (rapture) becomes apparent.

Erasmus was only too well aware of the gulf between his recommendation of 'personal' morality as a standard of political leadership, and the reality of social life. The masses, it went without saying, while they lacked the most elementary practical education (which the example of the prince was designed to supply), were filled with 'sordid desires'. The young prince, indeed, should be protected from their corrupting contact while his education was undertaken. And as few monarchs, even where they were insulated from the masses, enjoyed the civilizing benefits of the most rudimentary moral education, the majority were 'tyrants'. They were princes whose rule, that is to say, was neither softened nor justified by the exercise of virtue. They followed the 'unbridled will' of their own immediate inclination and, in common with the generality of their subjects, became slaves to 'lust, irrascibility, avarice, ambition; and all the rest of that malicious category'.[29]

Virtue, from being the realization of the divine order in fallen nature, had quite suddenly become identical with 'self denial'.[30] In the prince this self-imposed constraint manifested itself in his acting 'for the good of his country, not for himself'.[31] And, by implication, among the less exalted it was to act for the good of others through the subordination of immediate desires to a rule of conduct. It was no longer sufficient, therefore, to have collective salvation guaranteed by the devotion of religious experts. The religious quest became obligatory for all, and could not therefore be made the subject of a privileged way of life.[32] Religious seriousness, therefore, which found its natural expression in personal morality, was formulated in opposition to the emotional flamboyance of late medieval asceticism as well as to the absence of manners in secular life.[33] There was more than practical political wisdom involved in this urge to submit everyday life to the guidance of moral rules. The advantages in terms of the pacification of society were evident, but the real force behind the drive towards profane virtue lay in the relocation of Christianity's salvation myth necessitated by the collapse of its associated and previously authoritative cosmology.

CONFORMITY

A reformed society depended upon the practice of virtue. Although there was nothing inherently natural to such a condition, self-control had to become a spontaneous act of conformity to universal norms of conduct. Erasmus made plain the reluctance with which even the well educated embrace Morality. For the first time in western society, therefore, the necessity of 'educating' the populace, in addition to its prince, became apparent. The most rudimentary forms of self-control had to be learned.[34] The organization of emotion and feeling, traditionally contained within the symbolic hierarchy of feudalism (the knight was essentially courageous and just, the monk inclined naturally to humility), had to be redistributed and controlled ideologically.

A new moral economy of bodily functions had to be established as the precondition (the elementary rule) of a new society. Since the corporate identity of feudal society had dissolved and the locus of control shifted to the individual, the regulation of bodily functions gained a new meaning and significance. What was new here was not the imposition of constraint where previously there had been none, but the creation of an individuated and internal 'spiritual' power in place of such objective and external codification of behaviour as that contained in sumptuary regulations. And rather than declare a categorical rejection of the flesh in favour of the spirit, late medieval Europe saw a determined effort to spiritualize bodily processes. Shame, propriety and guilt, as interior and private forms of surveillance, became the new forces of self-regulation.[35] And in this process of interiorization and reconstruction Christian assumptions, whether or not they were directly allied to the church, maintained a pre-eminent position.

The need to 'Christianize' society had been evident to the Church itself and gave rise, amongst other movements of reform, to the foundation of the Dominican order at the beginning of the thirteenth century. Initially an extension of the Gregorian reform movement, and founded in part at least in response to the spread of Catharism in south-west France, it was an order devoted to scholarship and teaching. One of its major tasks had been the education of the clergy.[36] Progressively, however, it gained new responsibilities and, coinciding with the fourteenth-century 'crisis of feudalism', the task of the Dominicans was conceived in a much broader fashion. As the centralized and authoritative overseer of orthodoxy it became particularly concerned with the effort to control popular religiosity.[37] Since Christian orthodoxy was no longer built in to every aspect of organized social life, the church (and therefore society) could exist only through the inculcation of personal values that were in fact alien to the mass of the people. As the 'givenness' of the feudal–Christian order of things dissolved, 'popular' beliefs emerged as a dangerously explosive heterodoxy. Heresy, which in the pre-feudal period had been a problem only because, as it rapidly expanded throughout Europe, Christianity had remained doctrinally ill-defined, re-emerged in new and more menacing forms.[38]

The alternatives to, variants of, Christianity which threatened to take hold of the popular imagination were almost forgotten descendants of ante-Nicaean perversity given a new lease of life as popular millenarian 'ideologies'.[39] Faced with the apparent spread of heresy and the simultaneous politicization of the carnival tradition, the church responded by founding the Inquisition.[40] Indeed it is from the Inquisitorial records that the popular culture of the late medieval and early modern period is now being reconstructed.

A process of differentiation was taking place. Religious life, and the institutional complex of the church, from being an aspect of the totality of feudalism, was becoming a set of relations which defined a domain of activities and responsibilities which were uniquely its own. Religion thus occupied its own 'sphere' of life, separate from and related to a variety of similar spheres. Just as the market was establishing its own independence from political control, and the state was organizing its own secular administrative apparatus, the church, disengaging itself from its previous involvement in society as a whole, sought to establish its authority through the imposition of obligatory standards of personal Morality. The church came to define itself as the chief source and only effective guardian of virtue.

Its authority, however, was disputed by many. And to eradicate popular heresies secular and ecclesiastical authorities co-operated in a new way. The Inquisition established its own courts, and was, in many areas, the most effective of centralized institutions. It became, in some ways at least, the most progressive of post-feudal institutions. Its legalistic procedures, standards of evidence, and methods of investigation were, for the most part, more just than those of the secular states within which it operated.[41] The primary purpose of the Inquisition was to establish and maintain orthodoxy. Its first and preferred method was the use of reasoned argument. The Inquisitorial records provide detailed accounts of the extraordinary lengths to which at least some Inquisitors were willing to go to persuade individual heretics to recant.[42] But when the scale of dissent became more obvious, and (as had been the case with the Albigensians) there was held to be a distinct threat to all forms of established authority, secular forces were enlisted as a means to adequate repression.[43]

In both individual cases and in campaigns mounted against particular communities, it was the *moral* threat of heresy which was the main target. In Montaillou, as in northern Italy, it was the deviant behaviour of particular individuals which was seized upon (rather as it was to be in the later witch-hunting craze). Such individuals provided a convenient focus of resentment and frustration for the local populace; and, from the authorities' viewpoint, their prosecution and eventual punishment was an ideal form of mass education.[44] The pedagogical advantage of isolated and relatively infrequent heresy was obvious. The threat of a popular rejection of orthodox Christianity, of course, remained a different matter.

It was the popular revival, in a variety of forms, of dualistic heresies that posed such a wholesale threat. Deriving ultimately from early gnostic beliefs, the idea of the inherent evil of the material world, to those who suffered its worst hardships, is perhaps hardly surprising. To make of evil a wholly independent moral force provided a consistent and persuasive account of the rigours of everyday life for the mass of people. Its appeal, consequently, was widespread and it flourished additionally as a consequence of the protection afforded it by local (largely non-feudal) aristocracies keen to establish their autonomy from newly centralized authorities.[45]

From the dualist standpoint morality was part of the conventional order of things, and part, therefore, of the empirical world's spiritual dross. And as conventions had sprung originally from the same source as the rest of creation, to act conventionally was to collaborate with evil. To overcome creation, therefore, which is the real meaning of salvation, the true religion demanded conduct of just that sort condemned by the church. It was not to seek pleasure that the radical sect indulged in unrestrained sensuous gratification, refused to acknowledge secular authority, and lived in total disregard of family and kinship obligations; their incendiary antinomianism was, in fact, a form of asceticism. It was in order to reject it that the world was, so to speak, deliberately humiliated. In advance of any moralizing reform movement, then, a wide range of heretical sectarians had offered their own, anticipatory and practical, criticism of it.

To order and organize natural appetites, and to convert them into moral conduct, was to transform them in order that they might be 'consumed'. Morality might be likened to cooking; it transforms nature into an aspect of ourselves and makes it possible to ingest and digest 'alien' matter. It allows matter originating outside of ourselves to become incorporated, both physically and psychologically, into ourselves. Virtue transforms the natural functions and predispositions of the body into morally acceptable forms of behaviour. It spiritualizes the body and renders it safe for social life. But if nature is itself evil, then we are obliged to ignore such regulatory practices. We must endeavour to maintain, free from the contaminating touch of natural appetite (or the socialized virtues which contain them), the genuinely spiritual inner self. Virtue civilizes appetite by interiorizing the conventional rules through which they are ordered and disciplined. These rules become the new (and false) foundation of self-identity.

Thus, by ignoring such rules, the exterior and evil world which is inflicted upon us as natural human appetite is kept at safe distance. Rather than cultivate appetites, which inevitably introduce the principle of evil into ourselves, and make the corrupted world of nature and society an object for our satisfaction, the radical anti-moralist disregards all rules, and answers (without feeling) to the inescapable prompting of nature, in an undisguised and therefore less corrupting manner.

The careless sensuousness of the radical sectarians was, therefore, a strange ascetic practice. It signified a rejection of, rather than an enjoyment in, the immediate world of natural appetite. It represented, therefore, a profound transformation of the popular culture of the carnival. There sensuousness had been celebrated as a value, but for a rigorous moral dualism, sensuousness was indulged just because it was both dangerously evil and unavoidable. By allowing it to revert to nature appetite was ignored rather than controlled. Those who have viewed the immorality of some groups as indicative of political radicalism have, therefore, tended to underestimate the seriousness of their religious purpose.[46] Their challenge to established authorities and to existing conventions was not in the name of some secular vision of a better life or a more rational society. It flowed logically, rather, from a heterodox cosmological plan of salvation.

It was the transformation of social life which created (and was part of) a new form of religiosity. Not only in the context of orthodoxy, but also within a variety of heterodox traditions, the dominant conception of salvation was shifted from one founded upon Belief to one based upon Morality. This transition was connected particularly with a new distinction between 'public' and 'private' life, which was itself an aspect of a new division of labour. The order of society was guaranteed through its public institutions. One set of institutions, however, had been separated from the rest and was treated in a different way. Domestic life increasingly became a 'private' matter. This meant that at least a portion of the normal life of people was lived outside the direct controlling agencies of society. The task of insinuating the same order that governed society into the private realm, into the hearts as well as the minds of the populace, was the task of religion. Morality was primarily the order of private life, an order created in the image and in the interests of public life but essentially separate from it. Its maintenance, therefore, depended upon the self-control and self-policing of those who were its object.

CONSCIENCE

It was a Moral impulse of this new type which animated the Reformation. Luther's 95 *Theses* were nailed to the church door to announce a *Disputatio* (a public debate in order to establish a specific point), rather than as an act of defiance. His initial purpose, that is to say, was pedagogical rather than political.

Luther, priding himself on his lack of social ambition, was highly critical of particular ecclesiastical practices, not because they were unlawful or necessarily unreasonable, but because, as they were practised, they gave rise among the lower orders to dangerous misconceptions. His immediate target, the sale of indulgences, was attacked on the grounds of its presumed moral effects on the population at large. In fact Luther explicitly upheld the authority of the ecclesiastical hierarchy within their proper sphere of jurisdiction; that is in matters of canon law. And he went so far as to claim that 'God never remits guilt to anyone without, at the same time, making him humbly submissive to the priest, His representative'.[47] He is, initially at least, far less daring than Erasmus or More or others who had simply made fun of scholastic theological method and its abstruse justification of patently corrupt practices.[48]

The crucial point, in Luther's view, is the routinization of forgiveness which absolves individuals from any genuine sense of moral responsibility. The church used the device merely to raise funds, and the sinner, without contrition, was granted forgiveness. Luther insists on making the moral issue central. Thus, he emphasizes in particular the absurdity of the living having to pay in order to release those of their deceased relatives who were presumed to be detained in purgatory. He insists 'There is no divine authority for preaching that the soul flies out of purgatory immediately the money clinks in the bottom of the chest',[49] and announces unequivocally that 'Death puts an end to all the claims of the church'.[50] It is worth making the point again that this is far from a direct attack on traditional doctrine. The church is perfectly entitled to exact penance, but the question of 'forgiveness' is separate from this and, although it cannot be gained without the aid of the priest's intercessions, neither can it be guaranteed by him. Luther, therefore, rejecting radical attacks on the church, bluntly declares, 'Let him be anathema and accursed who denies the apostolic character of the indulgence'.[51]

He sees no contradiction, apparently, between this declaration and his equally forthright insistence that 'The pope himself cannot remit guilt'.[52] Luther in fact advises that 'Papal indulgence should only be preached with caution, lest people gain a wrong understanding, and think that they are preferable to *other good works*'.[53]

Indulgences are, in fact, just one form of penance, none of which unreservedly guarantees forgiveness. They are worthwhile only as outward signs of contrition and as such they constitute an indispensable precondition for divine forgiveness. Luther urges, just as vigorously, therefore, that 'penitence in one's heart' is imperfect 'unless it produces outward signs in various mortifications of the flesh'.[54] Indulgences are morally suspect just because they are inept signs. And the priest ought, therefore, to be more impressed by other 'good works' which, being less ambiguously indicative of true penitence, are consequently more deserving to be made the occasion for the church's intercession upon the sinner's behalf. 'Christians should be taught', he argues 'that one who gives to the poor, or lends to the needy, does a better action than if he purchases indulgences.'[55] Luther has no hesitation, thus, in recommending 'works of piety and love' as preludes to salvation.

He goes on, however, to make clear the uncompromisingly transcendental character of this salvation. The ultimate value cannot be purchased any more readily by good works than by indulgences. Salvation is 'beyond' any other value, and is not to be reached by any conventional means. The ultimate good cannot be consumed by taking possession of it as if it were a commodity of some kind. The foundation of all moral conduct, thus, cannot be found in merely human notions of goodness. It is only by embracing a transcendental value without regard to its place within the everyday rational calculus of valuation, that genuinely moral conduct can emerge at all. To act morally is to express a value which is held internally as an aspect of the personality; and the personality itself exists as an expression of a relation to a reality beyond all relative values. To raise the masses to such a form of conduct it is essential to attack their superstitious and magical notions of religion. In a letter to Albert of Mainz with which he enclosed a copy of his *Theses* he again makes the point that his opposition is to the 'mistaken impressions which the common people have gained, and which are universally current among the masses. For example the poor souls believe that if they buy these letters of indulgence, their own salvation is assured'.[56]

Where Cusanus had anticipated the implications for the traditional cosmology of the collapse of the feudal hierarchical conception of society, Luther's ethical Christianity just as presciently anticipates its implications for the notion of Happiness. The dissolution of the feudal hierarchy made everyone, at least every baptized male, a member of a new religious class. As baptism, gospel and faith define the Christian then 'are all equally Christian'.[57] And the religious functionary acts only with the authority of the faithful who have selected him. 'When a bishop consecrates, he simply acts on behalf of the entire congregation, all of whom have the same authority.'[58]

The education of the faithful, therefore, is seen by Luther, as much as it is by Erasmus, to be a vital necessity. Religious duty must be fulfilled in 'everyday' tasks. The universality of its moral claims makes the specialized functions of the monk, for example, plainly ridiculous. The fundamental instrument of education comprises the Ten Commandments, the Apostles' Creed and the Lord's Prayer. It is in these works that the entire *Moral* doctrine of Christianity is revealed; and it is of them that Luther is moved to remark: 'Surely it has been ordained by God that the people in general, who cannot read the Scriptures for themselves, should learn and know (them) by heart.'[59]

These are the essential works, they contain what 'a man should know in order to be saved'.[60] Luther's exposition of the Decalogue, in particular, reveals the broad range of his moralizing. The first commandment, we are hardly surprised to discover, applies to 'all forms of unbelief, doubt and heresy'.[61] Included among offences against the fourth commandment, however, we find 'To be disrespectful to the priesthood, to slander and insult it', and even 'All forms of pride and disobedience'.[62] Similarly all-embracing, 'Thou shalt not kill' is interpreted, subjectively, as an interdiction against 'all sins of anger and hatred'.[63] And the sixth commandment (thou shalt not commit adultery) is rendered as:

> Not to avoid whatever causes immorality, such as gluttony, toping, indolence, laziness, sleeping too long, and intimate contact with the persons of women or men. To use extravagant dress or gesture or the like to rouse others to sensuality.[64]

Luther, hardly surprisingly, claims that in keeping the commandments (that is to interiorize them as conscience) a person 'will be busy in good works day by day'.[65]

'Good works', for Luther, simply means living with strict regard to the Moral precepts of Christianity; observing the commandments which, without distortion, can be reduced to the single over-riding rule that 'forbids self-love'. This, superficially, is identical with medieval teaching and the practice of monastic humility. But the new social setting has transformed its meaning. Now salvation has become the personal responsibility of each believer, and cannot be granted either by an ecclesiastical hierarchy, or by a segregated section of the community acting as professional worshippers. And worship or penitence have a religious significance only when performed as an expression of private, inner conviction. In the new cosmos the spiritual centre of gravity turns inward upon each individual, who is liberated into the void of an infinitely extendable inner space within which he or she must attempt to form a personal relation to God. The church cannot fill this space, but it can provide the moral framework within which the organization of everyday life expresses the ultimate value of a religious truth.

Luther's celebrity, already encouraged by polemical reactions to his initial works, was enhanced by his increasingly direct, and at times strident, tone. His initial reservations, protestations of orthodoxy, and discretion quickly gave way to an outright attack on the traditional doctrine and practice of ecclesiastical authority. The sacraments, far more seriously than in the case of indulgences, had become a cash business. Making payments for special masses, baptism and so on, had the inevitable effect of turning 'the holy sacraments into mere merchandise, a market, and a business run for profit'.[66]

The venal motive of the priest is bad enough, but even worse is the encouragement, for the common people, of a semi-magical aura surrounding the sacraments. Attending a mass, the ritual of prayer, or other act of worship, is regarded by them as a 'means' to attain some particular goal. This is not only irrational (in a scientific sense) but irreligious. Luther makes absolutely clear that the duty to devotion is a primary religious task. This is an obligation imposed upon each individual in relation to God. The priest acts as mediator only in the very restricted sense of communicating the *signs* of God's promise, and emphatically cannot transmit its substance:

> the mass is a divine promise which can benefit no one, be applied to no one, intercede for no one, be communicated to no one, except only to the believer himself by the sole virtue of his own faith.[67]

Rather than to seek salvation through some special religious technique, the only means, in fact, by which to take possession of God's promise is to surrender to the inwardness of faith. Thus even prayer is ineffective as a means of gaining purely religious favours. 'For the mass, or otherwise, God's promise is not fulfilled by praying, but only

117

by believing; and it is as believers that we pray and do every good work.'[68]

'It is faith which prays', and as prayer is both inward and personal (or can be) it is a uniquely unmediated communication with God; it is 'its voice alone which is heard'.[69] The church, in its hierarchical structure, had replicated both the presumed cosmic structure, and the organization of social life within feudalism. The new religious situation, rejecting mediation and hierarchical authority, anticipated the 'freedom' that was to be instituted by capitalism. But, unable yet to discern its novel generative principle, the new doctrine was bound to appear negative and critical. From a traditional viewpoint it appeared to subvert the very idea of Christendom as a substantial community of believers. Luther's continual stress on moral duty, on the religious obligations which faith imposed upon each individual, was an essential piece of counter-propaganda. Indeed, it was more than that. Faith had lost, for Luther, the innocent joy in which (however rarely it had been thus experienced) it was first proclaimed. The Faith of early Christianity was an inwardness which expressed itself spontaneously in lawful acts. It made conformity to the conventions of social life both reasonable and effortless. For Luther, however, the matter was quite different. Faith was an interior abyss which could not be penetrated by rational means, and which kept within itself the secret of Divine Being.[70] Faith was inexpressible, but, at its most lively, might be felt as an inward qualification of the spirit. Faith was the innermost core of the person, and around it there had developed, so to speak, an interior 'cosmos'; an empty space had appeared which, if it was not to be seized by purely natural and destructive instincts, had to be filled with moral rules. The development of a doctrine of personal morality, therefore, even though it could not be logically deduced from the inner sensation of faith, was a proper theological task. It responded, no doubt, to a new social necessity, but more importantly right conduct provided a protective shell within which faith could be nurtured. Christianity, thus, while it was not to be identified with any specific code of Moral conduct, nevertheless in making conscience obligatory, gave to it a new ethical impulse.

The distinction between faith and works aimed at establishing a difference between a secular Moral, and a properly religious, sphere of existence. But Luther's own account of both, and of their relation to each other, is far from simple. Faith is at once an absolutely free inner spirituality, but at the same time it flows from the Moral compulsion to trust the Divine Will. Faith calls for unconditional obedience; and yet, at the same time, as the written word must be grasped intellectually rather than absorbed mystically, scripture must be critically scrutinized and doubted. Works refer at times to acts of worship, or charity, but frequently, and more profoundly, to the ethical impulse in conduct. Works can encompass, indeed, all manifestations of human will and personal volition. They have no differential quality of their own, they have no value other than the faith embedded in them. 'In His sight', Luther suggests, 'there is no difference between works except that of the measure of faith which they express.'[71]

Luther's use of the distinction, though it never remains quite fixed, is nonetheless a remarkable anticipation of the new reality (the commodity) which would come to shape the social world. While the medieval world, particularly in its feudal form, was conceived as a cosmos within which separate essences had been ordered according to the Divine Will, the modern world became dimly envisioned as a natural order of qualitatively identical matter 'contained' within an infinite and empty space.

It was the existence of 'qualitative' difference which had made a necessity of divine 'mediation' (and its earthly analogy in the church). God, absolute Being, in creating the world had created quite separate 'species'. The chain of being was composed of an almost infinite series of tiny linked gradations; the being of each one was conceivable as a kind of 'vassal' of the being immediately 'superior' to it in the chain. But there were real and essential differences which set each species and each level of existence apart from any other. It was only God, and within man the soul or mind, which was His 'likeness', that could bridge these qualitative differences. Man could thus surpass himself and elevate himself towards his divine origin. But within the new cosmology, where there were no such fixed gradations nor (although in Luther's time this was hardly realized) any fixed species or objects, there was no need for (and no realistic model of) the complex mediations of medieval theology. The new cosmological model was inherently indifferent to qualitative distinctions. The differences among things were only appearances which, properly understood, could be reduced to inessential quantitative gradations. Ultimately all substances were reducible to different arrangements of the same fundamental 'stuff' of nature. Analogously in the spiritual realm, Faith was the 'common value' whose presence lent significance to human action. The cosmos, thus, was a structure made up of substantially identical (and not merely analogically similar) bodies. And, in like wise, human society was composed of one basic ingredient, rather than of different types of human being. Within such a system of relations, human actions, however diverse, could have but a single universal meaning. All actions could be judged (in practice precariously) by the quantity of faith each 'contained'. The value attached to any action depended on how much faith it exhibited, on how much trust in God it poured into the world of mundane preoccupations.

The real strength of Luther's attack on traditional Catholicism lay in its systematic coherence rather than in its polemical aggressiveness. In three short works he presents us with an uncanny foretaste of the world beyond feudalism. The distinction between faith and works – which, in one sense, is simply the new categorical division between subject and object as viewed by the subject – is, in practice, difficult to make.[72] All the medieval theological categories had been abolished to be replaced by a single remaining qualitative distinction: that which was drawn between the 'inner man' in relation to which the person, who 'is sufficiently justified by faith', ought to reject all forms of external coercion;[73] and the outer world including bodily existence whose unregenerate nature provokes an urgent and endless need for good works. A man must 'rule his own body, and he must mix with other people'.[74] And it is to this dual necessity that good works are addressed:

> He must not be idle. Yes, the body must be disciplined and
> exercised with fasting, watching, labouring and all due training,
> in order that it may be obedient to, and in harmony with, both
> the inner man and with faith.[75]

It is only the 'inner man' which can be 'one with God', while, in his body, a man always finds 'a refractory will which wants to seek and serve the world, and which finds pleasure in doing so'.[76]

Luther sought to revive, as the goal of the religious life, a sense of inward release which had been typical of the doctrine (if not the practice) of primitive Christianity. Faith, protected by a 'sphere' of Morality which, in a sense never fully explicated by Luther, signifies its otherwise incommunicable presence, remains, for him, an ineffable and wholly private liberation from the burden of external command. But now the dialectic of Law and Faith has been interiorized as an inward spiritual relation between the 'inner man' and his own body. And in this relation all Moral obligations are subordinated under a single generative rule of conduct; that is, the obligation to have faith.

OBLIGATION

Calvin, elaborating on Luther's original programme of reform, construed the ideal of Moral constraint in a yet more thoroughly individualistic and subjective fashion. The spiritual being within man was justified by faith alone, but the experience of faith itself, and not just its psychic penumbra, was now endowed with a fundamentally Moral character.

Calvin holds that the greater part of sacred doctrine falls under two heads: 'knowledge of God and of ourselves'.[77] God is 'infinite wisdom, righteousness, goodness, mercy, truth, power and life'.[78] Self-knowledge begins in the acknowledgement of original sin, when 'the image and likeness of God was cancelled and effaced'.[79] Thus, 'all of us born of Adam are ignorant and bereft of God, perverse, corrupt, and lacking every good'; a condition of sin so thoroughgoing that 'if we outwardly display anything good, still the mind stays in its inner state of filth and crooked perversity'.[80] Progress in the life of the spirit does not come readily by a simple arousal of the soul against the flesh; as if the 'image and likeness' planted within us would be self-expanding after an initial, externally prompted, impetus to righteousness. The soul, however, is itself corrupted and rotten, the mind or inner man is infected with sin. Calvin is relentlessly consistent on this point: 'man will find in himself', he explains, 'only unhappiness, weakness, wickedness, death, in short, hell itself'.[81] Salvation depends, therefore, upon a gratuitous act of grace, which is experienced as the 'conscience', which 'sets before us good and evil'. Man in his state of sin is indifferent to this distinction and, 'blinded by self-love', remains ignorant (other than as an external compulsion) of the divine commandments through which the Lord 'engraved and, so to speak, stamped the law upon the hearts of all'.[82] Spiritual ignorance, that is to say, cannot be overcome by any self-motivated act, as all self-motivated acts further obscure the conscience which is the gift of grace.

Man can be made righteous only by faith; righteousness, indeed, is nothing other than human action suffused by faith. And faith itself is just 'a sure and certain possession of those things God has promised us'.[83] True faith is 'nothing else than a firm conviction of mind whereby we determine with ourselves that God's truth is so certain, that it is incapable of not accomplishing what it has pledged to do by his holy Word'.[84] Righteousness, that is, although it works through human activity, and may manifest itself in a certain type of consciousness, cannot originate with man himself. Righteousness is entirely

121

God's work, not ours. And we can do nothing to make ourselves deserving of such a gift; 'it can never be obtained except as a free gift'.[85] In fact we need do nothing (we *can* do nothing) to acquire faith but accept the promise through which it is offered.

From such a radical viewpoint it is clearly difficult to distinguish, in human moral terms, between 'good' and 'evil'. All human activities are morally dubious; the motives entering into them are seldom clear and never absolutely pure. Calvin points out that 'in the same work shines God's righteousness; their iniquity'.[86] And, even more fundamentally, since 'We indeed cannot comprehend God's incomprehensible wisdom, nor is it in our power to investigate it so as to find out who have by his eternal plan been chosen, who condemned', judgements of others' (or our own) culpability is never straightforward.[87] Thus, although it is clear that, ideally, 'the church is the people of God's elect', equally it is obvious that 'the elect cannot be recognized by us with assurance'.[88] Scripture describes 'certain sure marks to us' by which the elect may be recognized 'insofar as He wills us to recognize them'.[89] These marks are not the distinction brought by secular good works and charitable deeds, but comprise 'all who profess with us the same God and Christ by expression of faith, example of life and participation in the sacraments'.[90] Calvin, in the light of the uncertainty attaching to all human attribution of inner meaning is at pains to qualify this (generously imprecise) categorization; those, however they act in particulars, 'ought by some sort of judgment of love to be deemed elect and members of the church'. They should be so considered 'even if some imperfection resides in their morals (as no one here shows himself to be perfect), provided they do not too much acquiesce and flatter themselves in their vices'. Human judgement is, in principle, imperfect; 'For God, whenever it pleases him, changes the worst man into the best . . . And he does this to frustrate men's opinion and restrain their rashness'.[91]

Calvin, like Luther, rejects ecclesiastical authority and political coercion in matters of faith. But, to avoid some of the ambiguity involved in Luther's conception of good works, he feels obliged to make Morality an essential aspect of the notion of faith itself. However, also in anticipation of the developing cosmology of the capitalist world, and even more clearly than Luther, he insists upon the absolute transcendence, and therefore complete unknowability, of God. Moral certainty is thereby reduced to a faltering interior sensibility. We cannot, by rational forethought, act in such a way as to free ourselves from all taint of sin. Neither can we, therefore, through direct and indirect communicative acts, so express our inner faith as to make our membership of the elect indubitable.

Augustine had been able to elaborate a theory of communication between man and God in which scripture and sacraments could be conceived as authentic *symbols* of the Divine Will.[92] As man was joined to God by an unbroken chain of being, that element within man which preserved the likeness of God constituted part of his essential nature. It was just this natural basis for knowledge of Divine things upon which was constructed the elaborate analogical and anagogical structure of medieval thought and medieval Christian liturgical practice. The new cosmology, in breaking the chain of being, rendered fundamentally arbitrary the symbolic connection between man and god. Calvin speaks, therefore, of the sacraments as signs rather than symbols. Only baptism and the Lord's supper, having scriptural authority, should be considered authentic; the others (confirmation, penance, extreme unction, ecclesiastical orders and marriage) are signs which have been 'invented by the rashness of men'.[93]

Calvin is at pains to expose the residual superstition infecting the practice of these latter sacraments, the exercise of which has corrupted the real meaning of the former. The sacraments should not be considered as a *means* to acquire faith or grace. They are forms of human consolation, 'exercises which make us more certain of the trustworthiness of God's Word', and as such they are completely devoid of 'secret powers'.[94] At the same time we are told the primary sacraments represent a 'surer exercise of faith'.[95] Calvin's argument becomes obscure at this point. On the one hand he wants to sever any natural connection between symbol and the Divine Will represented by the symbol; on the other hand he insists upon preserving, for the authentic sacraments, an inner and authoritative meaning. The sacraments, in their outward form, and from a human point of view, are essentially arbitrary. However, in being *chosen* by God as the forms through which He might represent his will to men, they have an absolute claim upon our obedience and a unique capacity to act as vehicles for the public expression of our faith. The sacraments cannot create faith, or strengthen a faith which is feeble; they merely exercise a faith which is already present. This appears to be something we find necessary. We cannot help but 'express' through our conduct the presence of purely inward values.

Prayer, just as the sacraments, 'possesses no merit or worth to obtain what is requested'.[96] Prayer depends entirely upon faith. It is *'something secret*, which is both principally lodged in the heart and requires a tranquillity far from all our teeming cares'.[97] It cannot be a technique to coerce God, or to inflict upon Him the limitations of our own feeble will. Prayer is a temporary withdrawal from the tumult of everyday life; we should 'learn to persevere in prayer, and with desire suspended, patiently wait for the Lord'.[98]

The ideal of 'suspended desire' effectively captures Calvin's special brand of asceticism. The ascetic tendency is only an aspect, in his view, of the fundamental *freedom* of the Christian conscience. Because the inner world of faith is all-important, and, in its essential nature, incommunicable, no special effort should be made to harness it to a *Rule* proscribing specific 'gifts' which naturally satisfy human, bodily (and therefore inherently sinful) appetites. There is, in other words, a specific spiritual danger in self-denial. The genuine ascetic practises a form of *spiritual* self-discipline which is, in fact, endangered by the ostentatious prohibition of natural pleasures. All outward things are subjected to our freedom, and cannot therefore become the object of spiritual exercise. We ought to cultivate *indifference* to the world of the senses and satisfy our needs according to our station in life, the traditions of our community, and the availability of goods. To circumscribe our relations to the world of goods by religious rules is to enter upon an inevitably progressive asceticism: 'If any man think daintier food unlawful, in the end he will not be at peace before God, when he eats either black bread or common victuals.'[99] We should not give way to the easy comfort of an external authority, to the superstition of a *Rule*.

Extravagance and self-indulgence are, equally and far more commonly, spiritual faults; 'to wallow in delights, to gorge oneself, to intoxicate mind and heart with present pleasures and be always panting after new ones – such are very far removed from a lawful use of God's gifts'.[100] This is the more familiar side of Reformation moralizing. It is 'uncontrolled desire', 'immoderate prodigality', 'vanity and arrogance' which, more frequently than excessive and misconceived asceticism, enslave us, and entangle the spirit in worldly pursuits. That such phrases are even necessary is a demonstration of evangelical freedom. Faith and Morality are linked just because they are not identical, and the religious life is ordered as an expression of the relation between them.

The distinction between spirit and body, transformed within the new cosmology as a differentiation between 'inner' and 'outer', is replicated within the soul itself. Even as subject, that is to say, man, as

a consequence of original sin, is divided against himself. Philip
Melanchthon, one of the earliest and most articulate of Luther's
followers, provides a brief description of 'human nature' as conceived
within reformed theology. It is, first and foremost, a descriptive
psychology and not a philosophical account of the nature of man. The
long love affair between theology and philosophy has, he claims,
finally come to an end. Philosophy, the great rationalizing tendency
within western society, has all but destroyed authentic religious
sensibilities, and has corrupted people's notions of a religious life. 'In
general', he supposes, 'whatever has been handed down in the
commentaries reeks with philosophy'.[101] He is as astonished as
Erasmus or Vives, that anyone should prefer to instruct the philosophically naïve or the spiritually unwise by using Peter Lombard's
Sentences in preference to original Scripture. This is just an example of
the extent to which we have deluded ourselves into believing a
rational faculty of the mind can be held to be responsible for our
actions.

In fact, claims Melanchthon, man is (internally) divided into two
parts. A cognitive faculty, by which 'we discern through the senses,
understand, think, compare and deduce',[102] and, opposed to this, or
rather indifferent to it, a faculty 'from which the affections (*affectus*)
arise', and through which 'we either turn away from or pursue the
things known'. This latter faculty, sometimes called the will (*voluntas*),
is quite separate from intellect and resists union with the intellect as a
substantive power of reason in man. Morality is, thus, an aspect of the
affections, as is Faith which is its foundation; so that, shifting the
whole axis of religiosity, he can claim 'virtue and sin belong to the
faculty of the affections'.[103]

The fundamental Christian 'category' is defined by the opposition
of faith and sin. But both classificatory terms are subject to historical
transmutation. Melanchthon, in one sense completing the social (but
not the ideological) movement of the Reformation, identifies faith
with virtue, and by implication defines sin as immorality. It is the will,
or better the 'heart', which is the seat of conduct and the object, or
otherwise, of grace. The doctrine of predestination is concerned only
with the 'heart'. As there is 'no power in man which can seriously
oppose the affections' and 'the will (*voluntas*) cannot itself control
love, hate or similar affections, but affection is overcome by
affection',[104] God judges the heart and its affections which 'must be
the highest and most powerful part of man'.[105] Given that we cannot,
by the natural power of the intellect, control and guide the affections,

it is only through faith that they may be guided by God's power.

The Reformers, thus, in spite of insisting that 'faith alone, apart from any act of ours, makes us religious, sets us free, and saves us', came increasingly to stress the centrality of Morality to Christian truth.[106] The intention, clearly, was not to reduce spirituality to secular morality, but to draw out and illuminate the authentic spirituality of moral conduct. The Moral life is, in a rather special sense, a 'sign' of God's grace. It gains its meaning as a *consequence* of faith, and it is in this context that the Reformers invested personal conduct with its deepest significance. Salvation is a supremely irrational and undeserved gift; 'He brings with Himself all felicity, and takes away all infelicity'.[107] But this gift can be sensed as the 'release' into a new freedom in relation to the Law. It is an internal liberation that brings in its turn the necessity of a new discipline to ensure that '*only* the word and faith exercise sway in the soul'.[108]

The fundamental religious opposition no longer coincides, therefore, with the inclusiveness and exclusiveness of society. It is not sufficient to be an obligatory subject of Christendom. As a qualification of the heart, sin is universal and Christianity, far from being a truth within which a community can reside in complacent self-confidence, is a Moral obligation in relation to which the most ardent believer is found wanting. Belief in Christ loses its positive rational or interior voluntaristic (Augustinian) connotations. The irrationality of Belief is its real foundation, and imposes the most stringent obligation. Luther remarks that faith exists only 'where I do not merely accept what is said about God, but I put my faith in Him, I surrender myself to Him'.[109] And Melanchthon, in this context, makes a particular point of distinguishing religious belief from philosophical opinion. The scholastic notion of faith, he suggests, is defined 'as the assent to what is set forth in Scripture', and cannot be distinguished in terms of its inner quality from assent to any other proposition.[110] But even 'the godless have this faith'. Faith is not to be confused with an 'opinion concerning belief'; if it were no more than that it would have the subjective character of an 'uncertain, inconstant, and fluctuating deliberation of a mind on the Word of God'; which is just what, phenomenologically, it is not.[111] Faith has the non-cognitive character of the heart, it is *trust* in God, and cannot be assimilated to reason. It is in this sense that faith is the transcendental ground of personal conduct, and the real source of the aura of sanctity which accompanies the actions of an upright individual.

PIETY

Righteousness was an unattainable ideal. To be 'free from any temptation and selfish desire' was an attribution of Divinity which could never wholly apply to man.[112] We are commanded nonetheless to imitate God and would fall into despair over our failure to do so if it were not for the saving grace of Christ. This solution liberates us into a new form of inner obedience. The fundamental commandment remains, however, as equally obviously does our failure wholly to surrender our will to it. Nothing outwardly has changed. 'God commands what is appropriate to his righteousness; but we are incapable of keeping his commandments', and in consequence 'we are duty bound at all times to live as pure, clean, unspotted and right as God wants it.'[113] The obscure relation between faith and Morality is loosely interpreted as a 'reduplication' of the former in the latter. But as faith is not immediately knowable, and natural reason is not a sufficient guide to rectitude, 'God must draw up for man in black and white an exhaustive and authoritative code of laws'.[114]

A lesser 'human righteousness' thus becomes our actually realizable goal. God has already offered us this dispensation. In recognition 'of our broken nature' He has enumerated for our benefit specific commandments beyond the absolutely general but impossible injunction to love our neighbour as ourselves.

A life, calm, well-ordered, obedient to secular authority, the disturbing passions contained and controlled by marriage and domestic responsibility, mindful of public duty and above all guided by private conscience, should be the realistic religious goal of every individual. Everyday life should be the scene of unexceptional devotional activity, rather than a 'background' from which 'real' religious rites in some sense 'stand out'.

The major leaders of the Magisterial Reformation were concerned primarily with key issues of doctrine, interpretation and, increasingly, church organization and government.[115] They nonetheless made clear that the new religious movement had a popular evangelical appeal which made consideration of everyday life, also, a central theological interest. Their criticism of traditional orthodoxy was couched in the language of corruption. It was the organization of the church, and the interests and values bred through its introversion, that obscured the scriptural truth from the ordinary people. Education was, indeed, vital, but less in terms of the enforcement of orthodoxy, than through a critical re-examination of the origins of Christianity and the recovery of the original Faith of the church. On the other side the Reformers were vehement in their opposition to radical sects who confused criticism of ecclesiastical abuse with criticism of established secular authorities and thereby posed a threat to the social stability and ordered world which, far from subverting, the Reformers sought to inculcate in the heart of the masses.[116] Even at their harshest, the withering remarks the Reformers directed at the conceit of the ruling princes were never intended to arouse their subjects to revolt. They taught resignation, and the acceptance of just punishment sent by God, as an integral aspect of the liberated conscience.

In terms of Morality the Reformers were cautious and conservative. Yet, paradoxically, it is just here that Max Weber, in a justly celebrated essay, found the beginnings of a radically new rational attitude towards both the secular and the religious worlds. The depth of the paradox exercised a particular fascination for Weber, and for many of the subsequent commentators and critics of his thesis. The Reformation appears to be the very opposite of a process of rationalization. Was it not responsible, in fact, for replacing the identification of religious transcendence as Belief with an ethical and evangelical faith which is inherently irrational?

Weber uses the term rationalization in rather different ways. In a purely formal sense it refers to a process of progressive internal purification. Social action (including systems of ideas) tends to become internally consistent, and to be formulated with increasing self-consciousness. In terms of western Christianity this means the development of propositions consistent with its primitive assumptions about the nature of God. In this formal sense Weber claims that Calvin's theology is, in fact, the logical terminus of western religiosity. It represents the most rigorous exclusion of all magical or secular elements. The absolute transcendence of God, and man's helpless dependence upon His freely given grace, are stated with uncompromising clarity and made the centre of a system of rigorous deductions. The fact that the Reformers attacked a scholastic form of Christianity should not blind us to the fact that, particularly in Luther and Calvin, doctrine was stated with unprecedented philosophical rigour. In another connected sense, however, the process of rationalization refers to a general development of secular culture and the eventual 'disenchantment of the world'. Increasingly the 'ends' of social action are conceived in non-religious terms and, crucially, the choice of means in relation to such ends is freed from all traditional constraints. Self-conscious calculation of efficiency becomes the *only* guide in the organization of a social life dedicated to nothing other than material production by continuously improving means.

In both senses the Reformation is rich in unexpected ironies. The Reformation appears to be nothing less than the self-immolation of western spirituality. In finally clarifying all the implications of the primitive assumptions of a monotheistic, salvation religion, the Reformation created a psychological situation in which, shorne of its magical consolation, Christianity actually becomes powerless and, quite rapidly, loses any social significance. Weber's argument hinges on the reconstruction of the religious and moral world of an ideal believer. Such a believer, he assumes, has psychological needs ignored or undervalued by Calvin. The new doctrine, for all its anti-intellectualism, is more logically satisfying than it is psychologically realistic. The believer finds himself isolated in the face of an omnipotent and omniscient God whose Will he can neither know nor effect. The doctrinal insistence on the notion of predestination plunges the individual into 'an unprecedented state of inner loneliness'.[117] The single most important piece of knowledge a person might possess concerns the ultimate status of his or her soul, the probability of acquiring Happiness. But, in principle, no one can know if they are of the elect or not. As the link between belief (in a medieval sense) and moral conduct has been broken, personal conduct cannot be used as a means to acquire salvation. The only route to salvation is faith; the individual is therefore morally bound to have faith.

Faith is recognized as an 'inner certainty'. However, and again in principle, there is no absolutely reliable, 'mechanistic', causal sequence leading from a sense of inner certainty to positive knowledge of election. The certainty of faith is really a 'sign' of its presence in the human heart, and can never be a *means* of acquiring salvation. It is, therefore, an unreliable 'indicator' of spiritual status. God's will is utterly inscrutable and no definite deduction in regard to it can be made from the 'evidence' of individual behaviour. Weber argues that the 'extreme inhumanity' of such a doctrine is, in practice, intolerable. The doctrinal rigour of the Reformers is quite rapidly softened in the preaching and pastoral care of the Reformed Churches. The notion of a sign of faith is easily corruptible. Would God grant faith without also granting eternal felicity? Surely the inner certainty of faith is, in fact, a reliable indicator of ultimate salvation? The rational urge to link ourselves to God by way of the mind rather than by way of the heart proves too strong a temptation for the intellectual self-restraint of Calvin's followers. The ethical freedom of the believer is transformed into a repressive obligation to ascetic ideals in personal life as the approved technique of acquiring and maintaining the inner certainty which *is* faith.[118] The religious value of salvation is transformed into an end which can become the object of rational calculation; and ascetic morality is the means best adapted to the pursuit of this end.

It is this critical switch from inner, incommunicable spirituality to a rational sequence of causes, which is central to Weber's insight. Commentators have, understandably, concentrated upon the consequences of this transformation for the development of capitalism. This, after all, is the ultimate aim of Weber's work. But a central part of this argument concerns a purely 'inner' transformation of the meaning of salvation. In becoming an end salvation takes on the character of an objective reality in relation to which means can be fashioned. The Reformation, to put it another way, has been only partially successful. Belief still precedes and conditions Faith. The Puritan accepts the truth of scripture and the tradition of Christianity as a quasi-intellectual assent to a set of propositions. In the light of this conviction faith becomes the most valued of any possible end, and asceticism the means by which this goal can be reached. The Reformers' progressive development of the notion of spirituality as beginning in faith as the unconditional trust in God, which liberates an inner spiritual and ethical freedom, and drenches secular conformity with the potency of a religious sign, proved too rigorous for the vast majority of Christians. They were simply unable to free themselves completely from the long tradition of religious superstition which had infected western Christianity almost since its inception. Ascetic practices, rather than ritual observance, in fact, became the focus for a magical acquisition of salvation.[119]

The critical change wrought by the Reformation was not the rationalization of religious means so much as the breaking with traditional magical means in favour of novel, but equally magical, techniques for possessing ultimate value. In principle, Weber makes clear, religious goals cannot be conceived as objective ends. However, the general demand, which is the peculiarity of modern society, to render *all* social action rational encourages this misrepresentation of religiosity. It is *in order that* it might be subjected to the same universal criteria of calculation as all other aspects of social life that the Puritan divines so quickly compromised the Reformation.

A common view of Weber makes of his thesis little more than a contribution to economic history. Religion, in this view, becomes a 'prime mover' in the sequence of changes that led from feudalism to capitalism. The implication of his work, however, is quite different. Religion, as the Reformers claimed, has a symbolic priority over any other sphere of activity. If religion can become the object of rational calculation then *any* other aspect of social life, with less difficulty, can become so. We might see this in the context of Durkheim's analysis of primitive religion. If religion is a primordial rule, a rule which makes all other rules possible, then the radical rationalization of all conventions must begin with religion.

In the 'social theory' indigenous to the Reformation strict theology gave way to practical piety as a sign of election. The apparently slight hermeneutical shift from conscience to piety as the 'natural sign' of faith proved to be momentous. It is not just that this implies a distinction between an inward and invisible state in contrast to a publicly observable code of conduct; the form of signification has itself undergone a change. For the Reformation theologian, conscience was a sign just because it was separate from, and lacked all causal relation to, the inward sufficiency of faith. But among the Puritans of a later generation piety gained the indwelling power of an efficient cause. Faith was inner certainty, and piety could quite easily be viewed as the uniquely suitable means to acquire, rather than remain the passive sign of, this subjective disposition. It is this interpretive shift, more than the specific code of conduct recommended by Baxter, Mather and others, which is the real significance of the Protestant Ethic. The Puritan revolution, in setting apart the subjectivity of faith, made it possible to conceive its unique value as a rational object.

The affinity, as Weber termed the relation, between the Reformation and the rise of Capitalism, is therefore quite direct. In terms of the cosmological picture which is common to both this is hardly surprising. In both, therefore, a tendency towards individuation is well defined. Even more significantly, in both, an absolutely ruthless subjection of all ends to the calculus of efficiency in relation to their means brought all forms of social action within a single 'rational' framework. The more specific *historical* argument made by Weber, that a definite causal relation can be detected between the Protestant Ethic and the Spirit of Capitalism, must be seen in this larger, and more firmly established, context. Weber does not deny the possibility of other relations being causally effective in the rise of capitalism, or of there being other consequences of both the Reformation itself or the Protestant Ethic. It is only because it is part of a larger and more important argument that his thesis became so important.

131

The distinction between the Reformation and Puritanism is critical. It is just at this point that the inner meaning of religious activities undergoes a profound change. The Reformation declared the recovery of faith as the singularly irrational mode of justification. Yet the Puritan fathers found in piety a means to attain faith and thus subverted the 'spirit' of the Reformation.

Piety was responsive to the psychological needs of the common believer. And as it was effective as a means of acquiring faith, it could, equally, become an exemplary mechanism for displaying the fact. The hidden inwardness of the faithful re-emerged, so to speak, as the pious conduct which united the community of the elect into a church. The subversive genius of the Reformation, its political radicalism, and its spiritual purity, were easily compromised. Salvation, certainly, could not be earned, but its possession could be displayed. The hierarchical and authoritarian community of the traditional church, far from dissolving, found a new principle of organization. Faith might be a secret relation with God, but, truly held, it manifested its presence in an invariably pious way of life.

The association, to which Weber rightly draws attention, between progressive social developments and Puritan ethics, thus hardened into a social religion which became a new Christian orthodoxy. Civil religion is here a badge of respectability, the common property of all believers and the sphere of higher values within which social divisions could be reconciled or even dissolved.[120] Its fundamental value was that of self-control, a forceful and difficult subjugation of natural appetites to the dictates of convention.

CHRISTIANITY AND BOURGEOIS MORALITY

The transition from Faith to Belief was an expansive, outward movement, the objectification of an inward and incommunicable trust in God as an ideal cosmological structure symbolic of the Divine plan of salvation. The inner and hidden world of Faith was projected on to, and reflected in, the natural order of both human beings and things. The collapse of this structure of Belief, in both its cosmological and social dimensions, was inevitably viewed as a religious crisis. The underlying coherence of nature, and the firm promise of personal salvation, were simultaneously threatened. But while the cosmological crisis was resolved, in principle, by embarking upon a long-term process of secularization, the foundation of social order and the longing for Happiness clung together in a continuing religious embrace.

It was a religiosity of a new sort. Not the groundless, irrational and diffuse subjectivity of Faith, but the well ordered coherence of Morality was established as the new and radical form of inner religious life. A new ordering principle, which was itself an implicit expression of a novel cosmological vision, emerged through the systematic inculcation within individuals of self-motivating and self-controlling mechanisms. In the absence of a wholly objective structure of social relations such mechanisms had to be instilled as the universal and predictable springs of conduct. Each individual had to become aware, not so much of a complete map of the world with his or her location fixed upon it, as of generalized rules, akin to grammatical rules, which would condition their action irrespective of the particular circumstances in which people found themselves. In this way an ordered and peaceful society would be generated from a multiplicity of individuated moral acts.

The transcendental character of Belief was, thus, transformed and internalized as new, universal and unconditional Moral demands. And all hope of Happiness lay in the complete absorption of the claims of Morality. Individuals sought, thus, to consume new values, to make the generative rules of the new society part of themselves.

In this process of transformation anachronistic remains of the cosmology of Belief were attacked as 'superstition' and 'magic', and the form of religious consumption shifted. Rather than make liturgical and sacramental rites the focus of periodic contact with an ultimate value, this value became permanently present as the inner prompting of conscience. And these rites were transformed into signs of what the individual conceived to be an inexhaustible inner-obedience.

The asceticism characteristic of the Reformation and its aftermath was, then, quite unlike older Christian traditions of self-denial. It was not conceived as the exclusive and exemplary ordeal of a spiritual élite, nor, as Weber pointed out, was it expressive of a rejection of the world. It embodied, rather, a new universal principle of human self-control in relation to a ceaseless human need to act within and transform the world. In this context the underlying significance of ascetic practices changed dramatically. In Weber's view the ascetic morality espoused by the followers of Calvin served to relieve them of the anxiety provoked by their strict adherence to a doctrine of predestination. But self-denial quickly attracted to it an additional, and non-doctrinal, efficacy as a means of acquiring the inner certainty of Faith, which was subsequently interpreted as a sign of election. In effect it became a new quasi-magical technique of gaining salvation.

The historic success of Puritanism, however, need not be interpreted as itself a sign, magical or otherwise, of *its* causal efficacy. The emergence of ethical religiosity can be relatively clearly understood within the context of the decline of feudalism, but somewhat more precariously in the context of the origin of capitalism. Weber, in fact, talks only of an 'affinity' between the 'Protestant Ethic' and the 'Spirit of Capitalism'. The historical significance of Puritanism he sees in the emergence of an ethic which could be adopted as a self-justifying ideology of entrepreneurial activity. When the *religious* revolution had run its course the resulting ethical ideals could easily be identified with the emerging bourgeois class and its own secular aims. It is this coincidence of consequences (rather than accidental alignment of causes) which leant weight to Puritanism as the locus of what was to become the 'bourgeois morality' of capitalist society.

The period during which Morality constituted the promise of Happiness was, in fact, very short. It was the religious hope of societies in transition from feudalism to capitalism. Once that transition was completed the need for Morality as the guarantor of social order became much less evident.

'The Puritans wanted to work in a calling', Weber reminds us, 'but we are forced to do so.'[121] Capitalism quickly acquired a necessity of its own, a necessity which was independent of the moral language in which it had first been described. Social order no longer depended on persuading each individual to do the right thing, to give up some element of his or her own sovereignty in the interests of collective life. A new rationality had emerged. Society was established and persisted by 'amoral' action, by individuals selfishly following their own interests and applying to their behaviour the same standard of reason that had been established in the struggle to understand nature. And if Morality as an extra-rational standard of conduct was superfluous to the organization of social life, could not religion (as the source of such a standard) finally be dispensed with as an archaic illusion?

5

PASSION: DESIRE FOR HAPPINESS

The development of capitalism seems to mark a decisive shift in the spiritual history of the west. However vital a part the purely religious transformation of traditional values played at its outset, the subsequent growth of capitalism as a civilization apparently stands apart from any religious interest. In the face of capitalism, religion appears everywhere to be in retreat, and it is only because every society carries along with it debris from its own past that religion, in some anachronistic form, survives the capitalist upheaval.

Christianity as a cosmology was (in principle at least) swept aside even before the scientific revolution proper eclipsed the feudal view of the world. Even more significantly, the organizing principle of the new society was found to be independent of those Moral precepts with which the religious movement had filled the transition. Rather than lay the foundation for an unambiguously secular culture, however, capitalism fostered a new type of religiosity, and encouraged a new and determined search for Happiness. The specifically capitalist form of religious transcendence was found in a process of 'self-actualization', as opposed to self-denial, in Passion rather than in Morality.

THE AMBIGUITIES OF SECULAR CULTURE

The immediate impact of capitalism was, apparently, to inspire a view of human nature which was remote from religious assumptions. The early entrepreneur might have found spiritual meaning in an ascetic style of life, and in an obsessive work habit but, once established, capitalism engineered its own secular mechanism for self-reproduction. Capitalism 'worked' by divesting individuals of all means of satisfying their needs other than through the exchange of commodities, and made the initial surrender of labour-time in exchange for a wage its foundation. This most basic of social relations, unlike those from which other societies sprang, appeared to be both entirely 'natural' and perfectly 'rational'. As all other means of satisfying needs had been suppressed the exchange of commodities seemed, magically, to appear in direct answer to an inner appetite. Individuals need not, therefore, be persuaded of the moral superiority of capitalism. A minimal assumption of rationality was quite sufficient to guarantee its stability. The simple generative principle of capitalism was the assumption that society was composed of free individuals able to sense their own needs and capable of calculating for themselves the best way to satisfy these needs; a calculation which would inexorably lead them to make the elementary contract upon which capitalism was founded.[1]

Given that orthodox religion had become identified, in the post-Reformation period, with Morality, and that capitalism, as a social order, had freed itself from moral constraint and instituted in its place a new universal and formal principle of reason as its inner spirit, it followed that religion had become superfluous. Religion ceased to provide either the cosmic framework, or the moral context, for the organization of social life. In this sense capitalism was the first great secular civilization.

Sociologists and historians, as well as contemporary theologians and ecclesiastical writers, have, of course, not been slow to point out the shortcomings in this schematic picture of the formation of a modern pagan culture of Enlightenment.[2] Even if we concede to the eighteenth century an optimistic confidence (subsequently abandoned) in the power of human reason both to account for and control the domain of nature, it is clearly the case that throughout the formative seventeenth century *scientific* endeavour, as well as social thought, was still driven by religious preoccupations.

It was, paradoxically, just when nature began to be conceived as a self-moving mechanism that natural theology came into its own. The more the scientific revolution revealed of the intricacy and interconnectedness of natural phenomena the more indispensable seemed to be the concept of God as the fabricator of such a refined piece of clockwork. The assumption of natural theology was quite distinct, however, to the scholastic reliance on the cosmological argument.[3] It was the *design* of nature, rather than the alarming infinity of its efficient causes, which brought the secular imagination to its limit.[4] And we need not assume, therefore, that there was anything hypo-critical or merely conventional in, for example, Robert Boyle's protestations of Christian virtue.[5] To study nature was a religious duty; in revealing God's design, we become conscious, in a new way, of His divine majesty. We could not, certainly, know God, but we could know his works. There was no contradiction between religion and science; the latter could only illuminate, for reason, the faith which was held by virtue of unearned grace. Science did not 'lead' to faith in the traditional scholastic sense of arriving by means of its own concepts at the necessity of God's Being. Science prompted faith, rather, by its own insufficiency. By itself reason not only failed to 'arrive' at God, more significantly, it could not even 'arrive' at nature. The most fundamental concepts of the physical sciences remained empty without religious assumptions. Indeed, Newton's purely formal definition of 'gravity' had been criticized by some as scientifically incomplete, let alone as spiritually unsatisfying.[6] Scientists, for the most part, were not philosophical radicals, and, finding the design of nature inexplicable, were content to invoke God as a transcendental cause of natural laws.

This new relation between science and religion is most often viewed from the perspective of the new freedom of scientific enquiry it justified and encouraged. The ultimate cause of nature, the meaning of its observable regularities, the character of its primordial totality and simplicity, were all deemed to be scientifically incoherent questions. All such issues could safely be left on one side. A rational understanding of the cosmos had essentially more modest aims, but in fulfilling these aims it effectively filled with scientific discourse the enormous gulf between our immediate experience of the world and the assumption of transcendental Being. What was equally significant, however, was the new autonomy this view simultaneously extended to the domain of religious discourse. The religious sphere was not simply a residue of (currently) inexplicable mysteries that in some sense lay, for the moment, beyond the reach of scientific enquiry. It was, from its own point of view, an expanding inward cosmos, an interior world as extensive and many-sided as the external relations of nature.

Scientific rationality could not account for itself; *its* possibility depended upon conditions whose meaning and significance served to reawaken religious consciousness. This was nowhere more evident than in attempts to describe the conditions of personal, inward experience. In the context of established and self-sufficient capitalism religious assumptions appeared to be irrelevant to the conduct of everyday life. And in the face of expanding scientific ambitions God became an infinitely remote cosmological figure. Simultaneously, however, religious reality was reconstructed as the very foundation of selfhood.

The possibility of Happiness, superficially available within the limits of secular, civil society, still depended, in fact, upon a transcendental relation. As compared to the transcending reality of Morality, however, new conditions of existence allowed, indeed they required, the complete internalization of this relation as self-identity. Passion, then, might be conceptualized as the transcendental relation *within* the self, or, rather, as the experience of the self as a transcending reality.

The new relation of selfhood, which is simply religious reality within capitalist society, was partially obscured by the secular optimism of the Enlightenment. Particular and varied experiences of pleasure, however, should not be mistaken for the absolute value of Happiness; and, in spite of its association with completely secular ideologies, it was as an absolute and indestructible value that the 'self' emerged within capitalist society.

The specific character of Passion within capitalism can be illustrated with reference to a variety of psychological traditions which reflected upon it. It is, thus, to psychologists and philosophers, rather than to self-confessed theologians, that we must turn for a description of its inner forms. Passion, as a specifically individual and inward reality, appeared (too easily) detachable from any specific institutional context. And psychology consequently seemed, at last, able to free itself from the difficulties of an older theological language. The most acute psychologists of Passion, however, remained sensitive to this older language and, implicitly or in some cases explicitly, sensed their dependence upon a pre-modern tradition of thought.

The relocation of Happiness – the shift from Morality to Passion – can best be illustrated, then, through the writings, in successive centuries, of Pascal, Rousseau and Kierkegaard.

LONELINESS

It is in Pascal that we find the first fully developed expression of the religious spirit in capitalism. Among the most gifted mathematicians and physicists of the seventeenth century, as well as one of its most incisive moralists, the unity of his thought is revealed in his uncompromisingly religious vision of the world.[7] The communal and hierarchical cosmos has been radically rejected, to be replaced 'by the totally different concepts of the isolated individual and of infinite space'.[8]

Yet nature, even where we can grasp its superficial coherence as a mechanical system, is, from a deeper viewpoint, fundamentally incomprehensible; 'Why is my stature what it is and the span of my life one hundred and not one thousand years?' he asks, puzzled by such an incomprehensible limitation.[9] 'Why did nature give me this span of life, choosing it rather than any other from out of the infinite number available, where no compelling reason imposed on her this choice rather than another?'[10] The *religious* problem of modern life is here revealed in relation to nature. As a system of mechanical relations nature (and its personal subjective equivalent the ego) is an autonomously functioning, and meaningless, bundle of relations. The spiritual value of existence is revealed, not by a mind which mirrors God's structural plan of the universe, but in the spontaneous movement of the heart, in self-affirming, extra-rational activity.

Pascal is fully alive to the post-feudal conception of reason as a purely *human* faculty. The greatness of man lies in his capacity for knowledge, and above all for knowledge of himself. In the infinitely extended universe man has no option but to fasten upon himself as the root of existence. He cannot see himself, that is, as part of a cosmos, a division within a Divine totality. He must rather look out from his own, limited, prison upon the world at large and seek within himself a comprehensible order. From this perspective human knowledge stands apart from the world which it reconstructs in conceptual form; and, inevitably, we feel a sense of loss for this greater world. In a wonderfully dense expression Pascal writes that 'Man's greatness comes from knowing he is wretched'.[11] The peculiar privilege of reason is the knowledge of its own limitation; its fall from the ineffable self-sufficiency of its primordial state. Pascal elaborates the point by way of a celebrated metaphor:

Man is only a reed, the weakest in nature, but he is a thinking reed. There is no need for the whole universe to take up arms to crush him: a vapour, a drop of water is enough to kill him. But even if the universe were to crush him, man would still be nobler than his slayer, because he knows that he is dying and the advantage the universe has over him. The universe knows nothing of this.[12]

Behind, or rather within, his nostalgia for the security of the old cosmology (authority and community) lies a more general unease. It is not just a sense of dislocation and disorientation, but of estrangement. In his wretchedness, which is the unique attribute of human being, resides an unquenchable aspiration to experience once again his original nature. 'If man had never been anything but corrupt', he points out, 'he would have no idea either of truth or bliss'.[13] But in fact, as science and morals attest, we have a conception of both, so that 'unhappy as we are (and we should be less so if there were no element of greatness in our condition) we have an idea of happiness but we cannot attain it'.[14] We neither know God directly, nor are we condemned to eternal ignorance of His nature. God is hidden, rather than revealed, in his creation. And though 'God has appointed visible signs in the Church so that he shall be recognized', he has so hidden them 'that he will only be perceived by those who seek him with all their heart'.[15] It is, therefore, in 'sincerity of heart' rather than in natural reason that Happiness is discovered. In spite of his afflictions 'man wants to be happy, only wants to be happy, and cannot help wanting to be happy'.[16]

The condition of unhappiness is due in part to natural limitations. By reason alone man cannot 'cure death, wretchedness and ignorance' and he consequently seeks diversion from the preoccupation of naturally gloomy thoughts.[17] People seek in 'some novel and agreeable passion which keeps them busy, like gambling, hunting, some absorbing show, in short by what is called diversion' the consolation of perpetual and thoughtless activity.[18] And Pascal, human in his rigour, admits 'they are not wrong to want excitement'.[19] In wanting distraction, however, they paradoxically seek the cessation of the very activities by which they have become obsessed.

Distraction is continuous movement in the pursuit of absolute rest. 'We seek rest', but 'rest proves intolerable because of the boredom it produces. We must get away from it and crave excitement'.[20] Distraction is a continuous oscillation between excited activity and lethargy; it is boredom. Pascal is, in fact, the first to recognize the central significance of boredom as the immediate condition of human existence in post-feudal society. Boredom is inherent in the secular individualism which is the only moral foundation of capitalism. Although it always disguises itself in the particularities of an individual malady, it is a quite general disease. 'Man is so unhappy' he insists, 'that he would be bored even if he had no cause for boredom, by the very nature of his temperament, and he is so vain that, though he has a thousand and one reasons for being bored, the slightest thing, like pushing a ball with a billiard cue, will be enough to divert him'.[21] Man's capacity for boredom reveals a boundless spiritual reality.

Boredom is infinite, no secular diversion can finally assuage its restless inner movement, and stem its ceaseless craving.

Left to himself man continues to generate, from within his own soul, an image of fulfilment which he cannot reach. It is the persistence of this authentic longing for Happiness that renders everything unconnected with it dull and lifeless. 'We are full of things that impel us outwards', that drive us to express our nature.[22] It is in this sense that 'Man infinitely transcends man'[23] and now that neither public beliefs nor the institutions of morality or conscience provide a medium of transcendence the human soul must fashion it from the psyche itself, from the materials of self-awareness. Thus 'our instincts make us feel that our Happiness must be sought outside ourselves. Our passions drive us outwards, even without objects to excite them'.[24] Yet our Happiness seems to depend upon the discovery and appropriation of suitable objects for this inherent tendency towards self-expression. Thus we readily discover objects in the world which can act as the apparently rational 'ends' which stimulate our passion. What Pascal calls distractions are just so many 'accidental' objects to which we attach this outward drive. But, in treating these accidents as the objective causes of our Happiness, we deceive ourselves, and feel more wretched than ever.

The secular world of endless and fruitless diversions can be interpreted as a sign. 'What else does this craving, and this helplessness, proclaim but that there was once in man a true happiness, of which all that now remains is the empty print and trace'?[25] But the objects that excite our futile and vain passions cannot fill the emptiness of the soul, 'since this infinite abyss can be filled only with an infinite and immutable object; in other words by God himself'.[26] The immediate knowledge we have of ourselves, therefore, is knowledge of wretchedness and inconsolable cosmic grief. The soul lies within us, as the power of reason and thought, but gives us no joy. Its presence is a perpetual irritant, a continuously tormenting reminder of how far we have fallen beneath an ideal state of bliss. The more, therefore, that we use the natural power of the soul to direct our own lives the more we obscure our true end and the more firmly are we rooted in its graceless limitations. 'Our soul is cast into the body where it finds number, time, dimensions; it reasons about these things and calls them natural, or necessary, and can believe nothing else.'[27]

Pascal, thus, fully aware of the genuine triumph of reason in reducing natural appearances to a comprehensible system of relations, fastens upon its inherent limitations as a means of self-knowledge. It is not the inner certainty of faith, so much as the lack of it, that is a sign of God's presence within us. Our incapacity fully to comprehend ourselves, to reduce our passions to the ordered logic of a 'system of nature', is the point at which the spirit impinges on consciousness. He rejects out of hand, therefore, the cruder forms of materialist psychology which utterly fail to leap the abyss between matter and soul. Alluding to radical Cartesian materialism, he remarks: 'When they say that heat is merely the movement of certain globules and light the *conatus recedendi* (centrifugal force) that we feel, we are amazed'.[28] It seems absurd to him that pleasure should become a mere 'ballet of spirits'. To Pascal, 'the feeling of fire . . . the reception of sound and of light, all seem mysterious . . . It is true that the smallness of the spirits entering the pores touches other nerves, but they are still nerves'.[29] And we perceive the world, not the movements of our nerves.

Both real knowledge of God and authentic self-knowledge begin with this failure of reason. We cannot conceive of either as an 'object' with definite characteristics, magnitude, position and so on, but as 'infinite' subjects, as inexhaustible reservoirs of feeling. We know God, therefore, in our hearts. In a famous phrase he tells us that 'the heart has its reasons of which the reason knows nothing; we know this in countless ways'.[30] This is just another expression for faith, which Pascal defines as 'God perceived by the heart, not by the reason'.[31]

It would be just as misleading to view Pascal's thought at this point as a continuation of the medieval mystical tradition, as it would be mistaken to see his practice of natural science as a simple development of medieval scholasticism. Both are new principles, adapted to the new post-feudal cosmology and the social logic of capitalism. This is particularly evident in Pascal's own brand of intellectual asceticism. 'We must love God alone and hate ourselves alone', he remarks at one point,[32] the deep paradox of his instruction less evident to us than he might have wished. The point is that 'love of God' and 'love of self' can, for the first time, become identical. Pascal goes further and deeper in his rationalization of Christian categories than does even Calvin. He expresses with unrivalled eloquence and intensity the 'unprecedented inner loneliness' of the individual face to face with God. He cannot protect himself from the new cosmos; 'the eternal silence of these infinite spaces fills me with dread', he says.[33] And he seeks to resolve this tension by identifying the self with God, and God with the self. 'Self-hatred' is only hatred of what the self has become in the secular world. Authentic selfhood requires an ascetic rejection of diversion as an empty and futile pursuit, as boredom. There is here an implicit distinction between the 'self' (authentic inner being) and the 'ego' (the superficiality of an immediate experience, an illusory self). To turn the self towards God, to long seriously for the unique object which is the self's authentic goal, is to realize the self as well as, or even rather than, to overcome the ego.

Pascal's rigorous asceticism initially seems to be at one with orthodox Calvinism. 'The indulgence of self-will', he claims, 'never yields us peace, even if it procures for us the full measure of our desires: but we have peace the instant we renounce it'.[34] This is an absolutely general rule. The 'ego' is inherently sinful; 'denying it, we can never be unhappy: indulging it, never happy'.[35] This, however, is not the end of the matter. In a passage, remarkable even by the standards of the *Pensées*, he insists that 'The true and only virtue is therefore to hate ourselves, for our concupiscence makes us hateful, and to seek for a being really worthy of love in order to love him'.[36] He goes on at once to point out, however, that 'as we cannot love what is outside us, we must love a being who is within us but is not our own self'.[37] The real object of our love lies within us: 'Now only the universal being is of this kind; the kingdom of God is within us, universal good is within us, and is both ourselves and not ourselves'.[38]

The deeper meaning of the Reformation is revealed in the discovery of God *within* the subject, as an internal relation. Salvation no longer depends upon man being an integral part of the cosmic design through which God reveals himself. Such a design still exists, but God hides himself within it; a concealment which, never quite complete, urges upon the human subject the necessity of completing himself in the external expression of the inward movement of faith. Pascal is deeply conscious of the religious implications in his acceptance of the new cosmology. For him, paradoxically, the infinite is a relation that subsists within the finite. Human subjectivity tends towards spiritual elevation by passionate self-reflection, and not by a process of reasoning about the natural world. The infinite is not approached through an inconceivable expansion of the soul through the cosmos, as if, like some kind of spiritual balloon, it can come close to God by encompassing His creation. The infinite, rather, is discovered within the limits of a particular existence, as its precondition. 'Thou wouldst not seek me, if thou didst not possess me', he points out without fear of contradiction.[39]

The interiorization of God need not lead, therefore, to a purely secular psychology. Pascal hardly thinks it worth discussing the mechanistic psychology of Hobbes or the possibility of its ethical extension into utilitarianism. God's existence in the heart means that the human affections can never be reduced to a rational order of calculative advantage. Thus, even for those (that is almost everyone) who do not realize this, 'man infinitely transcends man'.[40] This is true, and not only in an ultimate metaphysical sense that might be realized in a moment of divine illumination; it is the mundane reality of human psychology.

Man is a passionate creature. This follows necessarily from God's concealment within the soul. We are consequently driven, by externalizing its inner movements, to discover the soul's hidden aspect. The urge towards self-expression manifests itself as love, which is the permanent condition of the soul: 'Disguise it, in fact, as we will, we love without intermission . . . we live not a moment exempt from its influence'.[41] In continually seeking that which is hidden we are conscious of the enormous gulf between our immediate experience of ourselves and the self-generating image of perfect Happiness. It is this disparity which drives our passions outwards. If we truly possessed God alone we would dwell happily within ourselves. But as 'Man cannot find his satisfactions within himself only; and, as love is essential to him, he must seek the objects of his affections in external objects'.[42] Man seeks 'beautiful' objects to satisfy his longing for Happiness, and, 'as he himself is the fairest being that the hand of God has formed, he must look within himself for a model of those beauties which he seeks elsewhere'.[43] It is the power of his own soul, casting about it as it were an aura of attractiveness, which confers upon external things their quality of beauty. Only those objects which 'partake of his own resemblance' have the power to attract, and this resemblance is just a consequence of a projective externalization of our own image of ourselves. All love is, in fact, a form of self-love, 'all possess in themselves the original of that beauty which they look for externally'.[44]

'Man is full of wants', of deficiencies rather than of needs; empty, and incomplete, 'he loves only those who can satisfy them'.[45] And what he loves in another are just those qualities felt as lacking in himself: 'we never love anyone, but only qualities', those 'borrowed qualities' which reflect our own wants.[46] 'And if someone loves me for my judgement or my memory', he goes on relentlessly, 'do they love me? *me*, myself? No, for I could lose these qualities without losing myself.'[47] The *individuality* which connects the various qualities of the self is, in itself, incommunicable and cannot be loved directly by another or, indirectly, as the image of another. This individuality is formed as the infinite relation of internal divinity and cannot be externalized because, when and if it comes into existence, it is complete and lacks nothing. It has the quality of God-like self-sufficiency.

It is Pascal, rather than the Puritan divines, who, in relation to Reformation theology and the post-feudal cosmology, establishes the fundamentals of a new religious psychology. The solitariness of the individual soul, fixed arbitrarily between 'infinity and nullity' is estranged from itself. Jesus, who 'is alone on earth', and 'totally abandoned' by human companions, is a spiritual paradigm. He alone can tolerate authentic selfhood.[48] In its struggle to free itself from its own limitations (sin) the self projects itself into the world and seeks to realize its inner value in activity. It fails; and in substituting distraction for Happiness discovers the empty pleasure of the ego. The link between Belief and Morality is shattered. In a society made coherent through the interaction of private interests rationally pursued there are no essential social and ethical implications of Christianity. God's transcendence need no longer manifest itself objectively as a *rule* of life, and no conventional sign need connect everyday life to the inner reality of faith.

Pascal is, of course, an unconvincing radical. His principled individualism, just because it is conceived as a wholly inward relation, is harmless. He elucidates, indeed, the positive side of an asceticism originally conceived within the framework of a social religion. The overriding religious obligation is experienced as the drive towards self-realization, the urge to express ourselves in relation to an ultimate value which is wholly interior. This ethic has social consequences, rather than a social content, as a mechanism which imparts value to mundane objects. The spirit *within* capitalism, that is, does not simply suppress enjoyment of the world; it organizes and controls such pleasure. It makes of consumption, as well as, and increasingly in preference to, production, an act of genuinely spiritual significance. In consuming objects we complete the self which is an inward relation to a transcendent reality. Consumption is the means of acquiring ourselves, of taking possession of our own nature. We ought, therefore, to consume only what is most valuable in ourselves. Now, in fact, we cannot externalize this ultimate value and, therefore, according to Pascal, all consumption is futile and pleasure is inherently self-destructive.[49] But in the everyday psychology of the capitalist world the matter was understood less rigorously. If the world is attractive because it reflects the light of our own soul, then consumption, as a discovery of the hidden self, is dignified with a new religious significance. The profane psychology of capitalism is, therefore, more a corruption of Pascal than it is a misreading of Calvin.

The more ardently Pascal sought God, the more completely did he discover himself. After an intense religious experience in 1654 he tried with increasing desperation to rid himself of the burden of his own body and its secular appetites. In imitation of forms of self-negation which were no longer appropriate and which took him further away rather than nearer to his goal, he lived with increasing simplicity and austerity. Fearful that the world might ruin the state of intense spiritual tumescence which he longed to make permanent, he withdrew from society, became suspicious of affection, and abandoned the love of friendship which, at one time, in common with Montaigne, he had held to be the rarest and most precious movement of the heart.[50]

The coldness of the intellect became a coldness of the heart, and Pascal inflicted upon himself an introversion that through time intensified to psychotic withdrawal from the world. The inner loneliness, the realization of which is the beginning of faith, became self-justifying. Christianity was seen as a religion of loneliness, the absolute and irrational ground of the self, the discovery of which threatened to plunge the individual into an abyss from which there was no return.

Pascal's criticism of the everyday psychology of distraction and idle pleasure is transformed into an affirmation of the religious value of rigorous solitude. The triumph of interior selfhood, in ignoring the diversion of sociable pleasure, confirms the spirit in its majestic solitude. It is a movement from concealed to open solitude. The consolation of society is abandoned for the consolation of spiritual self-consciousness. It is a movement few cared to imitate. Pascal can, nonetheless, serve as the prototype of a new religious personality. He reveals the hidden heart within capitalism, the distinctively human interior world of the passions. Human beings contain within themselves an entire universe of feelings. In seeking to express the unity of this inner world they form links with the world, creating an objective existence from which they derive pleasure. In his analysis of everyday psychology Pascal is supremely realistic. The vast majority of people would never feel moved to seek anything beyond this world. Distraction, most of the time, is an adequate substitute for genuine spirituality. But in allowing ourselves to be distracted, in forming attachments to the world, and in consuming it, we are unconsciously following the prompting of a hidden reality and seek, futilely, to establish, within the welter of sensation, the image of ourselves.

The creation of the self becomes, therefore, the new religious task; the vocation which, in complete disregard of all traditional assumptions, we pursue as a duty and with a fervour which mark it unmistakably as a spiritual quest.

SOLITUDE

Pascal bears eloquent witness to the seventeenth-century distrust of reason at the very moment it had claimed its greatest triumphs. The more common sentiment, represented for example in Leibniz's synthetic rationalism, was to seek a new philosophical language within which Christianity would find its appropriate 'place'. Religion, it seemed, could be subsumed within the ever-broadening compass of the human mind, and become just one other aspect of liberated reason. During the eighteenth century this metaphysical ambition, though it had never in fact been fulfilled, was somehow conceived as already in the past and provided an apparently firm foundation for the rejection of all conventional religiosity. This was not simply the rejection of an outworn cosmological plan, nor yet an attack upon all forms of religious moralizing in the name of personal freedom, but the more radical abandonment of the Christian hope of personal salvation. Pleasure, not Happiness, was conceived to be the only 'natural' human end. And the turmoil of civil society, rather than being a distraction, was the real stage upon which the human passions were acted out.[51]

The self which emerged in a religious guise through the Reformation and found its purest expression in Pascal was redefined in a seemingly harmless, and wholly secular, form. The self referred simply to the coherent bundle of intentions activated within the rational individual in pursuit of his or her own private interests. The psychological mechanism underlying capitalism was nothing other than private interest and individual need. Secular psychology, however, like the formalism of the natural sciences, could not properly 'reach' its object. The ego detached from any religious assumptions of selfhood proved to be equally as elusive as had been nature separated from God. The paradoxical tendency of secular psychology throughout the eighteenth century, therefore, was to recreate, in spite of its ideological commitment to empiricism, an ineffable 'spirit' as the irrational ground of consciousness.[52]

The bourgeois critics of utilitarianism in ethics, and sensationalism in psychology, thus, contrary to their initial intentions, sought out a deeper level of reality to explain the otherwise fortuitous coherence of experience. In consequently dragging the hidden spirit within capitalism into the light, they inadvertently became the severest critics of just those bourgeois values they had sought, in the first instance, to realize; values, of individuality, self-expression and self-fulfilment, upon which the everyday world had only ever, in fact, conferred an abstract and theoretical reality.

Rousseau, as one of the most unrelenting critics of eighteenth century rationalism, and, like Pascal, impatient of all pious, moralizing and sentimental religiosity, begins his analysis of personal experience within modern society from, what is for him, the glaring discrepancy between conventional morality and the actual conduct of everyday life. 'We no longer dare seem what we really are', he complains.[53] The 'mass' condition of modern society reduces all diversity to a single conventional response, and as everyone appears in society as if performing on a stage 'we never know with whom we are to deal'.[54] There is, as a result, no sure means of divining their real intentions or feelings. The heart remains locked up within itself so that one becomes uneasily aware that 'Jealousy, suspicion, fear, coldness, reserve, hatred, and fraud lie constantly concealed under that uniform and deceitful veil of politeness'.[55] The disparity he feels so acutely is not a logical or metaphysical difference – the disjunction between object and subject – but the dislocation of appearance and reality. The superficial world of appearances which ought to depend wholly upon, and grow naturally out of, a rational ordering of relations beneath or within it, has somehow escaped to form an illusory substance of its own. And it is the very work of enlightenment that has produced this 'veil of politeness'. The 'boasted candour and urbanity, for which we are indebted to the enlightened spirit of this age' is nothing but a secular piety, a conventional form emptied of real content.[56]

It was 'the scandal of deceit' that was Rousseau's initial target. He wished to free himself of the encumbrance of all those conventional forms of social discourse which had become detached from, and obscured, the reality of an inward truth. Even in terms of secular morality the duty to unmask and unveil the truth of existence was an urgent task. It was a task that required, first and foremost, that the writer unveil himself. In writing about himself, therefore, and even more in living, or trying to live, in conformity with the image of himself he portrayed in his writings, Rousseau became the first hero of the bourgeois psyche. He lived, unfortunately, in an unheroic age whose only deeper truth was hypocrisy, so that his gesture appeared ridiculous, and, when it failed, even dishonest.

Rousseau, in attempting to bring into the open the hidden and secret parts of himself, was acting with fearless honesty. His fault, which was in turn to afflict every 'serious' individual within the bourgeois world, was honesty. He tried to become the very individual which he believed he ought to be, the individual which existed secretly within everyone and to which bourgeois ideology paid lip-service. 'Society', however, preferred its individuals to be images of each other rather than expressions of a unique inner selfhood. Rousseau complains bitterly, therefore, of public opinion and the hold it has over people's conceptions of themselves and their conduct. Of course we all claim to live, or claim at least that we want to live, as Jean-Jacques: 'with all the courage of my soul I sought to break the shackles of opinion and to *do* with courage what seemed to me good, without giving the slightest thought to the judgment of men'.[57] Solitude is, for the capitalist age, the most basic of all ethical demands; it is the insistence on 'being free and virtuous, superior to fortune and man's opinion, and independent of all circumstances'.[58] We should disregard the opinion of others, even when, or especially when, it appears to come from within ourselves. We must be especially wary, therefore, of the inward prompting to virtue. Neatly turning Reformation piety on its head, he boldly declares that 'conscience is the vice of the soul'.[59]

To pierce the veil of conventional morality it is necessary only to recollect the history of the self, to observe the 'train of secret emotions' which formed the soul into the condition in which it now finds itself. Rousseau's is the first genuinely modern autobiographical project. Recollection is the 'method' through which the truth of the self emerges and becomes real. Following the train of recollections back to its earliest source Rousseau discovers a primal world of innocence, a paradise, unclouded by the deceit and dishonesty of society.[60] The unrestrained liberty of this world, its inner freedom, and at the same time its magical unity, its 'transparency' to thought, affected him deeply. All our later life, spent in false and wasteful diversions, is only so many failed attempts to reconstitute this spoiled paradise. The real object of our search, the search instituted in the disclosure of the gulf between appearance and reality, is the enraptured primal world. It is this primal world which constitutes, through recollection, the genuinely transcendental reality within us, and which conditions all our later experience. As 'true joy defies description', it cannot be fully recaptured, but as the intuition of Happiness it is permanently lodged in the heart.[61]

Rousseau, thus, absorbs the religious mythology of the Fall into his own biographical history and gives it a purely personal significance. At the beginning of his moral history stands the recollection of injustice. He was falsely accused of breaking a comb. His protestations of innocence were to no avail; he was not believed, and the transparent world of childhood was consequently shattered.[62] The incommunicable inner truth of his own experience was suppressed beneath the (more powerful) web of appearances which was spun from the rational convictions of adults who assessed the 'objective' evidence. Thereafter Rousseau finds himself drawn into this objective and deceitful world. The Fall is reinterpreted as a self-generated movement out of nature. It is experienced primarily as the birth of pride and, flowing from pride, the power of reflection and self-deception. After that actions become self-regarding in the narrow sense of supporting the pride which feeds upon the expectations and approbation of others. 'Selfishness perverts innocent love of self (*amour de soi* as opposed to *amour-propre*), vice is born, and society takes shape'.[63] The gap between appearance and reality is reflected in the 'ever-growing disparity not only between ourselves and the outside world but between ourselves and our own inner nature'.[64]

It is subordination to appearances (to society) which creates within him a host of 'artificial' desires.

> For his own advantage he had to make himself appear other than he really was. Appearance and reality became two entirely different things, and from this distinction arose insolent ostentation, deceitful cunning, and all the vices that follow in their train.[65]

It is this distinction and the subsequent growth of pride that 'explains not only the inner division of civilized man but also his subjugation to limitless desires'.[66] The continual renewal of want does not spring from nature; its ubiquity, rather, is a sign of man's attachment to the artifice of society. 'Desire is not a physical need; it is not true that it is a need at all.'[67]

Rousseau, thus, espoused the *immediacy* of the primal world against the illusions of society. To inculcate its virtue in others he withdrew

150

from society to lead an exemplary life of solitude. Society was the negation of authentic selfhood, the negation of nature; and Jean-Jacques must therefore negate society in order to reclaim the primal world concealed within the hectic passions of civil society. 'Rousseau made himself a stranger to men in order to protest against the alienation that makes men strangers to one another – a paradox for which he is still criticized.'[68] And it was only after he had freed himself 'from the social passions and their mournful train' that he was able to rediscover nature in 'all her charm'.

The primal world had slipped from his grasp, and what was left was an intuition of the Happiness which might be gained in overcoming the frivolous passions of social life. The world of the passions is inherently chaotic and self-destructive. Reflecting, towards the end of his life, on his own emotional history he despairs of grasping the reality of Happiness:

> Everything is in constant flux on this earth. Nothing keeps the same unchanging shape, and our affections, being attached to things outside us, necessarily change and pass away as they do . . . Thus our earthly joys are almost without exception the creatures of the moment . . . And how can we give the name of happiness to a fleeting state which leaves our hearts still empty and anxious, either regretting something that is past or desiring something that is yet to come?[69]

Happiness must be, in contrast, a state of rest and tranquillity, 'a state where the soul can find a resting-place secure enough to establish itself and concentrate its entire being there . . . where time is nothing to it . . . and no other feeling of deprivation or enjoyment, pleasure or pain, desire or fear than the simple feeling of existence, a feeling that fills our soul entirely'.[70] It is this state of 'fullness', of absence of desire or 'want' of anything beyond himself, that he experienced in his retreat on the island of Saint-Pierre. There, during his solitary reveries, he felt himself to be in a state of 'pure' and unmixed existence, 'self-sufficient like God'.[71] His heart was finally at peace, 'its calm untroubled by any passion'.[72]

It is necessary (and indeed sufficient) to cast off society to rediscover God within the soul. The social world is constructed, not directly from the interior selves of those who make it up, but through the mediation of a reflective logic and of affections which obscure the real nature of its individual members. In living through these relations man has become a stranger to himself. And by allowing himself the compensations of pleasure in these superficial relations he has rashly thrown away his only chance of genuine Happiness.

Salvation, that is to say, depends neither upon theological dogma nor upon conventional virtue, both of which belong to the alien world of society; it rests simply upon 'giving way' to the prompting of the heart. This is no easy *rule*, for everything tends to obstruct such a surrender. The heart, like anything else in the world of endlessly circulating passions, is never known directly. Its inclinations are always truthful but often appear to the normally socialized self in the guise of rational intentions, as the inner-prompting to all those activities which accumulate social honour. In patient solitude and reverie, however, the self is divested of all surplus affections and attachments. All our rationality makes this surrender difficult, and leaves us trapped in a set of social and conceptual relations which organizes our internal world according to its own, alien, rules. 'Thinking has always been for me a disagreeable and thankless occupation', Rousseau claims, but in reveries 'my soul roams and soars through the universe on the wings of imagination, in ecstasies which surpass all other pleasures.'[73] In such a state 'of blissful self-abandonment' the individual 'loses himself in the intensity of the beautiful order, with which he feels himself at one'.[74] The contemplation of nature's primordial state, which is really a merging with and participation in its unity, is quite distinct from the act of conceptualization, which separates and divides consciousness from the world; 'all individual objects escape him; he sees and feels nothing but the unity of all things'.[75] In blissful indifference, 'my ideas are hardly more than sensations now, and my understanding cannot transcend the objects which form my immediate surroundings'.[76]

The recovery of the primordial world *is* Happiness for Rousseau. He began with the ambition to awaken all to a universal salvation. 'I could be happy only in the happiness of all and my heart was never touched by the idea of a private happiness, until I saw my brothers seek their own happiness in my misery.'[77] He could neither deflect nor resist the corrupting power of the social order and its hectic passions. While he sought to make his voice heard among his fellow citizens, 'my entire being was in things that were foreign to me, and in the continual agitation of my heart I felt all the instability of human life'.[78] The artificial world of society oppressed him, and filled him with the demonic passions that obstructed the path leading back to the transparency of the primordial world.

152

Salvation is merely the realization of a state of inner tranquillity which already exists but is veiled by the necessary commotion of social life. But Rousseau claims to have learned 'to bear the yoke of necessity without complaining',[79] and in his voluntary withdrawal from society to find the real object of his search. He is 'reduced to my own self', an ultimate and inextinguishable value. This authentic self, like the object of religious value, is an unquenchable fount of life. It is an endlessly consumable value. Thus, it is true 'that I feed on my own substance, but this does not diminish and I can be self-sufficient even though I have to ruminate as it were on nothing'.[80]

The social world yet remains an inescapable evil. Human beings, inevitably feeling its wants stirring within them, cannot help but become its victims. They cannot settle for the genuine self-love which nourishes the instinct for preservation; rather, continually expanding beyond themselves, they are caught up, and lost, in the infinite web of selfishness. Rousseau admits, even after he has tasted its sweetness, that 'happiness is a lasting state which does not seem to be made for man in this world'.[81]

Rousseau's insecure Happiness is modelled on the exemplary and wholly successful solitude of Christ. It is not the philosophical meaning of the claim of his Divinity, so much as the human courage to become himself, which Rousseau regards as significant. For Rousseau 'the essence of Christianity lies in the preaching of a truth that is *immediate*'.[82] Christ's words are not to be analysed, they are simply part of his example, his witness, which directly affects the heart. Christ's presence, unlike the works of his modern philosophical critics, is effortlessly illuminating. Rousseau's contemporaries had reduced Christianity to nothing other than organized prejudice, a 'false consciousness' in which the evident injustice of naked interest was disguised. But this criticism, however much it might be an accurate indictment of the church, robbed man of any hope of genuine Happiness. Rousseau longs for Happiness; he passionately desires to be released from (secular) passion, and to discover Passion's real object. He takes God into himself and seeks to authenticate his own existence as His witness; that is, as a witness to himself alone.

Rousseau found, as by a different route had Pascal, a way of completing the Reformation. In the radical rejection of all mediators between the self and God, Christ may be dispensed with as a sign of Divinity, and becomes a Socratic genius, a teacher, who directly rouses the heart to its own inner reality. God is felt, inwardly and directly, as the absolute self-sufficiency of the self which spills over into the 'transparency' of primordial nature. Mediation (philosophy) is foreign to Happiness, and there can be no signs of salvation; 'happiness cannot be detected by any outward sign and to recognize it one would need to be able to read in the happy person's heart'.[83]

Rousseau expresses a subjective Christianity which is rather different to that of Pascal. Both find in a purely natural religion insufficient grounds for any rational system of Belief, and see in this limitation the real starting point of religious inwardness. But where Pascal seeks the self enraptured by its own transcendence, Rousseau holds on to an intuition of primordial reality freed from sin. He seeks nature *before* the fall rather than the piercing love that redeems it from corruption. Pascal's spirituality is tensed to breaking point; he is stretched, impossibly, between the finite and the infinite. Rousseau, in contrast, relaxes into solitude. Their rejection of natural theology, and of conventional piety appears similar, as is their flight from society into the seclusion of the study and the woods; but, from another viewpoint, they propose quite different solutions to the religious problem of capitalism.

Pascal confronts the new scientific cosmology squarely; and accepts it. More than that he admires its precision and potential completeness. But he knows its limitations. And he makes the hidden reality of the new world the resting place of his spiritual values. God is concealed in order to be preserved. He hides for his own protection. Rousseau, however, invokes a cosmology which, although it coexists with both, is neither scientific nor modern.[84] The vision of a primordial reality, which Rousseau is the first to associate directly with the experience of childhood, is nostalgia over a vanished world. The Platonic Christian tradition of separation and return is given an entirely new interpretation as an autobiographical journey from childhood innocence into adult sin, and thence to the hope of redemption in the recollection of our original and universal transparency.

The Christian mythology of creation is given fresh psychological depth as the ideal history of the self. But for both Rousseau and Pascal authentic selfhood is an entirely inward relation in which the immediate experience of the world, as an alien landscape of lifeless objects, is overcome in a process of demystification which strips appearance of every claim to independence. Rousseau is overwhelmed by recollection, by its ceaseless and boundless energy which continually 'breaks the bonds which confine it'. The infinity of God is transposed, through recollection, into a personal, interior infinity which 'the whole universe does not suffice to contain'.[85] The inner richness of human subjectivity cannot be directly voiced, even to oneself, and Rousseau is consequently forced to abandon the illusory intimacy of an authorial *I*: 'thy sentiments, thy desire, thy anxiety, thy pride itself, have another origin than this small body in which thou art imprisoned'.[86] To sense the incomprehensible immediate unity of nature, and dwell momentarily in its purified existence, is to *possess* the self, and to *consume* its inexhaustible variety.

The interior world is consumed without being diminished, indeed, it expands as it is consumed. Experience feeds off its plenitude. Genuinely inexhaustible, the self consumes itself by love. Innocent self-love enhances and expands the interior space of experience. Where an earlier age had talked of love of God as a surrender to the continuous outpouring of His divine love, as *agape*, Rousseau fashions a new language of selfhood in which these very qualities of transcendence come to characterize the soul. Self-love becomes the first principle of spirituality. God and self become identical, and neither, therefore, can be intellectualized as principles or categories. It is an immediately felt identity: 'it is, and that is enough for me; the less I understand the more I adore'.[87]

The problems of Morality are all problems of personal conduct, and they dissolve in moments of transparent bliss when the self, stripped of its social passions, becomes visible. Rules of conduct are not to be deduced from some abstract, axiomatic system: 'I do not derive those rules from the principles of the higher philosophy, I find them in the depths of my heart, traced by nature in characters which nothing can efface'.[88] The heart is never deceived, although it may be clouded by the affections and needs placed over it by social artifice. Accorded the freedom it needs to make itself felt, the heart is an infallible guide. Thus, 'our first duty is towards ourself', and it is only the complications of social life which have created the moral complexity which exhausts our conscience and colours every action with doubt.[89] However, even although, 'the decrees of conscience are not judgements but feelings', surrendering to them is no guarantee of justice. We may act spontaneously and honestly in conformity to our innocent feelings, but others, relying on the insecure evidence of language and reason which must always form a web of alien objective relations, around and within us, may nonetheless judge us to be guilty. Right conduct is no protection, in our society, against injustice, because language, which is the foundation of social life, is itself infected with corrupting passion.

Rousseau wrote his *Confessions* to correct the misjudgements of others, not to recollect a past which might otherwise be forgotten. But conventional moralizing plays no part in its plan. It corrects by abolishing, or attempting to abolish, the distance which rational discourse establishes between an author and his or her readers; a distance which originates in the conventional separation social life imposes upon individuals. Although its subject is unique, the peculiar and individual life of Jean-Jacques, its intention is not in the least egocentric. It aims, rather, to abolish the ego, to draw others close to him, to at once confirm the self which his solitude has allowed to grow, and abolish the loneliness which has been the only means of bringing it into existence.

Morality, he reveals, is no more able than Belief to furnish us with an objective reality in relation to which we might define ourselves. Happiness can be reached, in fact, only by the most determined opposition to either such illusory path in the inward liberation of the individual's primitive selfhood.

DESPAIR

Pascal and Rousseau chart the interiorization of Christianity in the post-feudal world. Neither, however, furnishes the new inner world of subjectivity with its definitive *bourgeois* expression, and it is to the writings of Søren Kierkegaard that we must turn to witness the authentic spiritualization of the modern ego.

Pascal, totally mastering and acutely conscious of the inherent limitations of the new rational cosmology, sought spiritual illumination in the heightened inward tension provoked in reflecting upon these limitations. The feudal hierarchy had been completely swept aside, but, rather than finding themselves at home in a newly defined universe, human beings continued to confront the otherness of God. The human and the Divine, no longer held apart spatially, all the more obviously constituted the intimate strangers, the incommensurable antitheses, of the inner life. A point of 'infinite inwardness', God, and thus the real self, remain unreachable. The nearest secular approach to Happiness is, thus, to feel the unbearable anguish and spiritual terror of the infinite. The human subject for Pascal is empty. Rousseau, on the other hand, finds his image of the subject in the actual content of childish and primitive consciousness. It is completely filled by the totality of nature. The enchantment of the primordial world, which is the universal experience of childhood, is a permanent but suppressed presence within the rational world of capitalism.

For both the bourgeois ego is the point of departure, rather than the *telos*, for a new religious sensibility. Pascal discovers an absolute but empty individuality, and Rousseau seeks to realize himself by letting his individuality slip from him in the recollection of a simple existence in the midst, and as part, of an undivided world of nature. Kierkegaard, however, mounting both a religious attack on the conventions of everyday life, and a psychological critique of orthodox religious life, found in the bourgeois ego itself the untapped spiritual potential of the age.

He expressed as uncompromisingly and as eloquently as Pascal or Rousseau a distrust of that tradition of rationalism which, intoxicating the *philosophe* even more than the natural scientist, had hardened into a purely intellectual instrumentalism.[90] In this context Kierkegaard levelled his attack at a new and more formidable opponent. Hegel's *Phenomenology*, by the time Kierkegaard became a writer in the early 1840s, had established itself at the centre of the intellectual world. Not only philosophers, but theologians, social critics and imaginative writers all looked to Hegel, and to the *Phenomenology* in particular, as the complete realization of the aims of the Enlightenment.[91] His history of 'spirit' had announced, apparently, the real vindication of philosophy. The religiosity of previous ages was assimilated to a universal development which terminated in Hegel's own philosophy. The entire dialectical movement of spirit, which Hegel's philosophy described, was itself the underlying reality which had brought forth that very system of thought. Hegel's philosophy, therefore, was at once the culmination of religious thought, and its secularization. In it religion was completed and became self-conscious.

Kierkegaard's radicalism was in complete opposition to the tendency of Hegel's philosophy. Christianity, in his view, was not, and never could become, an 'object' of philosophical thought. Any attempt to assimilate Christianity to the laws of thought was fundamentally mistaken; and in opposition to all such attempts he proclaims that 'Philosophy's idea is mediation – Christianity's the paradox'.[92] It is not simply that the two are incommensurable ways of thinking about the world – Christianity is not a 'mode of thought' at all. In describing Christianity Kierkegaard, of course, makes use of all the logical and philosophical means available to him (and he uses them with uncanny assurance); but this is forced upon him by the limitations of writing. In *representing* Christianity we always run the danger of turning it into an object of pure speculation, which is, in fact, the worst kind of misrepresentation. Kierkegaard tirelessly insists, therefore, 'that Christianity is not a doctrine . . . Consequently (since Christianity is not a doctrine), it is not a matter of indifference'.[93] And he takes an almost perverse delight in advertising its *paradoxical* character. We can represent it, most generally, as contradiction, absurdity, madness;[94] and it is only one of its minor paradoxes that Kierkegaard, in expressing this vision of a purely religious truth, should become one of the most philosophically gifted writers of his age.

The distinction between Christianity and philosophy is not that between two disciplines which are about different things and therefore, properly understood, have nothing to say to each other. There is between them, rather, a fundamental opposition, an antagonism which can never be resolved. By their very presence they confront the modern individual with an inescapable *Either/Or* – either the endless sequence of causes discovered by the natural scientist and made abstract and complete by the philosopher; or the irreducible dichotomies of existence. Kierkegaard's complaint is not only that the philosopher misjudges religion but that, in doing so, he loses reality.[95] The philosophical method, in which every reality finds its place within a system of mediation, is necessarily abstract. But we do not experience our own lives as abstractions, as parts of any philosophical system. We are only too acutely aware of the limitations and constraints of our actual existence. Mediation is not open to us; there are many things we cannot do. But the philosopher has unlimited power within his system of abstractions. He can move, ideally, from any starting point to any other, arbitrarily chosen point, without contradiction, without invalidating the grammatical rules of his system. Life, represented philosophically, is thereby likened to an arithmetic manipulation, or to a linguistic game. Not only Christianity, but all forms of actual existence, in themselves resist such systematic idealization. Christianity possesses this quality of irreducibility to an infinite degree; but all our experience is similarly composed of incompatible elements.[96]

The only valuable unity, in complete distinction to the abstract totality of the most refined of philosophical systems, is constituted by the existence of a 'single individual'.[97] *Either/Or* is a challenge to philosophy, not only because it refutes the complacent idealism of conventional bourgeois moralizing (in this regard, in fact, it is rather timid), but because it uses the most elevated of philosophical discourses, and the most objective and complete form of human knowledge, to express a purely personal truth. The ultimate aim of his writing is to edify, to arouse the singularity latent in the mass consciousness of modern society. And it is to this 'single individual' that all his works are implicitly addressed.[98] The lack of transparency in human communication renders futile a direct approach to this task. Obscurity, thus, is not, as it is for Rousseau, primarily a matter of personal regret, but, rather, the point of departure for a new *maieutic* (literally 'obstetric') art.

Kierkegaard's urge to explain himself to Regine and the world is conditioned by the even greater urge to arouse others to higher states of subjectivity and individuality. And it is controlled by Kierkegaard's clear understanding of the difficulty (amounting for practical purposes to an impossibility) of direct communication. Christ alone 'reveals the thoughts of the heart' which remain hidden to others, and even to the self.[99] We cannot easily become conscious of ourselves. It is pure philosophical conceit to assume the self develops by some ineluctable historical and biographical process. It is all too obvious to Kierkegaard that in contemporary society, self-consciousness is the curse of false-hood and deception, and that no amount of 'preaching' can rectify the situation.

Kierkegaard resorts therefore to indirect communication, to a whole series of works written under a number of pseudonyms, with the express purpose of deceiving the reader into the truth he would be unwilling to accept if presented with it directly. He begins therefore, in relating his own spiritual development, with a descrip-tion of personal existence under 'aesthetic' categories. The *Either* of *Either/Or* presents such an individual, that of the 'young man' who conceives of his life solely as a pursuit of pleasure. Every activity is motivated and judged by its capacity to bestow sensuous gratification. His whole existence is organized around the polarities of pleasure and unpleasure. The paradoxical result is a life of boredom. The 'young man', consequently, 'hovers over existence', he lives immediately and all his energies are dissipated in fruitless diversions. He is caught up in a self-defeating cycle of attraction and disillusionment. Nothing can hold his attention for long, nothing is capable of bestowing upon him more than a temporary pleasure. The tone of his life oscillates between lethargic withdrawal and frenzied activity. He is the victim of periodic fits of enthusiasm which, after a time, lapse and leave him more dejected than before. His personality is consumed by immediacy, by disorganized and accidental relations to the outside world, and 'loses itself in the multifarious'.[100] Gifted with extraordinary intellectual powers, and sensitive to every new artistic and literary movement, he is yet incapable of enjoying anything because as a self he has no more than a precarious existence in each momentary project. He lacks the coherence of a definite personality, that biographical consistency and persistence in time, which is essential to any more substantial pleasure. In identifying himself with immediacy he takes on the character of the world of appearances, and becomes estranged from himself, his personality is veiled and mysteriously inaccessible to himself. His spirit is no more than a potential reality.[101]

Pascal, schematically, and Rousseau, with considerable weight of circumstantial detail, had provided similar descriptions of the superficial forms of bourgeois egoism. Kierkegaard, however, quite apart from making his criticism the more telling by portraying the 'young man' as a genuinely attractive figure, makes this the starting point for a series of existential 'repetitions' unanticipated by his predecessors. The 'young man', failing to find pleasure, despairs. And despair, rather than intellectual doubt, is the beginning of authentic self-revelation. 'Despair is the doubt of the personality',[102] and when the 'young man' begins to 'despair seriously' he is, in reality already beyond despair.[103] Despair deepens experience and opens up a gap between the self and immediacy. And this is not a process of abstraction; quite the reverse, for it makes more concrete the individuality which had existed hitherto as a mere *possibility* that continually escaped into volatile and insubstantial projects.

There is, in spite of its groundless irrationality, a certain logic to despair; its every expression tends to intensify rather than to relieve the burden. Kierkegaard rejects, however, the notion of an inner dialectical necessity driving the personality beyond the aesthetic. Despair will bring the 'young man' to a point of ironic detachment, to an aesthetic recognition of the limitations of aesthetic existence, but no further.[104] *Or*, written apparently by an older friend, Judge William, is addressed to the 'young man' from an altogether different existential position. The judge lives under 'ethical' categories. His life is bounded by the polarities of good and evil, and his entire existence is subsumed under a purely ethical determination towards the good. From this standpoint he urges the 'young man' to make the 'repetition' out of aesthetic despair. In subsuming his pursuit of pleasure under an ethical value he will discover, the judge assures him, that 'nothing is lost'. The ethical defines the self in a more developed form: 'He who chooses himself ethically has himself as his task, and not as a possibility merely, not as a toy to be played with arbitrarily'.[105] It extends the self in time and gives it a purpose and a meaning beyond immediacy. It is just this condition which, in fact, makes aesthetic pleasure available to it. All those aesthetic experiments which failed when pursued for their own sake suddenly appear in an alluring new light. It is only in abandoning the aesthetic that pleasure becomes possible. The solution to the contradiction of immediacy lies beyond it. This, of course, to the person trapped in the immediate, sounds like a piece of philosophical sophistry. No amount of reasoned argument or moral exhortation can make the aesthetic individual desert immediacy in favour of what appears, from their point of view, to be no more than an illusory good. The movement of repetition, if it is to take place at all, must be self-willed. The choice of the ethical is not a choice of the good rather than the evil, but a choice of life determined by ethical rather than by aesthetic categories.[106] This transition, whatever necessity can be traced in its antecedents, is effected by an irrational 'leap'.

Ethical individualism is not, however, a solution to all the problems of existence. Ethical categories impose an inescapable obligation upon individual action. But, however much the good is made the object of action, the effects flowing naturally from every act cannot be rationally foreseen. The consequence is that the ethical sphere is coloured by guilt in the same way that the aesthetic sphere is coloured by boredom. Guilt is a higher form of despair than boredom or irony and makes ever more determined and concrete the specific characteristics of the despairing self. Guilt, Kierkegaard claims, reveals the self to the ego; 'so the essential consciousness of guilt is the first deep plunge into existence'.[107]

Either/Or is written indirectly and 'without authority'. In tracing, as it were from the inside, an existential map of personal life in the modern world it captures the attention of the reader and carries him or her forward to a point of decisive choice. In it Kierkegaard adopts the 'incognito' of a brilliant writer, but his real intention is not literary. Simultaneously with its publication he brought out, under his own name, the first of a series of *Edifying Discourses* which addressed the problem of becoming a Christian in a direct manner. They were written from the Christian viewpoint which was suppressed for the purposes of his *maieutic* art in the pseudonymous works. Yet even in his direct works Kierkegaard could not speak with authority. The powerful intuition of another 'sphere' of existence beyond the ethical, and of the redeeming power of this second 'repetition' fired his imagination with unrivalled spiritual eloquence. He could not, at that time make the final repetition into purely 'Christian' categories.[108]

Like Pascal and Rousseau, Kierkegaard experienced a heightening of religious sensibility through social isolation. His failure to marry Regine, which was the purely personal reason for his becoming an author and adopting an incognito through which he might, in spite of everything, explain himself to her and eventually to the world, exaggerated his melancholic longing for solitude and precipitated the crisis from which his wholly Christian writings emerged. His pseud-onymous works are, however, complete. They present a philosophical and psychological account of the Christian conversion he was later to experience as a direct spiritual shock. And in so far as it might be understood the religious exclusiveness of his last years must be grasped through the works written earlier for a non-Christian audience.[109]

The central problem is clearly presented in *Fear and Trembling* which immediately followed the *Either/Or*. The guilt of the ethical deepens to a point where the 'leap' into religious categories can take place. Kierkegaard illustrates the possibility through the story of Abraham's faith. For his faith Abraham is willing to sacrifice his son. From a human point of view this is indefensible, yet he is saved by his faith which is a 'teleological suspension of the ethical'.[110] Religion, that is to say, is a mode of existence which is 'beyond' ethics in the same way that the ethical is 'beyond' the immediacy of the aesthetic. And just as pleasure is accessible only from within the ethical, which absorbs and preserves immediacy, so the ethical is taken up and preserved in faith. Faith risks everything; all values are subsumed within it. Abraham is saved, not by sophisticated moral calculus which presents a point of view from which the sacrifice is conceived as right, but by a miraculous grace.

Religion, that is to say, has no more to do with Morality than it has to do with science; it is radically irrational. In both a logical and a moral sense, then, Christianity is an *offence*, and it is just this offence which is 'the Christian weapon of defence against "speculative comprehension" '.[111] It is a serious error, though the error typical of the age, to regard Christianity as a doctrine. But doctrine is in reality only 'a device to mitigate the shock of offence',[112] a rationalization of the absolute paradox which is the existential core of Christianity. The religious sphere of existence, which is contained within the di-chotomy of faith and sin, is beyond all understanding and all moral calculation. Incomprehensibility, which is characteristic of natural religion, is heightened and purified in Christianity, which makes concrete, as it were, the gross irrationality of its faith. 'The God-Man is the paradox, absolutely the paradox; hence it is quite clear that the understanding must come to a standstill before it.'[113] Kierkegaard often uses similar expressions to draw attention once again to the fundamental difference between Hegelian philosophical method and the actual task of becoming a Christian. Nothing can halt the understanding within Hegel's philosophy, yet Christianity not only insists upon the presence of discontinuities in personal existence, it refuses altogether the dignity of becoming a system. The two are so much at odds that Kierkegaard feels compelled to struggle continually against the self-delusions of the system. Hegel's writings, he argues, independently of the young Marx, amount to 'a deification of the established order'.[114] A deification which, in fact, 'constitutes the constant rebellion, the permanent revolt against God'.[115] Speculation renders the world immobile, transforming reality into a condition of lifeless perfection. Kierkegaard's critique of Hegel echoes a thought of Pascal's: 'Our nature consists in movement; absolute rest is death'.[116] It is a critique he might well have levelled directly at the natural sciences, which, assuming in fact that time had ceased in the arbitrarily chosen moment in which their equations were written, abstracted from the perpetual flux of impressions a complete system of interrelated laws through which the unchangeable totality of nature was represented.[117] All this, in fact, is nothing but 'the invention of the indolent worldly mind, which would put itself at rest and imagine that all is sheer security and peace, that now we have reached the highest attainment'.[118]

Faith, which requires absolute freedom from any outward constraint, stands aloof from both reflective and ethical seriousness. From a human and worldly point of view faith is necessarily an offence. In it there can be 'no defiling thought of anything meritorious'.[119] To appropriate religious categories the individual must, therefore, 'venture far out'.

Kierkegaard, expressing in his whole being the peculiarly modern collision between Christianity and orthodox values, directs his most withering remarks against the 'easy consolation' of conventional religion. The bourgeois piety which was so much a feature of Danish society, and was identified in particular with the dominance of the Lutheran Church, had removed the offence from Christianity and turned it into a harmless moral doctrine; 'People have quite forgotten what it is to "exist"'. In Christendom 'Christianity is done away with, for it has become an easy thing, a superficial something which neither wounds nor heals profoundly enough; it is the false invention of human sympathy which forgets the infinite qualitative difference between God and man'.[120] But Christ, he insists, is more than 'the gentle look' or 'the kindly eye'. He has nothing to do with this 'loathsome' and irrelevant 'sentimental frivolity'; echoing Rousseau, Kierkegaard declares Christ to be more than his teaching: 'He reveals the thoughts of the heart' which remain hidden to discursive reason.

The offence forces the individual to choose; either to continue to be offended or to will the Paradox as the ultimate object of faith. It is the function of reason and ethics to take notice of the offence, to feel the weight of its scandal. Christ, in existing both as a human individual and as God, is the Absolute Paradox. He is a 'sign of contradiction' and, like any other sign, is the 'negation of immediacy'.[121] The paradox exercises an irresistible attraction, but in eluding any form of rationalization it brings the fascinated subject into a more definite form of existence. In relation to the offence we cannot explain, we can only look, and 'while one looks, one sees as in a mirror, one gets to see oneself'.[122] Once again it is the act of choosing that crystallizes and perfects the self. 'The contradiction puts before him a choice, and while he is choosing, he himself is revealed.'[123] Salvation coincides with the absolute 'potentiation' of the self. Kierkegaard feels justified in saying, therefore, that 'Christ would first and foremost help any man to become himself'.[124]

Christianity cannot be communicated or taught directly as the fruits of reflection or as the lessons of history. The present age, which lacks passion, deludes itself in the conviction that it has domesticated the paradox; 'the tension of the paradox was relaxed, one became a Christian without noticing it, and without in the least noticing the possibility of offence'.[125] Kierkegaard, like Rousseau, pierces the veil of complacent appearances. He finds in Christ, as in ourselves, there is nothing but 'pure subjectivity and sheer negation carried to the utmost excess. He has no doctrine, no system, no fundamental knowledge'.[126] Religious truth cannot depend for its validation upon some contingent historical fact, or some limited human value. This is why there must appear to us 'something shocking . . . at the thought of bidding the poor, the sick, and suffering to come to him, and then to be able to do nothing for them but only to promise the forgiveness of sins'.[127]

God's transcendence, the 'endless yawning difference' between Him and man, is the offence which, taken to heart, 'proved to be an even greater torment and misery and pain than the greatest human torment'.[128] Far from being 'the gentle art of consolation', Christianity imposes upon the believer a consciousness of sin more terrifying than the pang of guilt which spoils the ethical life. The religious life intensifies rather than relieves the despair which had its previous incarnations in boredom and guilt. It is deepened to the specifically religious form of *Dread*. Generally through weakness, and more occasionally in the defiant choice of sin, the self perversely and paradoxically hides from itself. Dread is the religious form of what is normally now called anxiety. It is, literally, 'fear of nothing', it is 'nameless'. This is nothing but a fear of existence itself, an inability to 'will one thing' and actually to become the person one can and ought to be.[129] It is the inexplicability of dread (as incomprehensible as faith) which terrorizes the spirit. We suffer the irrationality of dread as a prelude to faith. And before we can overcome it we have to see it for what it is: nothing. However, just as Christianity appears in the contemporary world as a doctrine, as thought, and the unease of the ethical is betrayed in a continuous search for the origin of guilt in something outside and beyond the self, so dread precipitates another restless movement to discover the root of unhappiness in the accidental arrangements of the object-world.

The self is always beyond itself. This is despair; it is also the solution to despair because the beyond is finally discovered to be a wholly internal self-relation in which the unity of the personality and its reconciliation to the world is effected. But in the contemporary world, deceived by the power of reflective thought, the beyond is identified as nothing other than appearance, as objects, the possession of which is a token of an illusory happiness.

The deceptiveness of the contemporary world is not, however, a simple error. It has a deep psychological root in the need to communicate the reality of our internal state. A need which is itself the product of living in the falsity of the social world. Rousseau was not alone in feeling the urgency of this need. Yet, if we are to become Christian (and this is no different from becoming a 'single one') then we must assume an incorruptible *incognito*. The Christian accepts the suffering of the world more readily than could Rousseau (or Kierkegaard); the reality of truth is known only to the heart, and only then when it refuses the distraction of communicating, and thus falsifying, itself. The Christian is distinguished only by the sure possession within himself of his, or her, own identity. And the only signs of his inner exaltation are internal forms of communication which cannot escape the withdrawn interior.

THE SPIRIT IN CAPITALISM

The church, unable to make the transition to the new society, persisted by adapting, not to the underlying principle, but to the superficial 'ideology' of capitalism. But the spirit of capitalism, and later the bourgeois respectability of conventional piety, were, in fact, less in tune with the age than has often been supposed. Religion, from this standpoint, could at best be a convenient social mechanism, a way of 'oiling the machinery' of capitalist exploitation.

The value of individualism which was espoused as a religious goal within bourgeois society was, as Durkheim demonstrated, simply a reflection of a process individuation fostered by the 'organic' division of labour. In this there was nothing extreme or anti-social. Durkheim, indeed, was able to show that modern individualism, far from signifying the withering away, or even the complete collapse, of society, indicated just the opposite. A modern, complex society was ordered precisely through relations of individualism, and the characteristic subjective sense of uniqueness was only a particular aspect of the growth of the division of labour and the subsequent generation of solidary bonds among its separate units. Individualism was, in fact, the fundamental social institution of modern society.[130] Whatever Durkheim's own intentions, it is certainly possible to see his work as a clear statement of the purely secular foundations of modern, as opposed to primitive, society.

And in Weber's view, the process of rationalization which conditioned the entire development of western religion and its social environment culminated not only, with Calvin, in an internally consistent theology but, derived from this in relation to the psychological demands of everyday life, in an ethic which, for the first time, subordinated religious ideology to a universal secular calculus of personal advantage. In its degraded form this provided an ethical means to personal salvation, and therefore assimilated the most stubborn species of the irrational into the systematic completeness of bourgeois culture. Once established, however, capitalism takes on a purely objective reality of its own. The social world becomes independent of all *personal* moral presuppositions. Weber describes the resulting emergence of modern, secular, social life as the 'disenchantment of the world'.

Marx, from quite a different perspective, also draws attention to the pure objectivity of modern society. The world of commodities, appearing magically before us, holds us as if by a spell. We are bound to it by a superficially mysterious force. Once understood, however (as the alienation of labour), the religious 'halo' of modern society loses its fascination and melts into nothing. The 'critique of religion' gives way to the 'critique of political economy' just because the fundamental reality of capitalist society (as opposed, for example, to feudal society) is economic rather than religious.

In spite of their criticism of Enlightenment rationalism, that is to say, the classical authors of the sociology of religion tended to view religious consciousness within capitalism, whatever its relation to past societies might have been, as an empty illusion. Their justification for this rests principally on the view that religion is not an essential part of capitalist society. We can easily imagine a capitalist society in which all vestiges of religious belief and practice have been abandoned. Religion survives in its anachronistic forms simply because these forms have adapted to new, secular, requirements. It becomes the 'easy consolation' which provoked Kierkegaard's withering contempt. And the church, since Luther's time addressing itself to a 'free' people, self-consciously adopts the language of the marketplace. It offers something in return for the support of its congregation. But, in thus implicitly acknowledging itself to be just one good among other possible goods, it effectively negates the promise of salvation and accepts the complete triumph of the secular world. Religion is present in the modern world, then, only by ceasing to be, in some essential sense, religion at all.

This is a plausible argument only so long as it is assumed that religion has an essence which was in the past an inescapable feature of social life, and that, as society has now broken free of this inner connection with its religious form, the 'validity' of religion has been fatally impaired. Neither assumption is wholly reasonable. There is little evidence, beyond the mere fact of its presence within it, that religion was *ever* essential to the development of western society. And secondly, it ignores all modern forms of religiosity which take the social fact of secularization as their point of departure. Thus, while there is evidently a great deal of truth in the claim that a variety of religious forms persist by taking on a purely secular role, there is equally striking evidence of the creation of entirely new types of religiosity which, while predicated on the secularization of social life, are wholly spiritual in character.

In the emergence of passionate individualism, thus, we can detect a spirit *in* capitalism which is not the spirit *of* capitalism. Passionate individualism develops the Reformation to a new extremity of

167

inwardness. It sets itself not simply against the abuses of the church, or its tradition of authority and superstition, but against the idea of the church as such. The inwardness of faith, its absolute independence from historical and logical principles, its secrecy and confinement within the heart, isolates the individual in relation to God, and also in relation to other individuals. Within the passionate individual an absolutely pure but invisible soul is endlessly replenished. The self is endlessly consumed; and the more it is consumed the more fully it is developed.

A new religious sensibility, separate from and opposed to established ecclesiastical authorities of whatever sort, expressed the real value of capitalist individualism; but did so in such an uncompromising way that it appeared to be a subversive and atypical spiritual tendency. By the standards of bourgeois reasonableness, passionate individualism was a pathological version of orthodox values.

This intense inward spirituality might be viewed as part of the 'bourgeois critique' of capitalism. It adopts, and even celebrates, the values of bourgeois society, and quite self-consciously sets itself apart from the tradition of social criticism. It recognizes, above all, the significance of individual consciousness and individual feeling as the redeeming feature of humanity. It altogether fails to grasp, however, the secular tendency within capitalism. It takes value seriously and seeks to express the ultimate value of selfhood with reckless single-mindedness. The most severe critics of the hypocrisy, mediocrity and moderation of the bourgeoisie come from within this, rather than from any politically more radical tradition. Indeed it is hardly a tradition, but a series of rediscovered truths, excavated by the authentic psychologists of the successive phases in the development of capitalism.

Christianity, in advance of its modern apologists as well as critics, separated itself from reason and from morality, and discovered a sphere of its own. The more clearly it was defined within this sphere the less able was it to communicate with any other non-religious aspect of life. Religion thus became secure from any rash or speculative attack. It defeated its most sophisticated opponents of the Enlightenment; and disappeared.

But the promise of Happiness was rekindled in the search for authentic selfhood. From being 'hidden' in nature God was hidden in the depths of the psyche, a 'vanishing point of inwardness' towards which the self ceaselessly turned.

Passionate individualism was radically anti-social in its inwardness, its paranoia, its self-generating *angst*. And it was the most bourgeois of spiritual writers who, in fact, revealed the psychological depth of capitalism's inner contradictions. All values were conditioned by the transcending value of selfhood, but this ultimate value proved, in practice, to be unrealizable and inexpressible. The task of salvation had at last been placed in the individual's own hands, but in such a way as to guarantee that it could not be achieved. Historically, as the possibility of fulfilment had approached – national liberation, the pacification of society, the ideal of moral responsibility – true Happiness, keeping as it were one jump ahead, was removed to a yet more inaccessible distance. And when it finally devolved upon the self, it was as if the self, eagerly swallowing it up, lost contact with its (and its own) transparent unity. The world once again fell into obscurity, and the heart became opaque with wretchedness.

6

SENSUOUSNESS: HAPPINESS RECLAIMED

Christianity survived the emergence and development of capitalism. The historical forms of Christian transcendence – Faith, Belief and Morality – persisted, and, as they had in previous societies, attracted their followers. More importantly, however, Passion emerged as the unique religious spirit within capitalism.

It is only from the perspective of superficial secularism that Passion can seem to be the negation of social life. It is not so much a romantic complaint against a rational order of life, as the hidden mechanism which sustains such an order. This becomes clear as soon as religion is viewed in the context of consumption rather than production or exchange. The longing for things is a reflexive projection of the desire for the self. It is the inner movement of the heart, which, illuminating the world of potentially consumable objects with its discriminating beam of personal interests, is the source of attractiveness we discover in the external world. Capitalist consumption is driven by the need for self-actualization, by a religious love of self. In its classical phase this is conceived as a power of differentiation and distinction. The potential individuality of the soul confirms itself by 'defining' particular objects as desirable. And in subsequently consuming them the self acquires the solidity and substantiality, the thing-like particularity, of an object.[1]

The classical bourgeois view of the world corresponded to a society more or less accurately described by political economy. It was made up of individuals, each the centre of their own self-generated activity, prompted by internal needs and appetites, and guided by a more or less equally distributed capacity for rational calculation. In the process of exchange which comprised the content of social life the self emerged as a stable set of internal characteristics. It is this process which is given its radical religious form in passionate individualism.

170

However much this conception of the world might be regarded as an ideology, it took root in bourgeois consciousness just because it corresponded to an essential element in the social reality of capitalism.

Inasmuch as the bourgeois ego is still the immediate reality of capitalist society the religiosity of interior individualism remains as its ambiguous aftertaste. Classical bourgeois capitalism, however, has itself been transformed. 'Modern' society is still a capitalist society – it is built from commodities – but the social world erected from the commodity has altered in quite fundamental ways.

MODERN SOCIETY

'Modern' capitalism is a society in which quite different psychological assumptions to those institutionalized in its 'classical' predecessor are realized. The market, which had been the fundamental institutional expression of social and cultural individuality, has ceased to have any real independence from the process of production. Rather than being the pure dimensionality of exchange, its modality, the market has become an aspect of the way in which commodities themselves are produced. With extremely high concentrations of capital, large scale industry, mass production and 'scientific management', the ideals of entrepreneurial capitalism have given way to the monopoly capitalism characteristic of large corporate producers. Here, clearly, the rational calculation upon which production was founded can no longer be predicated on the independence of a pure market mechanism, and the powers of calculative self-interest inherent in the human individual. The demand for commodities, and the development of a market through which they are exchanged, themselves become an integral part of the exercise of corporate power. The consumption of commodities cannot, any more than can their production and circulation, be left to the 'sovereign individuals' of capitalism. The needs and appetites of the classically conceived bourgeois ego were continually self-renewing; but this is no longer sufficient. Such appetites have to be further stimulated, controlled and organized. The creation and satisfaction of appetites have to be freed from the rational individualism, and therefore the rational self-control and self-restraint, of the classically conceived marketplace.[2]

This transition found expression culturally as Modernity, as the liberation of the individual into a new form of subjective excitement. The subject, rather than being construed as a rational individual,

171

becomes a disconnected and unsystematic sequence of experiences, a fragment of himself or herself; or, rather, a web of such fragments within which the self is lost. The experience of modern life becomes evanescent, impressionistic, and incomplete; its ideal human subject is the 'man without qualities'. Beneath the superficial flux of experience, of course, everything goes on as before. Production is rigorously ordered, systematic and completely rational. But it no longer depends upon the subjective disposition of the individual members of society. Whether anyone likes it or not the production and exchange of commodities is the only means to life. So no one need any longer waste their time considering the matter. We can all, instead, indulge our imagination in frivolous and insubstantial reveries.

The new psychology found in fragmented experience, in dreams and in fantasy (rather than in reason), the key to understanding modern social activity. Subjectivity, once it had been anaesthetized into incommunicative inwardness and rendered completely safe as a hidden world of private thoughts and feelings, could be expressed phenomenally as a whole series of extravagant 'masks'. Superficially at least (and in modern society everything becomes superficial) subjectivity was no longer an interior and wholly private matter; it spilled over, so to speak, into the streets and coloured the most mundane of relations.[3] *Wishes* rather than needs linked the private world of the individual to the society of the commodity; the object-world became eroticized as the tools of wish fulfilment. The relation of individual to commodity was objective and rational in relation to production, and subjective and irrational in relation to consumption. And as the modern age became an age of mass production, the consequential expansion in consumption, rather than being tied to the rational development of desire, could only be fuelled by the boundless and effortless leap of the wish.

The individual, that is to say, no longer projects a potential identity into the world, attaches it to objects and then consumes these objects in order to validate himself or herself. The dialectic of Passion belongs to the classical world of capitalism, to the fiction of separated ego and individuated object. Modern capitalism creates an altogether more fluid and dynamic reality. The duty of the individual is to consume, not as a process of self-education and self-understanding, but simply in the hope of being excited.

The possibility of a momentary thrill is a sufficient stimulus to unbounded consumption. It is, in fact, a more effective and powerful driving force than the serious intention of self-fulfilment which lay behind the sober pursuit of pleasure within the classical bourgeois world.[4]

It appears that, socially, the subject is confined to the aesthetic sphere of existence, and (because the 'self' can no longer really exist) refuses the temptation of any higher categories. The fiction of salvation, as an illusory prospect of Happiness, has been finally abandoned in favour of an acceptance of the immediate world as a 'paramount reality'.[5] Advanced capitalism seems possible, in other words, only on the assumption that religion has come to an end. Negatively, religion has killed itself by 'proving' its own impossibility as passionate individualism. And positively, it is simply incompatible with the consuming demands of an advanced capitalist society. Even if we cannot adequately describe classical bourgeois capitalism without reference to a religious mechanism, its advanced or modern form seems possible only in a fully secularized form.

The real situation, however, is more complex. Excitement need not be promised, or at least not promised as the inevitable accompaniment to every act of consumption; its bare possibility is all that is required to prompt the enthusiastic but short-lived response that is the hallmark of modern consumerism. No rational connection links (and thus constrains) the relation between the commodity-world and the sensory excitement with which it is (arbitrarily) correlated. The self, that is, can be 'potentiated' into an 'excited' or more highly energized state by absorbing and reconverting the value alienated in the commodity. This process, however, is governed by an apparently unpredictable mechanism, or, rather, it is 'undetermined' in any mechanistic sense. It is as if we lived in a world in which the deepest levels of quantum discontinuity were realized in its everyday psychological forms. The psychological position of the modern consumer is consequently not unlike that of the early Puritan. Value is secreted in the commodity, but, as there is no rational means to appropriate this hidden reality, it exercises over the individual a dreadful fascination. Ignorant of which commodity will indubitably deliver, through its appropriation and consumption, the shock of energetic being, the ego is frozen in a state of anxiety. And to escape the pain of anxiety a popular compromise emerges. Rather than stand aloof from the commodity world, 'common sense' insists upon continuous and frenzied consumption as the (irrational) 'means' of maximizing excitement.

Viewing this from a somewhat different perspective it might be said that in modern society the fundamental *self-identity* of the commodity becomes a psychological reality. The phenomenal world has to be the way it is – the veil of illusion described by Rousseau and Pascal – just because it is the commodity, and not the self, which is its fundamental reality. It is a world within which the self will never find a home. But as the self crumbles and disintegrates the transcendental value of the commodity is fortuitously glimpsed in moments of decomposed subjectivity. And since the ultimate value stored in and released through the commodity is the formless and empty value of human creativity in general, decomposed subjectivity, which is no longer in search of its own finitude as personal identity, can absorb spirit without regard to the particular form within which it is, temporarily, embodied. Thus, in a quite real sense, every commodity becomes identical, the necessary but inconsequential carrier of ultimate value. As distinct from both the secular and religious psychology of the classical bourgeois era, modern psychology, and modern spirituality celebrate the authenticity of the moment. The religious quest for Happiness becomes the *wish* for contact with the actuality of the world. Wholeness, integrity, completeness and totality, rather than being the *telos* of the spirit, are transformed into the temptations of the modern age. They constitute the new metaphysical mythologies that, at all costs, should be resisted. And to resist the temptation of wholeness, a temptation that renews the lure of both philosophy and gnosis, the modern subject must consume, continually and thoughtlessly, the incomprehensible variety and vastness of the commodity.[6]

Happiness, that is, from being predicated on the Passion of a secret and hidden selfhood, is liberated into the commodity. This involves a complete revaluation of bourgeois categories. Nothing remains untouched in this revaluation; the entire map of experience is redrawn. In its place, rather than a new set of logical terms and divisions, there appears a set of *images* through which all categories dissolve, merge and are reformed. This process, which is the fundamental spiritual reality of the modern age, can be most readily described in the emergence of new images of nature, and of the human body, which are the privileged aspects of modernity's rediscovery of *sensuousness*. The historic gulf between flesh and spirit, reincarnated as the distinction between body and mind, seems to have dissolved in a new monism, an epiphany of the senses. Sensuousness becomes coextensive with reality itself; there is nothing 'beyond' to beckon and condemn, nothing from which we need feel separated or for which we need to long.

174

Thus, even more than in the case of classical bourgeois culture, the modern age presents us with a secular mask. Only, in this case, we insist upon there being nothing but the mask. Yet, as religion is only another term for value, for that which is sought in consumption, ought not the modern age, which is the era of consumption, be regarded as the most religious of ages? This seems incredible, a joke in bad taste. It is, however, one of the leading characteristics of modern culture that things can just as easily be represented by their opposite. The secular world, and not some imaginary hiding place from it, is, in fact, the real site of modern religiosity.

These tendencies, which stamp modern society with its characteristic *religious* meaning, as well as its distinctive secular culture, are evident, first of all, in new conceptions of the natural world. As in the classical period of bourgeois society, it is not from explicitly theological or ecclesiastical writings that we most readily discover the religious orientation of the age. But, whereas for that period psychology provides the most vivid description of religious Passion, it is scientific writers who first expose the Sensuousness which is the unique embodiment of spirit in modern society. The particular character of modern religiosity, therefore, can be discovered primarily in the emergence, at the beginning of the twentieth century, of a fundamentally new conception of nature, and subsequently in philosophical and psychological works which attempt to outline a new anthropology consonant with this vision.

RELATIVITY

Towards the end of the nineteenth century classical bourgeois orthodoxy rested with complacent certainty upon the foundation of human supremacy over nature that had been effected, it was thought, in the development of the natural sciences.[7] However, at the very moment when this development seemed on the point of completion, alarming paradoxes disclosed themselves in the most basic of the physical sciences. The scientific world-view, to which Pascal and others had responded by placing the religious out of harm's way in a personal and unreachable interior, became rich in transcendental oddities of its own.

It became increasingly widely recognized that the classical sciences succeeded only by ignoring nature. The Newtonian 'system of the world' was a supreme act of abstraction which not only left its fundamental mechanism (gravitational 'force') unexplained, but, what

175

was much worse, distorted the very phenomena it set out to explain. Classical physics described the cosmos at an arbitrarily chosen point in time. All its equations were ideally reversible, and from this mathematical idealization there was no way of predicting which way the universe would run. It froze the universe at a particular moment and made it stand for the system of nature as a whole. The physicist had reached fundamental laws only 'by violating nature . . . by isolating more or less artificially a phenomenon from the whole', and such laws, therefore, 'cannot directly express reality'.[8] This was, of course, a characteristic of bourgeois thought in general, but in the natural sciences, where a diachronic time-scale is vastly different to that of human history and even more to the biographical time-scale of everyday experience, the difficulties intrinsic to such a method remained undetected for quite some time.

Nietzsche, his comments ignored by scientists and philosophers alike, was the first to grasp the uncomfortable implications of the *failure* of the natural sciences. We had not 'reached' nature, we had succeeded merely in expressing ourselves in the language of science. In a striking passage he writes:

> We operate only with things that do not exist: lines, planes, bodies, atoms, divisible time spans, divisible spaces. How should explanations be possible when we turn everything into an *image*, our image! It will do to consider science as an attempt to humanise things as faithfully as possible: as we describe things and their one-after-another, we learn how to describe ourselves more and more precisely . . . in truth we are confronted by a continuum out of which we isolate a couple of pieces . . . The suddenness with which many effects stand out misleads us; actually, it is sudden only for us. In this moment of suddenness there is an infinite number of processes that elude us.[9]

The inherent directionality of nature only became represented by physical laws with the development of thermodynamics, which was, significantly, the first science to be inspired by the technology of industrialization. The energy loss involved in all heat exchanges was recognized as a fundamental fact of nature, and not simply as an imperfection in engineering. The resulting theory of *entropy* was the first time-sensitive physical concept. The 'system of nature' as a timeless equilibrium of forces lost its fascination. Ludwig Boltzmann, among the most eminent of nineteenth century theoretical scientists, spoke for a generation of bewildered physicists: 'one is amazed that, on the assumption that the world is a large system with a finite number of bodies . . . not even the world as a whole can be a *perpetuum mobile*'.[10] The long-term implication of the entropy idea involved a thorough reconstruction of cosmology. The universe as a whole might be considered as a thermal system and its dynamic history was fundamental to understanding any particular state in which it might, temporarily, be observed.

There was, additionally, no privileged point from which to make such an observation. The classical sciences had adopted the viewpoint of the isolated ego. An omniscient observer looked out upon the cosmos as if from a platform detached from, and unaffected by, the reality he or she observed. Again the unreality of such an abstraction, recognized in a formal way by Mach and Poincaré, demanded a fresh approach.[11] Relativity Theory began, thus, in socially realistic acts of observation. It was not the observation of an isolated ego, but the *comparison* of observations made by several individuals, each constrained by local conditions, that produced the basic data for which the scientist had to furnish a theoretical harmonization. Given this starting point, it was clear that no observations of fundamental physical quantities could remain independent of the position of the observer. Time and space could not, any more than the market, be treated as empty and independent dimensions.

Even more disturbing was the realization that *no* measurement of physical quantities could be considered independent of the act of measuring. Quite apart from the effects of the observer's position in relation to the object to be measured, the act of measurement was itself both a disturbing and a distorting influence on the 'system of co-ordinates' of which it formed a part. This problem went much deeper than might at first be supposed. There was no way of predicting what the impact of observational techniques upon the 'real' world might be. Indeed, at an atomic level, the act of measurement might even be construed as the very process which created the phenomena that were to be observed.[12]

The impact of the revolution in the physical sciences was profound, although for some time contained within its own recondite theoretical discourse. It was nonetheless clear that the very foundation of bourgeois thought – the idea that science could provide a complete and systematic account of nature – was not simply an unfulfilled project but a fundamentally mistaken conception. Any realistic notion of nature was in opposition to the ideal of scientific explanation. In the physical sciences, as elsewhere in modern culture, the desire for systematic completeness gave way to a new appreciation of 'the arbitrary, fleeting and contingent'.[13] *Any* scientific conception of nature was, in principle, rather than for practical considerations, incomplete.

Any particular and essential scientific concepts proved to be, even more embarrassingly, irreconcilable with other particular and essential concepts. It was necessary to conceive of light, for example, as *both* a discrete energy packet or *quanta, and* as a continuous and non-localized wave function.[14] Nature might still be presumed to be absolutely simple, but this simplicity was humanly inconceivable; so that in considering the most fundamental of natural processes we were confronted by paradox and contradiction. The *either/or* gave way to the *both/and*; it was no longer a question of choosing between a view of light, for example, as either a wave or a particle, so much as admitting that, paradoxically, it was simultaneously both a wave and a particle.

If reason could not render a complete account of itself in relation to nature, far less was it able to in relation to its own inner life as human experience. The modern psyche was split apart, fragmented and disunited. The long and exhausting search for personal identity, for the authentic selfhood that energized capitalism with its oddly calculative Passion, came to an inconclusive end. The conception of the self as a separate identity, the centre of its own moral universe and the point of integration of all personal experience, ceased to have any real meaning. Even as an unfulfilled religious ambition such a notion was suddenly anachronistic.[15]

The gulf between Kierkegaard's *Either/Or* and Dostoevsky's *Notes from Underground*, even though the latter precedes the revolution in the physical sciences, is as decisive as the distinction between the physics of Lord Kelvin and that of Max Planck. Dostoevsky's 'young man', like his counterpart of the *Either*, is trapped in the world of immediacy. 'I am a sick man', he declares with malevolent pride. He suffers from 'the sickness unto death', the despair of a purely aesthetic existence. It is in heightened self-consciousness that his most tempting symptoms appear. Because his capacity for self-understanding and self-reflection will not, even momentarily, leave him alone he cannot act. He sees through every possibility of self-realization; every possible line of action is imaginatively terminated before it can begin in actuality. His self-conscious despair cannot 'potentiate' itself beyond the point of lucid paradox. There is no saving possibility here of a 'repetition' into ethical existence. Underground Man is consistent and unrelenting in his despair. The search for authentic selfhood leads nowhere. And, rather as we cannot resist probing a sore tooth just to reassure ourselves that it still hurts, he cannot help tormenting himself with a perpetually subversive self-consciousness.

In Dostoevsky there is nothing 'beyond' despair. The catalogue of existential types that populate the cycle of mature novels that followed *Notes from Underground* is not conditioned by a transcendental *telos*. His 'polyphonic novels', whatever their author might have intended, implicitly deny any inherent developmental tendency within the psyche, or any (natural or transcendental) hierarchy of value.[16] All being is equivalent, everything exists at the same level. The clash of values, of life-experiences and of ideologies is unresolved and unresolvable. Higher and lower meet on equal terms. Underground Man reappears as Svidrigaylov in *Crime and Punishment*, as Stavrogin in *The Devils*, and as Dmitry in *The Brothers Karamazov*. There are no putative *Stages on Life's Way*; the developmental potential in aesthetic existence is a yet more self-conscious despair rather than the saving transcendence of ethics. And ethical characters, similarly, are deepened through the experience of guilt without the suggestion that they might resolve inner conflicts through the paradox of faith.[17] The irreducibility of existential possibilities to any single dimension of gradation or evaluation, their irreconcilable particularity, and the absence of any coherent framework of comparison among their life-views has the paradoxical result of establishing their fundamental human equivalence. Each stands independently on its own ground, and none serves merely as a prelude or introduction to a higher form. Each sphere of existence thus becomes a different version of immediacy, and simultaneously all forms of immediacy transcend the merely sensuous.[18]

In a world of decomposed subjectivity, and thoroughly relativized objectivity, 'duration' rather than 'system' or 'cause' becomes the fundamental self-generating and self-understanding reality. For both the science of nature, and reflective inwardness, the ambition towards logical completeness and the frozen abstraction of classical thought receded before a new evaluation of the momentary. And as in an impressionist painting the momentary in science and in psychology gained a new dignity. The meaning and significance of the merely actual now lay in its freedom from, rather than its revelation of, a past to which it had seemed bound by necessity and within which its presence had been already felt as a possibility. The present no longer offered itself as irrefutable evidence of an essential order relentlessly carried forward by time's own unshakeable continuity; each moment, rather, emerging miraculously out of nothingness, was an evanescent and unrepeatable actuality which was separate from, but formally identical to, an immediately preceding moment to which it bore a merely accidental resemblance. It was only the, seemingly magical, recreation of the world and of our consciousness within it, every moment, which gave rise to the illusion of 'time' at all. The 'actual' absorbs, as it were, the aura of nothingness. It becomes, more than ever, a world as if viewed through a partially obscuring veil. Its most truthful moments are, thus, shrouded in mystery: for Proust, for example, in the passage from sleep to waking, or for Bergson in the transition from memory to perception, and for Niels Bohr in the unpredictable emergence of physical events from the inconceivable flux of the quantum world.

DURATION

During the classical period of bourgeois culture efforts to understand nature and ourselves robbed both of their essential quality of duration. 'To perceive means to immobilize', Bergson tells us,[19] and, as we experience 'needs' which cannot be spontaneously fulfilled, we have no option but to tear ourselves free of primordial being, and immobilize it as the conventionally defined 'objects'. Thus, claims Bergson, 'whatever be the nature of matter, it may be said that life will at once establish in it a primary discontinuity, expressing the duality of the need and of that which must serve to satisfy it'.[20] Our separation from primordial duration is felt directly as the variety of human 'needs'. And, thus, 'our needs are, then, so many search-lights which, directed upon the continuity of sensible qualities, single out in it distinct bodies'.[21] The connectedness of reality, grasped and represented rationally as a system of necessary or logical relations, perpetuated the 'moment' to eternity. Yet nature is subject to change and the more deeply we understand this, the less able are we to render a rational account of its persistence.

'Duration' is the pre-conceptual being of nature, the pure sensuousness we misrepresent in both the systematic abstraction of the classical sciences, and in the variety of immediate appearances which result from the intervention of memory and perception. We can understand nature, that is to say, only by observing it, but each observation falsifies this very world by representing all its relations spatially, as if its coherence were concentrated into a single moment.

'Perception is never a mere contact of the mind with the object present.' It is, rather, a creative differentiation of the object from the wholly interconnected sensuousness of duration.[22] However meticulously, therefore, we describe the content of consciousness, however generously we expand the fullness of the moment, and however we may try to reduce the interval between moments to a negligible quantity, we never perceive the reality of duration. The real substance of nature transcends our immediate experience, that is, not because the world exists in timeless 'laws of nature' that the intellect can model by abstraction from immediacy, but more profoundly because empirical reality is itself an illusion of immediacy. Consciousness, in other words, even when it is content to relax into unreflective acceptance of sensations is, in fact, continuously analysing, organizing, isolating and rationalizing. This is just what we mean by the term 'consciousness'. However much science departs from the uncritical consciousness through which we normally experience the world, it is not fundamentally different; it merely refines and makes systematic the distortions essential to the art of mundane perception.

The transformation of the classical sciences, under the impact of powerful relativizing tendencies, encouraged a renewal of the 'cosmological argument'. Rather than conceiving of God as the terminus of an otherwise infinite regress of causes, as the first mover of the universe, He was invoked as the continuous miracle of duration.[23] God is, in this conception, first of all a process of continuous creation that underlies the discontinuity and randomness of nature. He is the essential glue that holds the cosmos together; or, rather, the absolutely simple substance from which we abstract the objects that can be grasped by the mind as an ordered and lawful cosmos.[24] There is, therefore, a sense in which the long process of interiorization of religious consciousness is suddenly reversed, and God reclaims His cosmological domain.

The classical bourgeois identification of God with a 'vanishing point' of inwardness has not, however, been superseded. Duration is at the heart of consciousness, as well as of nature. Indeed it is through considering the nature of consciousness that the reality of duration is brought to light. The unreachable reality of becoming conditions human experience (however much it departs from it) as well as the structure of the cosmos (which, similarly, is its falsification). God still possesses the quality of deep subjectivity; but now the external world of nature is bathed in this same attribute. The inwardness of God is projected on to the world, assimilating its incomprehensibility to His

181

transcendental obscurity. Human experience, that is, remains central to all distinctively modern forms of the cosmological argument.[25] And the experience of modernity is the root of contemporary religiosity.

The problem of personal identity is intensified and then trivialized, rather than resolved, by the social transformation announced in the new cosmology. The dissolving sensation that accompanied the rediscovery of genuine duration was not only a fresh vision of nature, it was, more immediately, the experience of personal fragmentation. Just as the scientist's *concept* of nature falsified what we intuitively understood of its simplicity, so the self was necessarily an unrealistic abstraction from the real duration in which our existence participated. The real problem of personal identity in the context of modern society is, thus, rather different to that encountered in bourgeois ideology. It is not the nature of the reason characterizing each separated individual which is at issue, but the very possibility of personal consciousness; how, in fact, is personal experience related to authentic duration? Conventional views of the person as maintained by the power of memory are viewed as superficial and inadequate. Once again it is the 'movement' from moment to moment which involves a miraculous *leap*, a continuous transition which cannot be grasped in rational concepts, and which depends for its coherence on the fiction of a permanent and unchanging ego.[26] In fact, this substratum of continuity is illusory. 'The truth is that we change without ceasing' and, therefore, 'there is no essential difference between passing from one state to another and persisting in the same state'.[27]

The conscious memory of self-composure and calculative rationality is continuously undermined in the human propensity for 'recollection', in the spontaneous dissolution of the self and its internal order in the unpredictably lucid moments when our past becomes immediately present to us once again. Bergson, thus, distinguishes two distinct types of memory, one founded on 'motor mechanisms' and the other contained in purely 'personal memory-images'; 'The first, conquered by effort, remains dependent upon our will; the second, entirely spontaneous, is as capricious in reproducing as it is faithful in preserving'.[28] In dreams, reveries and fantasies we are, for more or less long periods, 'absent' from ourselves. Yet no one regards these temporary states as forms of despair. In them we are not ourselves in a wholly innocent fashion. The self is temporarily abandoned, not because it has lost itself within a (socially necessary) veil of illusions, but because it has gained a privileged participation in the primordial pre-conceptual reality from which the personality is a temporarily differentiated segment. As we have no concepts through which to assimilate this experience to the normal (and artificial) continuity of the self, we interpret its subversive liberty as memories of childhood (Freud), or artistic inspiration (Proust). David Hume's powerful philosophical criticism of the Enlightenment is finally and fully acknowledged. The uninterrupted sequence of causes we imagine to be the coherence and continuity of nature, and the persistence within our own memory of a self which carries our personality from moment to moment, are revealed as illusions made necessary by our particular way of life. And, as the modern way of life has significantly departed from its classical bourgeois antecedent, the ego 'has become a fable, a fiction, a play on words'.[29]

Truth, made permanent, but distant and obscure in being grasped indirectly through rational concepts, becomes fortuitously and unpredictably accessible to immediate apprehension. *Afterwards* – its threatening selflessness already overtaken by the arousal of the personality – the shock of contact with the underlying simplicity of being is interpreted (illogically) as the memory of a pre-conceptual past. The Proustian reverie of dissolution and reawakening, the Freudian reconstruction of symptom-formation, Bergsonian duration, all seek to establish a relation between the conscious rationality of the remembered self and the more primitive experience of the world from which it sprang. This relation is conceived only because the primitive has received new value, and can once again be admitted into existence. It has a being of its own, quite apart from the undertow it effects upon our consciousness. As something more than a degraded version of the illusions of consciousness, duration claims our attention as a source and repository of value. We can consume this value and become happy only by *relaxing* the demands of selfhood. It is a sphere of existence which is reached only by unburdening ourselves of our selves, and, since time and the self have formed such an intimate alliance, its briefest occupation has the invigorating intensity of eternity.

The separation which creates the self is experienced internally as a loss of, and consequently as the wish to be united and merged once again with, its own primordial reality. It is not the self's potentiation but its (temporary) negation which is sought in the spirit of modernity. The self is no longer construed as desire, as a want which establishes a reciprocal relation with its image projected on to some particular object beyond itself (and towards which it is attracted in order to complete and actualize itself). It is filled, rather, with nostalgia, with a melancholic sense of loss over the Paradise which it cannot remember but which, in unguarded moments of recollection, is still *sensed*.[30] The self *wishes* but does not any longer desire, and all wishes return to the past and to the pure sensuousness of duration. This is the quite positive sense in which we might view the 'death instinct'. It is the wish to do away with the self and to return to the greater freedom of an existence we imagine as our own childhood.

God, having vanished inside the subject as the ground of authentic selfhood, found an insecure resting place. Once interiorized, the self had sought, as it were, to keep God at arm's length. But no sooner was He coupled to the pure interiority of the subject than the unconditional relation of inwardness thus established dissolved into nothing. The absolute negativity of the God idea was, as it were, too powerful for the ego to tolerate, and, in consequence, it perished.[31] 'God is dead', Nietzsche's madman tells himself, 'and we killed him'; yet, such is the indifference of the modern world that we might put it another way: 'we are dead, and God killed us'. We could not tolerate salvation and rejected it as a permanent possibility. This is the fundamental truth of Ivan Karamazov's poem, 'The Grand Inquisitor'.[32] If Christ were to return the church would have to destroy him; not to perpetuate its corrupt authority, but, more profoundly, to continue the work of consolation which is its real source of legitimacy. Rejecting 'the servile rapture of the slave', Christ wanted to be followed freely by human beings 'captivated and fascinated' by him.[33] It proved to be a terrible liberation; 'instead of taking possession of man's freedom you multiplied it and burdened the spiritual kingdom of man with its suffering for ever'.[34] Christ would be destroyed, that is, to save humanity from the insupportable torment of continuous contact with the truth of Being. He would be destroyed for profoundly religious reasons, and the Inquisitor would have been justified in doing so; 'I do not want your love', he concludes simply.

By making the self a transcendental category the bourgeois psychologist was bound, sooner or later, to destroy the objectivity of the psyche. God is the source of all difference, but is Himself indifferent. The character of the self, however, is just to stand out from and even against the world. Its fundamental principle is pure distinction. In Durkheimian terms, therefore, the self exists as the religious prerequisite of all experience and action. It is the rule which makes all other conventions possible, a wholly arbitrary division within duration from which emerges the rational relations of self-identity and object-world.

The modern search for the authentically human has become identical with the religious demand for salvation.[35] He is the universal solvent within which the bourgeois ego merges with a pre-conceptual, undifferentiated, soup of Being. From this perspective we can see how mistaken is the notion of capitalism's regrettable secularization. The real difficulty with capitalism is just its unrelenting religiosity, its spiritual tyranny, which has insinuated itself into the heart of subjectivity and ensnared the soul with its cunning. Each liberation from oppressive religious categories turns out to be a yet deeper and more subtle form of oppression. In claiming its autonomy from religious prejudice the self performed a decisive act of the spirit; it was a fundamentally *religious* protest. And, finding itself no better off, was seduced by the idea of doing away with itself completely. The truth was that the location of Happiness had moved, and salvation had once again been claimed by new categories. The mythology of the self could be acknowledged because God had already deserted its illusory citadel and left it vacant for the secular psychologists to rummage among its ruins.

SENSATIONS

The modern world is marked above all by the *dissolution* of distinctions once held to be unambiguously natural. The differentiation of object and subject, form and content, self and world, accentuated as logical and categorical oppositions and contradictions, gave way to new, mobile relations. All contemporary distinctions lack the logical necessity characteristic of their bourgeois antecedents. The antimonies of bourgeois thought seem, in fact, to be on the point of giving way completely to the indifference of the modern age.

The illusion of space, like the other illusions of the sense world, had been supported and maintained by the fundamental social division, which reappeared, over and over again, between exchange and use. Upon this division was erected the whole social world of capitalism and its utilitarian ego psychology. Society appeared to be a set of necessary relations predicated upon a natural order existing among commodities. The activity that went into the creation of society, and the social relations through which this activity was accomplished were obscured by this division. Social relations were themselves subsumed under the 'rule' of nature, alienated into the irresistible logic of production and exchange. The commodity itself contained the whole objective power of society as if it were a fact of nature. It was as part of this alienated world of objective relations that each ego looked out and weighed up its prospects of survival. Every other person, and every other thing had received the stamp of objectivity and naturalness. Subjectivity had as it were been condensed into the ego, which became a second (but not secondary) cosmos.

Human experience in modern society, however, begins with a softening and merging of these distinctions. This fluidity is nowhere more marked than in the overcoming of the historic Christian separation of spirit from flesh, a division which had its secular equivalent in both ancient and modern philosophies as the disparity between mind and body. A powerful impulse to overcome this antithesis (or rather to reach back into a primal and undivided reality prior to its emergence) was already evident in Feuerbach. Anticipating both the most penetrating attack upon, and the most committed defence of, modern Christianity, he erected a new theological anthropology in the name of pure sensuousness.[36] Marx at once claimed that Feuerbachian terms remained as metaphysically laden as had Hegel's. Sensuousness proved to be, for him, an *idea*, a concept as remote as any other from the immediacy of life. However justified the objection in relation to Feuerbach's writings might be, it could hardly be levelled at more modern authors.[37] By the close of the nineteenth century sensuousness, as a living reality, had literally broken into the timeless void of pure ideas and infected every bourgeois category with its subversive genius. The fixity of nature and of the ego had broken down. Intellectually the only possible way to grasp the new reality of modern life was as continually creative duration. Every thing and thing-like quality was, so to speak, sucked back into the primordial sensuousness from which it had, momentarily, separated itself. Sensuousness, that is to say, unlike older concepts or ideas of a body, was essentially unbounded, playful, infinite in its inner transformations and metamorphic diversity. There was, thus, no body which was not, simultaneously and more profoundly, spirit, and no spiritual reality other than in relation to a body. Sensuousness was *both* flesh and spirit, body and mind.

The senses – those privileged terms within the classical scientific conception of human nature and human activity – recovered in the modern period, therefore (or were described as recovering), some of the quality of real life of which they had been drained by science and its method of rational abstraction. Bergson, for example, insisted that every act of perception contained memories, and was therefore indicative of a particular disposition towards the world. There was no such thing as a simple sensation, passively received. The phenomenon of attention, the mode of experiencing the 'outside world', the complex associations set up by an initial recognition of some detail in this world, all combined to make perception a spontaneously creative act.[38] And, before Bergson, Nietzsche suggested that, in modern society, 'sensitiveness is infinitely more acute', and that 'the abundance of different impressions is greater than ever'.[39] There is now, he claims, 'a certain hypersensitiveness, even in morality'. No sphere is free of sensuousness: 'the spiritual tempo has altered; the pleasure which was begotten by spiritual refinement and cleverness has given room to the pleasure of colour, harmony, mass, reality etc.', all of which point to a new *sensuality in spiritual things*.[40]

Sensations, as synthetic acts the mechanism of which generally escaped our attention, were rich in interpretation, in memory, and in intention. We do not, for example, 'see a tree exactly and entire with regard to its leaves, branches, colour, shape; it is so much easier for us to put together an approximation of a tree'.[41] In defining and ordering a world separate and independent from itself, all the spiritual qualities of the subject come into play. And, more than this, in assimilating that world, they occasionally succeed in piercing its newly contrived objectivity, recovering from a fortuitous combination of sensations the primordial flux which informed them. Rather than confirming the rational objectivity of the self through interaction with the world which was not the self, the Proustian moment of recollection returned the subject to a point prior to this distinction, bathing both self and world in the glow of pure sensuousness. We are reminded in such moments, which are always connected with a particular unexpected scent or taste, a specific tint of hawthorn blossom, or some odd visual sensation, that what had seemed so natural to classical bourgeois psychology – the separation of ourselves from the world – was, in fact, a continuous and problematic act of differentiation. The moment of lucid self-consciousness was, at the same time, the moment of the self's reabsorption into the flux of Being. Sensuousness has become the epiphany of the modern age.

Perception ought to be seen, therefore, as a perpetual division and differentiation. Having divided the world and thus created ourselves we move about within it as the interactive unity of direct experience. But, just as the scientist discovers that, strictly speaking, he cannot separate himself from the object he would like to measure and define, so, when properly understood, ordinary non-reflective acts of consciousness emerge from and merge with a continuous flux of possible sensations. Consonant, then, with the most profound tendencies of the new cosmology – tendencies which overcame the distinction between matter and space – the immediate experience of the modern world must be understood as a particular, and ultimately arbitrary, interactive arrangement, a field or manifold within which all distinctions are fundamentally conventional.

For the psychology of modern life the body was redefined and given a new prominence as the natural symbol of pure sensuousness. The classical bourgeois conception of the body had suppressed the chaos of spontaneously generated feeling beneath every development of the spirit, and every progressive discovery of reason. Codified, ordered, self-controlled, the shelter and temporary housing of the self, the body had been as alien to sensuousness as had the most refined of abstract thoughts. In this context, Bergson's merging, in a new interactive psychology, of the polarities of sense experience and ideas, of the objectivity of the outside world and an inward spirit, is not an isolated example. Similar literary and philosophical experiments abound in *Fin de Siècle* culture, and come most prominently to notice in the writings of Freud and Proust. For both memory is a rejection of the body, an attempt to escape into the timeless realm of pure ideas, while recollection draws the body back into the midst of Being. Recollection is the body's attending to itself. It makes the body once again the central preoccupation of consciousness, and of feeling, and the core, therefore, of the *spiritual* world.

THE BODY

The chaos of modern thought is symptomatic, then, of a recollection of the body, a stirring of sensuousness which could not be seen, at first, as other than disorderly. 'The "spirit" is more like the stomach than anything else', Nietzsche remarks approvingly, making the connection explicit.[42] 'Perhaps the whole of mental development', he goes so far as to suggest, 'is a matter of the *body*'.[43] This should not be mistaken for a materialist manifesto. He claims this only because the body has become the spiritual *topos* of the modern world:

> Granting that the 'soul' was only an attractive and mysterious thought, from which philosophers rightly, but reluctantly, separated themselves – that which they have since learnt to put

188

in its place is perhaps even more attractive and even more mysterious. The human *body*, in which the whole of the most distant and most recent past of all organic life once more becomes living and corporal, seems to flow through this past and right over it like a huge and inaudible torrent: the body is a more wonderful thought than the old 'soul'.[44]

Bergson concurs:

> At certain moments, in certain points of space, a visible current has taken rise; this current of life, traversing the bodies it has organized one after another, passing from generation to generation, has become divided amongst species and distributed amongst individuals without losing anything of its force.[45]

Where Feuerbach's 'pure sensuousness' retains an air of conceptual unreality, the *body*, which has become its natural symbol, *contains* the infinity which is man's real nature. There is nothing inevitable about this. Indeed, our conscious activity takes place in relation to an ordered *mechanism* of bodily functions, and expresses itself through rules of comportment, which have a conventional, social foundation. The body, therefore, is part of history, and is always experienced in terms of specific conventions and meanings which belong to the estranged world of social forms. Our bodies are never our own; chosen from a few basic types they allow us only the illusion of an inalienable inner space.[46] The socialized body-form, which is remote from the pure sensuousness of which, in modern society, it seeks to remind us, *is* a concept, and is experienced conceptually. Yet it is just the historical peculiarity of modern society to allow the body, from time to time, to emerge in another way – as the natural symbol of sensuousness. In such moments it then regains the entire world of possibility, and, consequently, becomes a mystery to itself.

Sensuousness, that is to say, is at one and the same time within and beyond us. It can neither be assimilated to the pure objectivity of the outside world, nor can it assume the deceptive subjectivity of ideas. The body, the most privileged concretion of, or rather within, the interactive perceptual field, is not just a meeting point, but a solvent of all such dichotomies. It is neither myself, nor my world, but 'my present', that 'consists in the consciousness that I have of my body'.[47]

Even in its aspect as a fully socialized and completed image, the modern body-form is quite different to its bourgeois antecedent. The modern body, the exterior shell of the 'man without qualities', is nothing but a reflecting surface. It has no insides. This is simply because social life is no longer, as it was for the classical humanist, a matter of controlling disruptive internal processes. Nor is it even a matter of appetite or desire which begins from an internal movement which is felt as a partial emptiness. The process of emptying has been completed, and the interior can now be ignored, or, if considered at all, reduced to an undifferentiated soft substance, the indifferent 'heavy mass of the body'.[48]

The body becomes ideally superficial. 'My body', says Bergson, 'acts like an image which reflects others.'[49] The theme of self-reflection, which had been a central motif of classical ego psychology, is transposed and dissolved into a new psychological disposition towards 'mirroring'. This, in turn, is a transformation of a much older tradition in which the human body was viewed as a microcosm – a specific and finished structure modelled on the cosmos of which it was a symbol – and the human soul was conceived as an interior mirror conformed to the divine structure of Being in whose image it was made. The 'mirror' of modernity, however, is simply a reflecting *surface* alert to every deformation of the relational field within which it is a temporary condensation. In the modern world everyone must become adept at reading these reflected images. Nietzsche brilliantly expresses the idea; he describes an ideal modern subject

> . . . lacking any other pleasure than that provided by knowledge, by 'mirroring', he waits until something comes along and then gently spreads himself out, so that not even the lightest footstep and the fluttering of ghostly beings shall be lost on his surface and skin. Whatever still remains to him of his 'own person' seems to him accidental, often capricious, more often disturbing, so completely has he become a passage and reflection of forms and events not his own.[50]

The, largely hypocritical, drive towards self-actualization has been abandoned. The modern person 'no longer knows how to take himself seriously, nor does he have the time for it'.[51] All sense of inwardness has been drained of real content. There is no depth to the void enclosed by the body; 'His mirroring soul, for ever polishing itself, no longer knows how to affirm or how to deny'.[52] The 'objective man is an instrument', but no longer an instrument of his own rational ego; he is, rather, a precious, easily damaged and tarnished measuring instrument and reflecting apparatus which ought to be respected and taken good care of . . . a delicate, empty, elegant, flexible mould which has first to wait for some content so as 'to form' itself . . . a 'selfless' man.[53]

Modern psychopathologies might, thus, be viewed as anachronistic, and incompletely emptied, body-images. The psychotic is afraid of 'losing himself' , of 'letting himself go', and is terrified of flowing out of his own body. He therefore makes of its surface a hard and impenetrable barrier between a residual inner selfhood and the outside world. His body surface is unpolished, dim, absorbent; his life is withdrawn into 'the soft muffled gloom of the interior'.[54] Its mirrored surface is turned inwards so that all he can see is an endlessly multiplied self-image. His bodily shell has been taken off, as it were, and put back on, inside-out.[55] His body becomes an enclosure, a prison within which his soul dies from loneliness.

The neurotic, on the other hand, wants to be rid of everything that is on the inside because she (in the mythology of modern life – which is still related to an earlier Christian ideology of sexual differentiation – psychosis is a male disease, neurosis a female complaint) feels an over-abundance of content. The body shell literally cannot contain the highly excited and energized interior, which sends out highly charged 'cathexes', like solar flares, from its surface. The neurotic glows with excitement, radiating waves of bodily energy. Her surface is unfinished and incomplete; it is too open and acts as a transmitter, rather than as a reflector, of prodigal images.[56]

In modern society the body is ideally superficial, a sensitized surface enclosing a more or less lifeless void. As living beings we identify ourselves with the energetic boundary enclosing this emptiness. We exist, like molluscs, just behind a protective, reflecting surface.[57] The psychology of modern life, indeed, is comprehensible, in large measure, as the, superficially contradictory, techniques of body maintenance.[58] To prevent ourselves being absorbed into the continuous flux of external stimuli we enclose a portion of these mobile stimuli within a hard casing.[59] But to prevent ourselves being sucked into the central void we have to establish and maintain, through consuming, a subcutaneous layer of sensitive living flesh. Our interior organs remain a mystery to us and come into prominence only as the seat of 'illness', that is a disruption of the normal body-image. Inside we routinely imagine an undifferentiated soft substance that we feed and energize through continuous absorption of additional material from the outside world.

Yet the body, as an integrated whole, hardly exists for us any more. It emerges, rather, in a series of different, overlapping and contradictory forms. The body-image, and it is as an *image* that we are aware of the body, is a moving and dynamic force. It expands and shrinks, orients itself in innumerable ways, and takes up a hundred ghostly positions as we try to discern its outline more clearly.[60] Sensuousness is contained within and pours forth from the body. But it is only from an extraneous and naturalistic standpoint that the body possesses even a morphological unity. In this century, indeed, reviving a tradition inaugurated by Goethe, but still-born in his intuitive 'anti-science', the morphological unity of the body was briefly recognized as the long-sought synthetic a priori. Not only the human body, but the other species that could be distinguished within a rational order of nature, were conceivable as so many alternative body-forms each marking off one possibility of subject–object integration within the infinite possibilities of pure sensuousness.[61] We could not directly experience any such unity other than our 'own', and even then, when we made the effort to become conscious of our body in its unity and wholeness we found it to be a chaos of alternative and contradictory images. This tendency to fragmentation, as much as any scientifically principled rejection of Bergsonian vitalism, put an end to the brief flowering of romantic biology and the effort to grasp the scope and inner nature of 'sensuous spirit' as the variety of naturally occurring bodily forms.

Sensuousness appeared, thus, in two distinct spheres of existence. It was, first of all, a kind of condensation of subject and object which constituted itself as an outwardly reflective and inwardly irritable body. There, taking on all the rigour and deceptiveness of philosophical language, it adopted the reality of an image or representation. Perceived as an object it appeared to be ordered, differentiated, controlled, inter-related and self-sustaining in both its adaptation to the environment, and as an internal equilibrium of forces.[62] But within and as it were between these rationalizations, grasped in the fullness of its subjectivity, it offered glimpses of itself as pure duration. Then, abundant, unlimited, unfinished, endlessly flowing, inherently irrational, and indifferent to all distinctions it radiated the aura of spirit.

In both senses the flesh is, literally, made spirit and the spirit made flesh. Whatever sociological interpretation of transcendence we care to adopt, it is, in modern society, most fully applicable to the body-image. As the distance between individual consciousness and collective representations, or as the difference between culture and nature, or as the estrangement of appearance from reality, bodily awareness simultaneously divides and conjoins two realms of being. The body is both an immediately given assembly of mundane objects, and an inescapably transcending presence. The Logos of society, thus, is inscribed upon us as a transcending conventional order of bodily signs. But this is an order which is itself spontaneously dissolved in the mystical contact with the undiluted sensuousness from which it was originally, and arbitrarily, distinguished. Ideas no longer escape into a realm of their own but retain their character as aspects or gestures of the body. Nietzsche never tires of tracing every concept to a 'physiological' root, not to unveil and unmask so much as to ennoble their faded and pallid forms. At the same time sensations become indistinguishable, or at least inseparable, from the spiritual realm of memory and imagination in which they have their real being. It is as if the soul, having fled the outside world for the safer haven of inwardness, expands once again to fill up the space it has appropriated. It expands to the limit of the body's surface and sensitizes its boundary with the outside world.

EPIPHANIES

The body has ceased to pose a problem of control or identity; it no longer offers any serious resistance to the self-composure of good manners, nor does the continuous miracle of its personal signature throw the intellect into a state of exhausted bafflement. It no longer has to pretend to be a single thing. It may appear, from the outside, that it continues to force itself upon our attention as a natural symbol of wholeness, but from the inside we have become aware of the illusory nature of such a claim. It continually breaks down into parts, and rebuilds itself according to a slightly different plan. Or, rather, it dissolves itself not into parts but into

> *partial views* of the whole. And, with these partial views put end to end, you will not make even a beginning of the reconstruction of the whole, any more than, by multiplying photographs of an object in a thousand different aspects, you will reproduce the object itself.[63]

The modern body is not a unitary structure but a multiplicity of contradictory *images*. It contains, so to speak, the infinity of its own possibilities. A sensitive and irritable substance coated with a reflective and protective shell, it exists only through a continuous process of construction and deconstruction.

The body, thus, never completely grows out of, or forgets, its previous forms. Indeed, it carries with it, as if entertaining on a purely playful basis the notion of a completeness that it knows to be illusory, the stored-up images of its own past. The body casts multiple shadows; it cannot simply abandon older conceptions it had of itself. The body in modern society, therefore, can still seem to be driven (indeed, it still is driven) by Passion, or appear to furnish the self with its natural appetites, or pretend to be nothing but the instrument of the mind's intentionality, or perhaps it recalls being a 'machine that winds itself'. It is continually adding to its repertoire of images, continually augmenting its store of memories.[64]

Modernity, thus, consists above all in the relativizing of succession. Where exclusivity and wholeness marked the bourgeois body, sensuousness was forced into a single and definitive form alone, and was, because of this, no more than an abstract idea of itself. But, so long as all images of the body are thoroughly relativized, those that, because of their failed integrity, have been thrust into the past to form a sequence of rejected conventions can be retrieved and laid alongside freshly emerging possibilities.

This continuous accumulation of past images enriches the present moment with the entire suppressed structure of *Time Regained*. It is the experience of duration, a continuous, fragmented and contingent present, in which everything that has gone before, as well as the addition of all that is genuinely novel, has become overwhelmingly immediate. The absoluteness of *Time Regained* should not be mistaken for the unchangeableness of a remote truth; it is, rather, the presence of reality unobscured by intellect or habit. Such a presence, once dimly sensed, subverts the naturalness of present conventions and floods the body with its own past.[65] We become, in consequence, composite beings: 'The past of every form and mode of life, of cultures that formerly lay close beside or on top of one another, streams into us "modern souls" thanks to this mingling, our instincts now run back in all directions, we ourselves are a kind of chaos'. The spirit therefore has 'access to the labyrinth of unfinished cultures'.[66]

The philosopher, as the heretical Christian of an earlier era, little realizing that the infinite has come to rest there, longs to leave the body. He wishes to be rid of it in favour of the world of pure ideas. He is 'prejudiced *against* appearance, change, pain, death, the things of the body, the senses, fate, bondage, and all that which has no purpose'.[67] The madman, more profoundly, believes he has already been fully restored to the equally 'pure' flux of sensuousness within which the body is a temporary concretion. The latter experiences the world directly as the endless fluidity, absolute generality, essential interconnectedness, and inexhaustible generative power that the former tries and fails to represent in thought. The madman, in other words, follows the mystic road to salvation, while the philosopher still insists upon the path of reflection.

What is new to the modern age is the eccentricity of either ambition. There is no need to follow either route because the spirit has come to rest in an everyday epiphany of the senses through which the body-image is continually created and destroyed. It is the *appearance* of reality, rather than its underlying 'essence', that has taken on the aura of spirituality. Spirit, consequently, is 'liberated' for the first time into sensuous categories; and, because of this, sensuousness has acquired all the characteristics of spirit. In this process the conceivability of spirit is altered in conformity with the character of sensuousness. Thus, rather than exist as frozen and changeless nature – the necessary being beyond the actuality of mere becoming – God pours himself into duration. God is suddenly conceivable *only* in terms of a process of continuous creativity. He realizes Himself as perpetual Becoming, as a continuous outpouring of novel forms of being, an unrestrained and unquenchable flow of creativity. He is forever *new*, eternally creative, a *living* God.[68]

It is his profound grasp of sensuousness that forces Nietzsche into the paradoxical expression for reality as the 'endless recurrence of the ever same'.[69] Spirit is both new and, as necessary Being, always identical with itself. In flowing into new forms it does not alter itself, it does not *become* one thing rather than another, it merely chooses to exist in all possible ways, to fulfil through superficial metamorphoses its potentiality for unconstrained freedom. Consciousness, which is limited to the particularity of a chosen form, is nonetheless able to sense its inner-connection with the unlimited series of forms from which it temporarily distinguishes itself.

Sensuousness is momentary and fragmented, but an eternal moment and a complete fragment; for the moment exists only as a possibility instigated by a fortuitous act of will. It has to be torn by memory from the pure stuff of duration. Kierkegaard, indeed, was correct to designate the sensuous by music. Its fundamental character is its transitoriness. But, properly understood, the transitory is an echo of the eternal. The succession of notes may be captured and turned into the spiritual quality of harmonic relations, recognized and responded to in incipient bodily movements, in an appreciative flicker of the organism itself.

Modern sensuousness is continually 'beyond itself', in the same way that, for the period of classical capitalism, the self was continually beyond itself. Endowed with spiritual qualities, it cannot any longer be self-contained, or exist as a division of the natural order of things, or fit into a fixed and arbitrary category. Its abundance, its plenitude, presents to everyone a series of quite different faces. We are swept along, simultaneously present and absent in a flux of contradictory experiences. There is now *only* the immediate, because the immediate has gathered everything up into itself and released it into the world, little by little, without regard to sequence, or gradation, or development.

Modern philosophy, therefore, if it is to grasp reality, must exploit the conceptual distinctions implicit in bodily forms. A new philosophical language is born; heaviness and lightness, coldness and warmth, excitability, cleanliness, and, above all, health and sickness provide the irreducible vocabulary of modern terms. The modern European was first of all a 'sick man', oppressed by a diseased self-consciousness. Unable to grasp even what was immediately available to him, he languished in the morbid self-pity which was an 'expression of the physiological over-excitability pertaining to everything *decadent*'.[70] It was as if the elusiveness of the spirit, in becoming sensuous, had hidden the body from itself. The simplest of experiences thus becomes perplexing, and worse, provokes feelings of estrangement, incompleteness and sorrow.

Nietzsche, as later Proust was to do, translates metaphysics into bodily experiences. And they do this, not from wanton originality, but to unearth the spirit from its latest hiding place; and not to destroy, but once again to reveal, its truth.

Dostoevsky, similarly and perhaps less self-consciously, discovers the soul within the flesh, and the flesh within the spirit. Older conceptions of spirituality cannot withstand the spontaneous destructive power of the author's psychologizing. The Karamazovs are sensualists: it is not only Dmitry for whom sensuality is 'the definition and inner essence of him'; in the whole family 'sensuality has reached a point where it becomes a devouring fever'.[71] In the Karamazovs sensuousness has evidently become a demonic power, a force no less spiritual than that embodied in conventional religious forms. Dmitry, who always speaks 'with extraordinary excitement, almost with irritation',[72] refuses to recognize the legitimacy of any constraint upon the satisfaction of his bodily wishes, but it is before him, as if acknowledging the authenticity of this spiritual *hubris*, that the saintly elder Zossimov prostrates himself. And Ivan, in spite of his consciousness of despair, wonders if anything 'would overcome this frenzied and, perhaps, indecent thirst for life in me'.[73] Their father makes no apology for his dissolute existence: 'I intend to carry on with my filthy kind of life to the end'.[74] Indeed, he defends himself against all hypocritical censure; his 'absolute' sensuousness is, he claims, the real value of modern life. 'This filthy kind of life is sweet, sir: everyone abuses it and everyone lives it, except that they all do it surreptitiously, while I do it openly.'[75] It is significant that the supposed hero of the work, Alexy, is not simply less sensuous and more conventionally spiritual a character, he is also markedly less 'real'.

The destructiveness of the sensual in characters such as the Karamazovs, or in Nastasya Filippovna, appears in a completely novel way. It is not the privation of spirit (the flesh), but an overwhelming and demonic force, uniting spirit and flesh, which crushes conventional morality and conventional wisdom. It is their warped spiritual power, rather than any lack of sensibility which is so destructive. Their demonic sensuality is, therefore, a perversion of the spirit, rather than an unnatural predilection of and for the flesh. It is the spirit, rather than the flesh, which tempts.

The merging of all categories within modern subjectivity prevents the differences between Myshkin and Nastasya, or among any of the Karamazovs, being developed into 'logical' oppositions. There are only relative degrees of health and sickness; a terrifyingly arbitrary line is drawn, or rather not so much drawn as provisionally suggested, so that on either side an area of ambiguity exists. All differences are assimilated to divisions within the same reality. Dostoevsky, as Nietzsche, who claimed the great novelist to be the only psychologist from whom he had learned anything, dissolves the hermetic boundaries within Kierkegaard's *Stages on Life's Way*. There is no incipient arrangement, or developmental sequence, no enlightened procession through the aesthetic to the ethical to the religious.

In modern society the sensuous appears to be dangerous just because it has become identical with the spiritual. And it is only because the spirit has expanded to fit the body, that our bodies can become estranged from us. The otherness of spirit confronts us at the level of simple sensations. Spiritual suffering, so well described by Kierkegaard from a psychological viewpoint, becomes so many bodily complaints. Symptoms are 'misrelations' of the spirit, a kind of false synthesis of the body. The first and most noticeable aspect of nervous disorders, therefore, is their interference with normal bodily functions. In Freud's first case studies, for example, a local paralysis, bouts of sickness, or attacks of dizziness, are the tokens of a more general and 'deeper' malady.[76] The charm of discovering that these disorders have a spiritual meaning should not obscure the form in which they find expression. These bodily signs at once conceal and reveal something in the patient's past, an incident, or more frequently the fantasy, of a sensuous event. And the fantasy is no less real than the event to which it falsely alludes because both are bodily dispositions carried forward in memory to become an aspect of contemporary sensuousness. As recollection it already has a place in the bodily economy; but when it finds a place in the active, conscious memory, a conflict is set up, the temporary resolution of which is a symptom. Such symptoms, along with parapraxes too minor to rank as symptoms, display by their slight misrelation the fact of the normal integration of spirit and body in contemporary sensuous immediacy. Other, more disturbed patients either drive the spirit beyond the body and live as deadened mechanisms, or become so spiritualized themselves that they cannot bear to be *touched*.[77]

Every place in which the spirit locates itself becomes infected with its unassimilated irrationality, its strangeness. In the newly relativized body, sin is transformed into the temptation to illness, and faith becomes an unreflective bodily ease. Our body can appear as a stranger, even as an enemy. It falls ill, it refuses to express our wishes, not from the meaningless resistance of dead matter, but from a deep cunning of its own.

Jaspers's *General Psychopathology*, therefore, which contains the fullest catalogue of distortions in the modern body-images is, at the same time, the most complete encyclopaedia of modern spiritual perversity. Meticulously detailing the martyrdom awaiting every spiritual extremist, it has something of the appeal of both hagiography and heresiography. 'In psychotic reality', he tells us, 'we find an abundance of content representing fundamental problems of philosophy; nothingness, total destruction, formlessness, death. Here the extremest of human possibilities actually breaks through the ordinary boundaries of our sheltered, calm, ordered and smooth existence'.[78] Psychopathology becomes a theology of modernity, rooting out every heretical transgression in order to establish the naturalness of what, in fact, cannot be any more than a conventional order. Jaspers is, then, from this point of view, a modern Ireneus; and Freud is the Augustine of a new age.

THE SUBLIME COMMODITY

The fundamental problems of post-Reformation theology, particularly since the writings of Hegel and Schleiermacher, have been connected with *anthropology* in its broadest sense. *Man*, not God, poses the basic religious problem. As 'the animal that is not yet established', man is continually beyond himself.[79] As 'the being which is superior to himself and to the world' he is ignorant of his own nature, and estranged from the world which that nature has produced.[80] Human self-transcendence follows necessarily from man's formal and limited likeness to God, and God's absolute otherness from Man. 'God is the unknown God', so that the consciousness of His abysmal presence, even more than the awareness of his absence, is felt as painful self-alienation.[81]

The modern theologian has thus joined forces with the secular critic of human self-estrangement. The progressive absorption of the transcendental structure of Being into the frame of humanity which, more than its progressive rationalization, has characterized the history of western Christianity, has culminated therefore in the fundamental identity of secular and theological anthropology. For *both* the aim is the liberation of human being from the 'misrelation' of his corrupted nature. Modern society is unique in its radical separation from the natural world, in its technological mastery of the means to life, and in the self-consciousness of its conventions. Yet (quite apart from any particular issues of its resulting injustice!), the emergence and expression of a new level of human freedom in the fundamental arbitrariness of modern society has not meant the recovery of fully human being. On the contrary, the detachment of humanness from the natural world is a process which has increased, rather than diminished, the distance between living human beings and the realization of their true, but hidden, humanity.[82] The *religious* goal of life, however, has been painfully clarified. It is to be found in the completion of this movement, in the establishment of a way of life which is 'infinitely concerned' over the human.[83] Pascal's 'hidden God' reveals Himself in the urge towards *human* self-expression. The human, further, should not be mistaken for an inward, personal and ultimately empty selfhood. Nor should its transcendence be viewed, religiously, as merely the ideal characteristics that human beings project, as it were, ahead of themselves. The human, rather, manifests itself in every aspect of our being, and most fundamentally in the barely conscious separation of our bodily experience from purely natural organic processes.

The obstacles to the complete emancipation of the human no longer lie in the weight of fallen nature in which human existence was once implicated, but in the disordered structure of his chosen way of life. The religious call to obedience is transformed, therefore, into an obligation to defy the law and live humanly.

'Man is a synthesis', writes Kierkegaard, a synthesis 'of the infinite and the finite, of the temporal and the eternal, of freedom and necessity'.[84] The condition of modern living has revealed that both poles of this synthesis, the finite *and* the infinite, are contained *within* the purely human. The human, therefore, properly conceived and properly lived, is an 'infinite relation to the infinite'. The purely human is a religious phenomenon, and religion is a wholly human phenomenon. Thus while the experience of the modern world can be described as the secularization of older forms of religiosity, it can with equal validity and greater pathos be characterized as the consecration of the profane world.

This 'theological circle' cannot be broken. A correlation between religious and secular language is inevitably part of human self-understanding, and of the practical grasp of human reality as a phenomenon *sui generis*. The incompleteness of such self-understanding (which is the same as the complete understanding of our own unfinished nature) is the foundation of all religious knowledge of man. And, on the other hand, the reality of God is grasped in the continuous unfolding of human duration. It would be fruitless to claim either Man or God as the ultimate ground of the Other. The *sociologically* interesting aspect of this correlation, however, does not require this circle to be broken. Starting from *either* God or Man the peculiar nature of modern transcendence as sensuousness can be discovered.[85] For both, the body becomes a potentially whole, but actually fragmented, form of Being.

The human quality of being is recovered from the fragments of everyday life by simple immersion in its duration, rather than through any forced reconstruction of its presumed totality. The sensuousness which is the religious expression of modern social life, and the social form of modern religiosity, can be characterized as the playful transformism of the 'primary process'. Any residual prejudice against bodily forms, therefore, must be overcome; we cannot 'consider our instincts as too impure, the sensuous as too peripheral, or our emotion as too fleeting – everything must be included and integrated. What is wanted is not the abstracted self but the whole, undiminished man'.[86] 'The soul and not the spirit is the true centre of man', and the soul can be identified with the 'primary process':

> Here is the deep centre, in this seeing, this awareness, this feeling, we are close to the primal reality, to that existence and life which has no contradictions, which has not yet been differentiated, the 'immediate'.[87]

True being is not a unity or totality in the usual sense. It is not a finished structure but continuous metamorphoses whose infinity of possibilities is preserved in each of its arbitrarily divided parts. The totality of sensuousness is present in its smallest fragment, its entirety reappearing in a single fortuitous sensation. Ivan Karamazov, as much as Proust's Narrator, or John Cowper Powys's Wolf Solent, is conscious that 'however much I may disbelieve in the order of things, I still love the sticky little leaves that open up in the spring'.[88]

The body knows itself only in relation to a world towards which it is infinitely open, a world which it has, in fact, created for itself.[89] In modern society, natural objects, like the 'sticky little leaves', are not inherently different from the commodities which more obviously form man's 'second nature'. The commodity is the relation through which the world, including the natural world, is conceivable.[90] It is also, therefore, the relation through which human beings encounter their own bodies, whose transcending sensuousness can be understood sociologically as a living paradigm of the commodity form.

The emergent modern correlation between religious and bodily language – their coincidence as sensuous being – finds a third, mediating term in the commodity. Indeed, the transition from Passion to Sensuousness is comprehensible as the most recent episode in the secret history of the commodity relation.

The commodity is generated by bodily activity, by labour, but in becoming part of a process of exchange which is in principle infinite it acquires an objectivity which is alien to its origin. Marx described this process as the 'fetishism of commodities' which is an inversion of the true relationship between man and his world. The quality of timeless necessity which the commodity realm acquires, and in relation to which man appears to be a wholly dependent subject, is in fact transferred to it through the process of labour. In capitalism this process is perversely set free of any guiding human needs and becomes subordinated to an abstract principle, the law of capital accumulation. The commodity, which is by definition a useful object, is of no intrinsic interest to the capitalist, who organizes its production with a view solely to its value in the general process of exchange. The world produced by capitalism is, therefore, a world abstracted from human needs and human relations. It confronts human beings as 'an entire system of estrangement', and its inversion is the reality (of timeless, necessary and reversible relations of exchange) upon which the classical scientific view of the world was modelled.[91]

Marx identified the representations of this 'fantastic' reality both with the classical sciences, particularly political economy, and with the 'alienated consciousness' of religious thought. As soon as an object enters into the system of exchange, that is, as soon as it 'emerges as a commodity, it changes into a thing which transcends sensuousness', and becomes 'a very strange thing abounding in metaphysical subtleties and theological niceties'.[92] It acquires its 'mystical character' in being exchanged, in becoming part of a transcending system of obligatory relations.

Marx is interested above all in the *production* of this perverse reality, and he interprets religious ideas as eccentric representations of the alienation of labour. It is an abstract and symbolic description of the process of alienating human value (labour) into a world of objects which are then treated as if they were the autonomous source of this value. The *secret* of religion is traced to the slow emergence of the commodity form of production; to the suppression of use-value in favour of exchange-value. This, however, is to interpret human reality from one side only. Western Christianity has always held personal salvation to be of central religious significance, and this has usually been conceived, implicitly, as a process of consuming, rather than of making or of producing the world.

The religion associated with classical capitalism, therefore, is Passion, a specific 'mode of consumption' through which the self projects and then absorbs its own authenticity. Now, as the only source of value is human, and the commodity world is a collection of individuated objects, value is conceivable (superficially) as the object itself, or (profoundly) as an image of the self alienated into the object. Religious existence is the potentiation of the commodity relation viewed from the side of consumption. It grasps the value hidden in the commodity to be human value in general, and therefore to be an infinite value. All consumption becomes a 'search' for the self, the validation of the existential self as identical with this infinite value.

Religion does not disappear with capitalism; it simply accommodates itself to the new realism of political economy.

In modern society, however, the commodity world, particularly viewed from the perspective of consumption, is no longer the perfect mechanism of exchange which, during most of the nineteenth century, it had appeared to be. The law of capital accumulation has not ceased to condition the process of production. Indeed, it is to satisfy its necessity that the consumer must be liberated from the artificial constraints of selfhood, and the entire ego psychology of consumption based upon it. The commodity world, to exist at all, must continually expand. It must endure, propelling itself forward with the force of its own inexhaustible novelty.[93] Thus, rather than being invested in the qualities of particular objects, 'ultimate value' is now so to speak scattered randomly throughout the commodity world in discrete packets or *quanta*. The appropriation of value thus depends upon chance. And it is the resulting uncertainty which provokes a wishful relation to the commodity, supplanting, as a more powerful stimulus to consumption, any rational utilitarian, *or* passionate, form of want.

The consumption of ultimate value is, thus, no longer the validation of selfhood, mirrored in the commodity's external and objective form, but the displacement of the self into the pure sensuousness of duration from which the commodity itself springs. The transcendence at which modern religiosity aims is no longer the ideological truth of capitalism (changeless Being) but the reality of which society is a falsification (restless Becoming).

The modern religious disposition no longer exerts itself in the search for a hidden and obscure reality. It longs neither for the mystical simplicity of preconceptual being, nor for the dogmatic clarity of an individuated inner-self. It gives way, rather, to the overflowing abundance of things, and rediscovers a primitive trust in their immediacy as the source of an endlessly replenished store of value.

CONCLUSION
The End of *Happiness*

'Transcendence itself has a history', remarks a contemporary theologian.[1] And its history, like any history, is both a part of, and a comment upon, a changing reality. Transcendence is, so to speak, an active ingredient in the creation and preservation of the finite and limited present; yet the manner in which it is conceived (or rather misconceived), and the peculiar necessity of its ineffable presence, grow out of these very contingencies.[2]

In western society transcendence makes itself felt with peculiar intimacy as Happiness. Strictly speaking, of course, the transcendent cannot 'make itself felt', and the theologian must be content with the pure negativity of God. Yet the conviction that, while the transcendent reality of God can never be reached, His presence can nonetheless be felt as the pang of Happiness, is an ontological model of human being institutionalized at almost every level and every period of western history. Thus, while we may no longer feel the need of a cosmological God, and may be able to describe our personal existence in terms of wholly secular psychological concepts, our relation to the realm of value (and in particular our activities as consumers of value) reveals the fundamentally religious structure of our everyday lives. However reluctant we might be to use the term, our lives are conditioned by the possibility of Happiness. Human being in western society is defined and redefined primarily in relation to Happiness; the *end* of Happiness has survived the end of *Happiness*.

Happiness is a relation, a relation of finite and infinite, time and eternity, freedom and necessity. This relation is embedded in, and expressed through, the changing forms of western society which reveal the inner-transformations of its polarities. We now take for granted the fact of human history, and no one is any longer rash enough to claim for its subject a fixed and unchanging nature.

Somewhat less obviously, the God who cannot be known or defined can certainly be talked about, and participates in this same history. The God of Faith, thus, is not the same as the God of Belief, or the God of Passion. Both the social form of ultimate value, and the modality of its relation to us, are subject to the continuous revision of history. Happiness, thus, is not a fixed category within the development of western society, but a series of different forms for the expression of relations of transcendence.

Relations can only be conceived and expressed socially. It is (from the viewpoint of our own existence) the necessary but contingent fact of society that defines reality. We cannot conceive anything other than this reality.[3] Yet we can become aware of its conventionality, and even of its arbitrariness; and whatever else it might be about, it is this relation of practical transcendence which is expressed in the history of western religiosity. The emergence of each new social form, therefore, has been the starting point for a thorough reconstruction of the traditional truth of Christianity, and the occasion for a fresh vision of Happiness.

Every social relation is touched by transcendence, each exists in the face of the possibility of being other than it is. Any social relation, therefore, can find its own religious expression. But it is in the sphere of value that the most consistent religious forms are developed. This is not because value defines the good (as opposed to either the bad or the evil), and religion is in some sense an essentially moral discourse, but simply because value is the language of relative worth. It is, thus, a meta-language of relations, a category within which all other relations can be caught up and ordered. And, in the west, absolute value, as the source and standard of all relative values, can be conceived religiously by an act of theological abstraction. The apparent incompatibilities among values, their incommensurability one with another, are apparently resolved in a theological harmonization or mediation. It is a characteristic of western religion that, in addition to the 'natural religion' which springs from the partial realization of the conventionality of all social relations and, therefore, of all values, a theologically defined 'absolute value' is formed into the possibility of human Happiness, and as such is the guarantor of the worth, and the conditioning *telos*, of all subordinate values.

This entire development rests on the purely objective character of value. It is because value is alienated into *things*, and is, therefore, distributed throughout the object-world, that both the necessity of a general system of exchange, and the problem of incommensurability within it, arises in the first place. The religious problem is intimately bound up with this emptying of value into things. The immediate world is diminished to the extent that value, rather than being directly present within it, is confined to an artificial realm of social institutions which, in being constructed from more or less extended sequences of exchange, is not directly available to human consciousness.[4] Christianity as the mediation of absolute value can be viewed as a statement of the human interest in this alienated value. It expresses, in its various forms, the possibility of reclaiming not only lost value, but with it the generative source of all value. Christianity is, in this sense, the religion of absolute consumption.

Western society conceives of the relation of transcendence in terms of (a changing) ultimate value, and throughout its development Christianity has insisted upon the infinite abundance, and the nearness – the consumability – of this value. But it has done so in a variety of ways. The distinctions among Faith, Belief, Morality, Passion and Sensuousness define the shifting location of, and appropriate mode of consuming, such ultimate value. They are the relations, therefore, through which, in its various stages, western society becomes most fully present to its members.

In the social world of a declining ancient empire, Faith is an irrational expression for the estrangement of value. Through Faith lost value can be replaced and overwhelmingly augmented in an act of internal liberation. Society exists in the imposition of Law; and Christianity expresses itself, therefore, as both the culmination of, and freedom from, the Law. Society is wholly internalized and free subjectivity becomes the source of that order which was previously guaranteed by coercion. The Law is consumed in order that human dependence upon it can be overcome. Provided only that an individual has Faith, the transcending value of Law becomes intimately present as spontaneous conformity.

In the new barbarian society of the west, and in its successor feudal states, ultimate value was embedded in a cosmic reality of which they were held to be imperfect copies. First as a general notion of hierarchy, and then through the hypostasis of personal dependence, Happiness was symbolically linked to the completed structure of creation. The diversity of such societies, and the variety of social experience which had to be integrated within the universal truth of Christianity, meant that Law became a relative rather than absolute value. Additionally their shrinkage and relative closure, their less extensive commercial, manufacturing and trading activities, made

Belief rather than Faith the core of religious life. Faith had made society inwardly real, consuming the externality of Law and converting it to free subjectivity. Belief, combining both objective and subjective aspects of value, was the form in which God's *asiety* was expressed, and the medium in which His presence was most intimately disclosed, to a later and more diverse body of followers. In consuming Belief the individual knew both society and God. The mind, that is to say, was conformed to the reality expressed equally in creed, cosmos and society. Happiness, therefore, resided in the *contemplation* of God.

The collapse of feudalism, before it could be viewed as the precondition of a new age of universal reason, appeared as the chaotic disruption of the medieval world. The transformation of cosmology rendered Belief just one other, and therefore dubious, theoretical vision of existence. The locus of transcendence shifted decisively to a new inwardness, conceived as Morality. Society existed in a new, individualized and universalized, moral order which was consumed as the absolute obligation of self-control.

The moral reality of religion deepened during the development of capitalism into Passionate individualism. The religious reality of selfhood was yet a further transformation in the mode of consumption. The dialectical psychology of desire, through the mediation of the commodity world, sought to establish absolute value within the self.

The rationality of the self, by the end of the nineteenth century, collapsed in solipsism and lost its power to act as a bearer of reality. The locus of transcendence once again shifted, keeping as it were one jump ahead of all attempts to finalize, and thus abolish it from, the social world. Now pure sensuousness, historically the antithesis of spirit, has undergone an epiphany of its own. Ultimate value now resides in the rediscovered primary process, made permanently available as religious representations, that is, as the abundance of commodities. This is part of a new psychology of consumption, one which is freed from the constraint of moral concepts, but one which is still driven by the spiritual power of transcendence.

This perspective is, in some respects, at odds with conventional approaches in the contemporary sociology of religion. Religion in contemporary western society, it has been argued, is comprehensible only in the context of a general historical view of the formation and development of that society. Yet the dominant tendency in contemporary sociological studies of religion remains unhistorical. The result of this neglect has been the persistence of 'one-dimensional' general theories of religion. Overwhelmingly, thus, religion is viewed as a symbolic means of 'making sense' of the world. In the broader historical context of western Christianity, however, such a view is difficult to sustain. Christianity has never been an exclusively cosmological religion, and, in terms of its recurrent promise of personal salvation, it might well be seen as 'making nonsense' of the world.

Even less tenable is the view, which seems often and unjustifiably to be attributed to Durkheim, that the most (or even the only) significant feature of religion in western society has been, and continues to be, its moral content. Religion, in this view, is primarily the legitimating mechanism of a secular social order. The period during which Christianity conceived of itself as Morality, however, was, in the context of its entire development, relatively short, and, more significantly, the conception of Morality it espoused was part of a vision of personal salvation, of Happiness, rather than directly of a collective obligation towards sociable conduct.

The perspective adopted here is, of course, equally opposed to all attempts to understand western society, and particularly its modern age, as a process of secularization. It is characteristic of each of the religious transformations of western society that they can be described (especially, but not exclusively, by their opponents) as the secularization of a previously 'more' religious age. But there is no need to see in each of its phases an inevitable loss of religious consciousness, or the wilful destruction of a religious truth, far less the emergence of an unobscured and rational human reality. In each succeeding transition, rather, we can find expressed, in the manner most appropriate to its particular and characteristic social relations, a formula for ultimate value.

The religious transitions within western society should not be viewed as partial transformations of any one particular aspect of social life. On the contrary, such transitions reveal the depth and generality of the internal social dynamics of western society. Nothing remains untouched in these transitions; everything is renewed and requires fresh forms of understanding. The identity and continuity of the west is not to be found in some 'underlying' and unchanging substance, nor can it be described as the continuous unfolding of a single 'spirit'. The continuous preoccupation with Happiness in western society is, in fact, a purely formal and empty designation which takes on a meaning only in the context of specific social relations. It is a radical possibility that has been re-created, time and again, in western history; yet it does not really have a history of its own. It does not persist, as if by some kind of spiritual inertia, from age to age. Nor does its reappearance, however transformed, in the midst of each new form of social life, allow us to claim Happiness itself to be the thread upon which the diverse societies of the west are strung. The continuous reconstruction of Happiness, like the idea of the continuity of the physical world within modern cosmology, is not so much something we feel obliged to explain as it is a phenomenon we are forced to accept as the starting point of any enquiry.

It is clearly also difficult, within this relativized perspective, to describe the Christian west as undergoing, in any systematic and sustained fashion, a process of rationalization. Within each of its phases the search for Happiness might well be conceived as falling under increasingly well organized and rationally ordered means, but the transitions from any one phase to any other phase belong to no such universal process. The notion of the long-term rationalization of western culture, in fact, assimilates all change to a providential movement of secularization. Yet, even in modern society, human activity is a continual denial of such a movement. Sensuousness is not the destruction of religious preconceptions, but the absorption into everyday consciousness of the ontological structure of Christian transcendence. In the perspective of its entire history the more fundamental movement of Christianity seems to have been from an outer/cosmic to an inner/psychic form of religiosity. But this, too, is an oversimplification. Primitive Christianity was ideally inward and subjective, while modern Sensuousness is a partial projection of a previously wholly interiorized form of religious consciousness. So, more precisely, there has been a double oscillation, a kind of religious respiration, between an inner and an outer religious reality.

An unresolved ambiguity in the social logic of transcendence has encouraged the development of two fundamentally different ways of conceiving of the acquisition of Happiness. That is, irrespective of its historical phase, a positive, ecclesiastical and intellectual tradition has been to some extent opposed by a negative, mystical and emotional variant of Christianity. The first has taken the distinction between individual and society as its starting point. Transcendent reality is thus represented authoritatively as the *structure* in relation to which the individual can become conscious of himself or herself. It runs the risk of deifying what is, in fact, only the connecting thread that mediates between man and God. The second route aims ideally to abolish this intermediary zone and feel God's presence directly. It models transcendence on the distinction between any social convention and an *undifferentiated* preconceptual and unthematized nature which it presupposes. The mystical way to God, by seeking Him directly, therefore runs the risk of compromising God's absolute otherness. The first tends to a view of Happiness as the completion of an inner structure, a 'copy' of God's design for the world, the latter prefers a vision of union which overwhelms and annihilates any mundane consciousness. Of course the dangers of either are recognized by their most enthusiastic advocates. Aquinas, for example, wholeheartedly proclaims the otherness of God, and Saint Bonaventure insists that, in transcending all vestiges, images and similitudes, the Mind is not thereby emptied of content but fixes itself upon Christ as the Redeeming Mediator. In this way the structure of consciousness is not so much dissolved into nothingness as acutely focused on its natural object.[5]

For neither tradition has Christianity ever been fundamentally ascetic in character, though powerful ascetic tendencies are, at various stages, evident in one or the other. From its early development, however, when radical gnostic asceticism posed a real threat to the establishment of Christianity as a world religion, orthodoxy has always declared the world to have a positive value. And the Augustinian synthesis was re-established at various critical points thereafter. God created the world, which depends for its existence upon His goodness. Therefore the world is not, in itself, evil. However, the aim of the Christian life, which is Happiness, is gained by consuming ultimate and absolute rather than secondary and relative value. As all values express, in their relation to its transcendence, ultimate value, some religious 'benefit' ought to be derivable from consuming any value. The Christian, however, is intent upon consuming the greatest concentration of being; this is, simple spiritual economics. And as historically the transitions in western society have thrown up first one and then another apparently privileged sphere of value, Christianity has successively cultivated an insatiable appetite for these privileged spheres, while at the same time it has affected indifference, though not necessarily hostility, to all others. The 'age of Belief' was suspicious of the enjoyment of any value other than belief. Conscience, for example, was likely to be regarded as a form of self-indulgent pride, and an obstacle, therefore, to the attainment of authentic religious goals. And, on the other hand, for the Passionate Christian the acceptance of conventional morality is to give way to a cowardly distraction from the religious task of inner self-realization. And in modern society, where Sensuousness has become the privileged realm of value, the Christian must practise a mild restraint upon every enjoyment *other* than that of the senses.

Human beings are 'unfinished animals'; they are continually going beyond themselves. They cannot prevent their activities alluding, therefore, to a reality which is not yet fully disclosed, or to a future which can be brought into existence only as an act of faith.

NOTES

INTRODUCTION: THE *END* OF HAPPINESS

1 Augustine (1873), vol. V, p. 3.
2 Ibid., pp. 3–4.
3 Ibid., p. 4.
4 Ibid., p. 5.
5 Ibid., p. 6.
6 Ibid., p. 9.
7 Ibid., p. 17.
8 And 'Following after God is the desire for happiness', ibid., p. 13. It is
  certainly possible to trace back to Aristotle's *Nicomachean Ethics* a secular
  tradition in the idea of happiness: McGill (1967), Tatarkiewicz (1976),
  Telfer (1980). *Eudaemonia* is related to the establishment of a particular
  scheme of values, and, unlike hedonism, is clearly related to what is here
  termed Happiness. The peculiarity of the *western* tradition of happiness
  only emerges, however, when this idea is brought into contact with a
  distinctively religious form of salvation.
9 Boethius (1969), p. 79.
10 Ibid., p. 101. Boethius, in identifying Happiness with Goodness is more
  openly Platonic than Augustine. But the central psychological point,
  that transcendence is implicated in human Happiness, remains the same.
11 Aquinas (1911), vol. 16, pp. 95, 105.
12 Pascal (1966), 134 (all references to Pascal's *Pensées* are to the numbered
  entries in Krailsheimer's translation).
13 Ibid., 373.
14 For a recent example see Polkinghorne (1986), and more generally
  Davies (1984).
15 Quite apart from the revival of interest in the historical dimension in the
  writings of Weber, for example, Schluchter (1981), the pioneering work
  of Pirenne (1936, 1939) has been particularly influential in the re-
  emergence of 'Europe' as an historical problem, notably in Herrin
  (1987), and should be set alongside the very different but equally
  impressive studies of Ste Croix (1983), for an earlier period, and Braudel
  (1981, 1983, 1984), for later developments.

16 The phrase is from Laplace, allegedly in reply to a question from Napoleon.
17 As we study history 'in order to attain self-knowledge' – Collingwood (1946), p. 315, and history is a particular form of that self-knowledge, these methodological difficulties point to distinct and irreconcilable tendencies in our experience of the *present*, rather than to purely logical problems.
18 Blumenberg (1983), p. 4. For conventional sociological accounts of secularization in the context of *Enlightenment* see Martin (1969, 1978); Wilson (1966); MacIntyre (1967); Luckmann (1967); Greeley (1973); Towler (1974); Acquaviva (1979); Gilkey (1981). The historical and philosophical issues are brilliantly explored, from opposing viewpoints, by Lowith (1949) and Blumenberg (1983, 1987).
19 It is the fact that Happiness is not *contained* in a fixed structure of relations that allows such differing judgements of the present age to be made. It can appear, depending on the model which is applied (as in Nietzsche's writings, for example), as both wholly secularized and spiritually intense.
20 Parsons (1937) remains the fundamental interpretation.

1 HAPPINESS: BEYOND THE SOCIOLOGY OF RELIGION

1 David Hume's *Natural History of Religion* (1757), and Lord Kames's (Henry Home) *Sketches of the History of Man* (1813) are notable, and exceptional, among Enlightenment authors for their positive interpretation of religion.
2 Durkheim has particularly in mind the German philological school as exemplified by Müller (1898). See W. Schmidt (1931), pp. 93–9 for a still useful discussion.
3 Durkheim (1915), p. 35.
4 Ibid., p. 37.
5 Ibid., p. 38.
6 Ibid., pp. 38–9. Hence (ibid., p. 38), 'The traditional opposition of good and bad is nothing beside this'. W. Robertson Smith (1907, first edn. 1888) had drawn a similar distinction between the *holy* and the *common*, but in the context of developed religions only: 'Religion in primitive times was not a system of belief', he claims (ibid., p. 20). For his influence on Durkheim see Lukes (1973), pp. 238–9, 450–1, Beidelman (1974), pp. 59–61. John H. King (1892), on the other hand, traces all religion to the distinction between *luck* and *ill–luck*, which he interprets in terms of the general evolution of 'sentiments'. Durkheim's theory might be seen as combining the sociological insight of Robertson Smith with the generalizing ambitions of King. The most fruitful application has been in the reconstruction of 'archaic' religious consciousness, see van der Leeuw (1963), vol.1, pp. 47–8, Eliade (1959).
7 Ibid., p. 40.

8 Ibid., p. 41.

9 Ibid., p. 41.

10 Ibid., p. 43.

11 'Magic, too, is made up of beliefs and rites . . . The beings which the magician invokes and the forces which he throws in play are not merely of the same nature as the forces and beings to which religion addresses itself; very frequently, they are identically the same.' Ibid., p. 42.

12 Ibid., p. 43.

13 Ibid., p. 43.

14 Lukes (1973), pp. 477–84; Pickering (1984) for clear and sympathetic exposition.

15 A development already evident in Mauss (1954, original French edition 1925). Generally, see Levi-Strauss (1968), Part One.

16 An interpretation that owes most to Parsons's (1937) authoritative study, though enjoying something of a history of its own in British social anthropology, see e.g. Radcliffe-Brown (1952).

17 A common 'evolutionary' perspective dominated all aspects of social thought during the latter part of the nineteenth century. For a clear general discussion see particularly Burrow (1966), and for popular 'scientistic' applications Haeckel (1879), Gould (1977), and Turner (1974). Durkheim was not uncritical of this framework, but his 'bookish ethnography', it was claimed by critics, suffered the defects of equally untested theoretical ideas; see van Gennep, in Pickering (1975), pp. 205–8.

18 Durkheim (1915), pp. 101–13.

19 Ibid., p. 102.

20 Ibid., p. 147. See also Durkheim and Mauss (1963), pp. 3–11.

21 Ibid., p. 147. And (ibid., p. 145), 'It is because men were organized that they have been able to organize things, for in classifying these latter, they limited themselves to giving them places in the groups they formed themselves'.

22 On this understanding, in fact, he opens himself to damaging criticisms. See Needham's 'Introduction' to Durkheim and Mauss (1963).

23 Durkheim (1915), p. 167.

24 Ibid., p. 119.

25 Ibid., p. 188.

26 Ibid., p. 189.

27 Ibid., p. 190. 'All the beings partaking of the same totemic principle consider that owing to this very fact, they are morally bound to one another; they have definite duties of assistance, vendetta, etc., towards each other; and it is these duties which constitute kinship.'

28 Ibid., p. 206.

29 Ibid. p. 207. Both Tylor (1871) and Frazer (1900) had traced 'primitive' religion to 'fear' of nature. See Ferguson (1990), ch.2. But Durkheim insists that religion is rooted in the *moral* supremacy of the collective over the individual. 'Respect is the emotion which we experience when we feel this interior and wholly spiritual pressure operating upon us.' Durkheim (1915), p. 207.

30 Ibid., p. 218.
31 Ibid., p. 225. And it is thus that 'Religion ceases to be an inexplicable hallucination and takes a foothold in reality'.
32 Ibid., p. 419.
33 'In fact, *petitio principii* is, in a sense, a feature of the book as a whole, for Durkheim begins it with his conclusion, building it into his very definition of religion and then seeking to prove it by finding examples.' Lukes (1973), p. 481.
34 Durkheim (1933), pp. 181–3. And, p. 228, he declares: 'Every society is a moral society. In certain respects, this character is even more pronounced in organized societies. Because the individual is not sufficient unto himself, it is from society that he receives everything necessary to him, as it is for society that he works. Thus is formed a very strong sentiment of the state of dependence in which he finds himself . . . In reality, co-operation also has its intrinsic morality.'
35 Ibid., pp. 174–81, and, in the context of classification, Durkheim and Mauss (1963), pp. 6–7.
36 Durkheim (1933), p. 79.
37 His view of 'primitive' society seems closely related to Rousseau's imaginative reconstruction of human prehistory. See particularly Rousseau (1984), pp. 81–107, an author who was central to Durkheim's Latin thesis, and influential in the development of Durkheim's views on education. See Lukes (1973), pp. 125–8.
38 Bergson (1935), p. 18, expresses the same idea; in society 'only one thing is natural, the necessity of a rule'.
39 There can be no society sustained by 'mechanical solidarity' alone. Division and interdependence are part of the *definition* of society. The 'unity' of society is always the recombination of parts.
40 Augé (1982), p. 91, perceptively comments that 'one cannot find social activities that are strictly speaking outside the sacred'. A difficulty alluded to by Durkheim himself: 'since no known thing exists that is not classified in a clan and under a totem, there is likewise nothing which does not receive to some degree something of a religious character'. Durkheim (1915), pp. 153–4.
41 The connection between the growth of 'organic solidarity' and the development of individualism is brought out particularly in Durkheim (1915) chs. 2 & 3.
42 Rousseau (1984), p. 109.
43 'Egoistic' suicide is wrongly named; the predisposing condition is not one of egoism, which is a typically modern social relation, but *isolation*.
44 The first described in exemplary fashion by Freud, vol. 21, pp. 64–5. And the second most notably by Otto (1959) and William James (1960), pp. 366–413.
45 Marx (1975), p. 244.
46 Feuerbach (1957, first edn. 1841), p. 122, quoting Sebastian Frank: 'God is a tear of love, shed in the deepest concealment over human misery. "God is an unutterable sigh, lying in the depths of the heart"; this saying is the most remarkable, the profoundest, truest expression of

Christian mysticism.' For the development of Marx's ideas about religion see Turner (1983), and Ling (1980).
47 See Marx and Engels (1955); Ling (1980); McLellan (1969); Lowith (1964), pp. 53–136; Kolakowski (1978), vol.1, pp. 81–95. And for a useful selection of original texts Stepelevich (1983).
48 Marcuse (1955), p. 260.
49 Marcuse (1955), pp. 150–1.
50 Both Christianity and philosophy, argues Feuerbach ' . . . in this development of the supersensible as what is alone essential, and of the sensible as non-essential . . . become world denying'. Quoted in Wartofsky (1977), p. 57. Though, in this context, it is worth recalling Hegel's own early, radical, theological works, particularly *The Positivity of the Christian Religion*, in Hegel (1948), in which 'Spirit, not thought, is life'.
51 Wartofsky (1977), p. 1. Barth (1972), p. 534, argues that for Feuerbach 'even Kant, Fichte and Hegel are still supernaturalists, to the extent that they are seeking the divine Being in reason, separately from man'.
52 Ibid., p. 198.
53 Feuerbach (1957), p. 1.
54 Ibid., p. 2.
55 Ibid., pp. 12–13. 'Consciousness of God is self-consciousness, knowledge of God is self-knowledge.'
56 Ibid. 'Man has given objectivity to himself, but has not recognised the object of his own nature.'
57 Ibid., pp. 29–30.
58 Feuerbach makes a somewhat misconceived effort to identify this infinity with the actuality of history.
59 Marx (1959), p. 244.
60 Marx (1975), p. 244.
61 Ibid., pp. 57–198. See also Marx (1970), pp. 57–60; Hyppolite (1969).
62 Marx (1975), p. 243.
63 Ibid., p. 244.
64 Marx (1970), pp. 39–52.
65 See, for example, Kolakowski (1978), vol.1, pp. 182–233.
66 Marx (1975), p. 256.
67 Marx (1970), pp. 42–8; Ollman (1971), pp. 168–75.
68 Marx (1975), pp. 322–34.
69 Marx (1976), vol.1, pp. 163–77, for classic analysis of the 'fetishism of commodities'; and Avineri (1968), pp. 86–95 for a useful discussion of Marx's conception of communist society.
70 'The mysterious character of the commodity-form consists therefore simply in the fact that the commodity reflects the social characteristics of men's own labour as objective characteristics of the products of labour themselves, as the socio-natural properties of these things.' Marx (1976), vol.1, pp. 164–5.
71 Marx (1975), p. 323.
72 Marx (1976) vol.1, p. 163. C. F. von Weizsacker, quoted in Blumenberg (1983), p. 79, remarks acutely that 'In modern times, the

world takes over this attribute of God: infinity becomes secularized. Under this aspect it is most remarkable that our century has begun to doubt the infinity of the world'.

73 The aim of a *critique* is to reveal the truth hidden in perverse and mystified forms of human (and therefore ultimately valid) consciousness. Thus, for example, 'The categories of bourgeois economics consist precisely of forms of this kind. They are forms of thought which are socially valid, and therefore objective'. Marx (1976), vol.1, p. 169.

74 Ibid., p. 163.

75 Sohn-Rethel (1978) for a general discussion of this perspective. Marx (1973), pp. 150–2.

76 Ferguson (1990).

77 A possibility which depends, of course, on the genuine, as opposed to merely formal, freedom of labour.

78 Weber (1965), p. 1.

79 Ibid.

80 See, generally, Weber (1978) vol.1, pp. 3–24.

81 See particularly his famous essays, 'Politics as a Vocation' and 'Science as a Vocation'. Weber (1948), pp. 77–158.

82 Weber (1963), p. 1.

83 Burrow (1966).

84 Weber (1963), pp. 27–8.

85 Ibid., p. 28.

86 Ibid., p. 29. These distinctions, it should be noted (unlike Durkheim's) are fluid rather than categorical.

87 Ibid.

88 Ibid., pp. 46–59; and Weber (1952), pp. 267–335.

89 Weber (1963), p. 59.

90 Ibid.

91 Ibid., p. 75. He notes, indeed, that 'Pastoral care in all its forms is the priests' real instrument of power, particularly over the workaday world'.

92 Ibid., p. 144.

93 Ibid., pp. 144–5.

94 Ibid., p. 145.

95 Ibid.

96 Ibid., p. 146.

97 Weber (1948), pp. 324–30.

98 Weber (1963), p. 171.

99 Ibid., p. 173.

100 'Unwillingness to work is *symptomatic* of the lack of grace'; Weber (1930), p. 159 (emphasis added).

101 Weber (1963), p. 80.

102 Ibid., p. 85.

103 Ibid.

104 Ibid., p. 95.

105 Ibid., p. 97.

106 Weber (1968), vol.2, p. 953.

107 Weber (1930), p. 181.

108 Mitzman (1970); Mommsen (1974); Brubaker (1984). A fruitful comparison with Marx from this perspective is provided by Lowith (1982).
109 There is a remarkable parallel between Weber's social theory and Harnack's (1894–99) *History of Dogma*. They both consider western Christianity to be characterized by a long-term, and ultimately destructive, process of rationalization. Harnack, however, views this process as the progressive assimilation by (irrational) Christianity of Greek philosophical discourse, rather than as a general feature of all aspects of social development which has a particular 'affinity' with the formal characteristics of western Christianity. On Harnack see Pauck (1968).
110 That is to his essay *The Protestant Ethic and the Spirit of Capitalism*. For a guide to the various controversies it has sparked off, see Marshall (1982) and Poggi (1983).
111 To avoid any form of 'Hegelian' immanence, Weber insists on discovering the process of rationalization in the *transformation* of a decidedly 'irrational' phenomenon.
112 Harnack (1894), vol.2 viewed the route from classical Greek culture to North African Christianity as the more direct path of rational development in Western religion. A view that finds strong contemporary support among historians of Christianity in all its aspects. See, for example, Pelikan (1971), vol.1, and Daniélou (1964), vol.2.
113 Ferguson (1990), ch.7.

2 FAITH: HAPPINESS PROCLAIMED

1 Troeltsch (1931), vol.1, p. 31.
2 Ibid., p. 39.
3 Ibid. A view recently confirmed from quite a different perspective in Ste Croix (1983), pp. 418–52; ' . . . it was precisely the exclusive concentration of the early Christians upon the personal relations between man and man, or man and God, and their complete indifference, as Christians, to the institutions of the world in which they lived, that prevented Christianity from ever having much effect for good upon the relations between man and man', ibid. p. 439. This indifference was itself, as Ste Croix points out, conditioned by and part of 'the institutions of the world'.
4 Kautsky (1925).
5 Troeltsch (1931), vol.1, p. 43.
6 Ibid., p. 48. Troeltsch (1972) takes up the methodological implications of such a view. Thus, e.g. 'It is impossible to construct a theory of Christianity as the absolute religion on the basis of a historical way of thinking or by the use of historical means', ibid., p. 63.
7 See, generally, Robinson and Koester (1971); Koester (1986).
8 Nock (1933), p. 10.
9 Ibid., p. 17.
10 Burkert (1985), p. 189.
11 Nock (1933), p. 18.

12 Burkert (1985), p. 109.
13 Ibid., p. 119.
14 Fox (1986), p. 325.
15 Cumont (1956), p. 28; Altheim (1938) for a survey of Roman religion.
16 Ibid., pp. 29–30. Reitzenstein (1978), p. 32, concurs: 'The climactic point of the religious life is formed by the ecstasy which reaches its fullest and most unerring form in the mystery'.
17 Dix (1953), p. 5; Reitzenstein (1978), p. 17.
18 Dix (1953), p. 10. On the significance of the 'axial-age' as a transition from 'primitive' static to 'advanced' dynamic religions see Hick (1989), pp. 21–35; Bellah (1970), ch.2; Eliade (1979); Bloch (1986), vol.3, ch.53.
19 Nock (1933), pp. 171–80, and (1972), vol.1; Ferguson (1987), pp. 155–6; Wilken (1975), pp. 161–2, points out that Philosophy 'required discipline, the forming of habits, the slow, gradual transformation of one's life'.
20 Ibid., p. 179.
21 Ibid., p. 171.
22 Scholem (1941), p. 7.
23 Rist (1982), p. 38.
24 Ibid., p. 20.
25 That is actually 'divine', as the gods, for Plato, are not transcendent. Rist (1964), p. 17.
26 Nygren (1953), p. 174.
27 The phrase is Plato's, from *Theaetetus*, quoted in Dodds (1965).
28 Nygren (1953), p. 51.
29 Nock (1933), p. 27.
30 Rist (1964), p. 197.
31 Chadwick, in Armstrong ed. (1967), p. 137, for example, claims 'The history of Christian philosophy begins not with a Christian but with a Jew, Philo of Alexandria'. Dillon (1977), pp. 139–83.
32 Philo, ed. Winston (1981), p. 15. He continues, 'Thus ever thinking he creates, and furnishes to sensible things the principle of their existence, so that both should exist together: the ever-creating Divine Mind and the sense-perceptible things to which beginning of being is given'.
33 Ibid.
34 Ibid., p. 127. See Onians (1951), pp. 11–13 for a discussion of the association between breath and thought.
35 Ibid., p. 138.
36 Ibid., p. 127.
37 Ibid., p. 138.
38 Ibid., p. 164.
39 Ibid., p. 65.
40 Ibid., p. 168.
41 Plotinus (1969), p. 1.
42 Ibid., p. 70.
43 Ibid., p. 73.
44 Ibid., p. 50.

45 Ibid., p. 61. Blumenthal (1971), p. 20, points out that, for Plotinus, 'The soul *uses* the body as an instrument, just as an artisan uses his tools'.

46 Ibid.

47 Ibid., p. 63.

48 Ibid.

49 Just as it might be mistaken for the Platonic Good. On the Plotinian misreading of Plato see Rist (1964), p. 43.

50 Weber (1952), pp. 114–16; Dix (1953), p. 11.

51 Derrett (1970) emphasizes the significance of the Judaic conception of Law for the teachings of Jesus: 'The laws are the requirements of God', so that 'What God demands is good, but this is to be done not because it is good but because God demands it', ibid., p. xxii. See also Schillebeeckx (1979), pp. 230–56. For Weber's views see (1952), pp. 297–335. Zeitlin (1984) p. 282, concludes his reassessment of Weber's monograph by claiming that it seriously underestimates the ethical significance of the *priest* in favour of the prophet.

52 Scholem (1941), p. 24.

53 Ibid., p. 20.

54 Ibid., p. 34.

55 Quoted in Daniélou (1964), vol.1, p. 163.

56 Ibid., p. 195.

57 Ibid., p. 9. Zeitlin (1988) stresses the proximity of Jesus to a variety of Judaic traditions.

58 The basic texts are conveniently available in James M. Robinson ed. (1988); Foerster (1972). Significant discussions of the sources include Wilson (1958); Jonas (1958); Grant (1958); Nock (1972), vol.2; Pagels (1979); Perkins (1980); Logan and Wedderburn (1983); Rudolph (1983); Hedrick & Hodgson Jr. eds. (1986); Filoramo (1990).

59 Hedrick & Hodgson Jr. eds. (1986), p. 9.

60 Quoted in Jonas (1958), p. 137.

61 Ibid., p. 269. Rudolph, in Logan and Wedderburn (1983), p.31, provides an authoritative summary of the leading characteristics of gnosticism: 'Impelled by an anticosmic dualism, which also dominated its anthropology, early Gnostic thought, as far as we can tell, concentrated on the liberation of the hidden, divine core of man (the *pneuma*, the 'self'); despite all that happened in the world and history this core remained secretly united with the original above the heavens, of which it was a copy (it is 'speculation about the self'). This involves belief in the original fall of the (secret) core and its eventual rescue ('ascent of the soul'); this belief is made possible by the 'knowledge' of this complex of ideas, 'knowledge' which is a response to the redeeming 'call' of the Gnostic prophet or revealer (revelatory texts with exegetical methods are one of the main types of Gnostic writings). The usual response to these concepts is ascetic or encratite behaviour, but the Gnostics could also dispense with the customary moral and (Jewish) legal teachings. The 'kinship of souls' provided the ideological basis of their communal life; their community centred on the redeemed or 'spiritual' people (pneumatic), while the rest were either redeemed or

still on the way to 'liberation'; thus two sets of moral standards were involved'.

62 See particularly Stephen Gero's essay in Hedrick & Hodgson Jr. eds. (1986). The 'asceticism' of the gnostic should not be assimilated to the later Christian monastic tradition; 'Marcion's asceticism, unlike that of the Essenes and later of Christian monasticism, was not conceived to further the sanctification of human existence, but was essentially negative in conception and part of the gnostics' revolt against the cosmos'. Ibid., p. 145.

63 Pagels (1979) interprets gnostic disregard for authority, private property and the sexual division of labour to be a 'radical' ideology subsequently repressed by the development of the Christian church. It is important to emphasize that these are profoundly antinomian, rather than 'progressive', features.

64 Quoted in Jonas (1958), p. 137.

65 Bowker (1978), pp. 77–96.

66 Bauer (1971). Robinson and Koester (1971), p. 62, referring to problems of classifying the earliest 'Christian' texts, conclude: 'Not only have orthodoxy and heresy not yet separated into different ecclesiastical organizations; they have not yet separated their theological conceptualizations. Rather, from a common body of traditions, ambiguous in their concrete meaning, each side transmits interpretively, in terms of understandings that only gradually come to objectify themselves into fixed positions that could be branded as rights or wrong in and of themselves'. Thus, for example, Grant (1971), p. 88, stresses the polemical character of St Paul's theology. On organizational variation see particularly Brown and Meier (1982).

67 Gunther Bornkmann, quoted in Robinson and Koester (1971), p. 164. Koester (1986), vol.2, p. 64, is similarly forthright: 'The quest for the historical kernel of the stories of the Synoptic narrative materials is very difficult. In fact such a quest is doomed to miss the point of such narratives, because these stories were all told in the interests of mission, edification, cult, or theology (especially christology), and they have no relationship to the question of historically reliable information'. That there might still be some point in writing an historical 'Life' of Jesus has been demonstrated by Schillebeeckx's (1979) monumental volume. The religious point is made all the more definite by his subsequent, equally monumental study on 'Christ' (1989). On Wisdom literature and its relation to the Gospels see Wilken ed. (1975), and for the apocalyptic tradition, Dewick (1912), Rowley (1947), Aune (1972).

68 Robinson and Koester (1971), p. 164.

69 Ibid., p. 215.

70 Ibid., p. 227.

71 Theissen (1978), pp. 10–15; Stanbaugh and Balch (1986), p. 102; Gager (1975), p. 24. It is worth noting, as Boring (1982), p. 93, points out, that asceticism as a 'life-style was integral to early Christian prophetic eschatology' and owed nothing to a 'renunciation of the world as inherently evil'.

72 Meeks (1983) is particularly valuable in this respect. See also Malherbe (1977); Fox (1986), pp. 265–335; Frend (1980), pp. 25–42.
73 Quoted in Meeks (1983), p. 51.
74 Weizsacker (1894), vol.1, p. 33; Vermes (1973); Bowker (1978), pp. 132–3.
75 Ibid., p. 3.
76 Ibid.
77 Ibid., p. 34.
78 One is reminded of Durkheim's understanding of the 'interiorization' of social norms. Bultmann (1935, 1956) stresses this is a radical call to unconditional obedience to a purely formal authority, and not the anticipation of a humanistic ethic. See also Goguel (1964), p. 421.
79 Weizsacker (1894), vol.1, p. 123.
80 Ibid., p. 146.
81 Ibid., p. 147.
82 Ibid., p. 136.
83 Pagels (1975), traces a variety of gnostic influences in Paul's Letters. More generally on Christian and gnostic tendencies to asceticism see P. Brown (1989).
84 'It is not the physical in man which is evil – the *whole* man is evil if his will is evil'; Bultmann (1935), p. 48. Equally, the Kingdom should not be regarded as a state of mystical rapture, 'He promises neither ecstasy nor spiritual peace'; ibid., p. 47.
85 Pelikan (1971), vol.1, p. 125.
86 Ibid., pp. 187–8; Dix (1953), p. 78.
87 As it was to be for Augustine.
88 On the grounds that his theory of the 'multiplicity' and migration of the pre-existing soul introduced alien elements of Greek philosophy into Christianity. See Barnes (1981), pp. 198–9.
89 Clement, Roberts & Donaldson eds. (1867), vol.1, p. 69.
90 Ibid., vol.1, pp. 389, 416. This collection of miscellaneous remarks , the *Stromata*, 'will contain the truth mixed up with the dogmas of philosophy, or rather covered over and hidden, as the edible part of the nut in the shell'; ibid., p. 359.
91 Justin (1861), p. 18. And more warmly, 'Philosophy is indeed the greatest of treasures', ibid., p. 71.
92 Clement (1867), vol.1, p. 135.
93 Ibid., vol.1, p. 366.
94 Ibid.
95 Irenaeus (1868), p. 12.
96 Clement (1867), vol.1, p. 381.
97 Ibid., p. 372.
98 Ibid., vol.2, p. 220. Tertullian, of course, took the view that we must believe *because* it is absurd.
99 Clement (1867), vol.2, pp. 18–20.
100 Justin (1861), p. 74.
101 Ibid., pp. 72–3.
102 Origen (1869), vol.1, p. 12.

103 Ibid.
104 Cyprian (1868), vol.2, p. 20.
105 Ibid.
106 Ibid., vol.1, pp. 180–8. See also, in particular, the influential account of the martyrdom of Polycarp, Robertson and Donaldson eds. (1867), pp. 87–102.
107 Fox (1986), pp. 419–92.
108 Clement (1867), vol.1, p. 118.
109 Origen (1973), p. 11.
110 Ibid., pp. 9–10.
111 Ibid., p. 12.
112 Ibid., quoted p. xviii.
113 Origen (1869), pp. 132–3.
114 Augustine (1873), vol.1, p. 6. On the continuous nature of conversion in Augustine see Brown (1967), p. 59.
115 Ibid., p. 55.
116 Ibid., p. 75.
117 Ibid., p. 126.
118 Ibid.; But again it is important to note the difference between Christian and neo-Platonic 'asceticism'. The Christians 'do not wish to have no bodies at all but rather incorruptible and most agile bodies . . . they do not strive to destroy themselves'; Augustine (1958), pp. 20–1.
119 Ibid., p. 171.
120 Ibid., p. 214.
121 Ibid., p. 215.
122 Augustine (1873) vol.V Works p. 6.
123 Ibid., p. 134.
124 Ibid., p. 141–2. On dependence upon, and difference from, neo-Platonism see Bonner (1986), pp. 193–236.
125 Augustine (1873), vol.VII, p. 1.
126 Augustine (1873), vol.V, p. 141.
127 See Nygren (1953). Cyprian (1868), p. 4, sees 'righteousness' as the continuous availability of an endlessly circulating ultimate value; 'there is not, as is the case with earthly benefits, any measure or stint in the dispensing of the heavenly gift. The Spirit freely flowing forth is restrained by no limits, is checked by no closed barriers within certain bounded spaces; it flows perpetually, it is exuberant in its affluence'. 'Self-reflection' thus becomes the focal point of the Christian life, and 'an immense reality appears in self-consciousness, and this knowledge swallows up all interests in studying the cosmos'; Dilthey (1988), p. 234.
128 Augustine (1873), vol.V, p. 141.
129 Harnack (1894–99, 1957). Harnack traces the rationalization of *dogma*, rather than, as Weber proposes, religious life in general.
130 Rostovtzeff (1957); Ste Croix (1983), p. 439.
131 Rostovtzeff (1957), vol.2, p. 1046.
132 Ibid., p. 1046.
133 Ibid., p. 1050.
134 Just those forms of 'valueless' consumption which Augustine was to

inveigh against.
135 Rostovtzeff (1957), vol.2, p. 1053.
136 Ibid., p. 1099.
137 Ste Croix (1983) pp. 133–74 re-emphasizes the central role of slavery in the ancient world.
138 Rostovtzeff (1941), vol.2, p. 1017.
139 Nietzsche (1967), for the original argument. Scheler (1961) and Nygren (1953) for responses rather than outright rejections. Nietzsche's great psychological discovery tells us more about 'modern' religiosity than it does about the origins of Christianity. Modern academic social psychology has hardly fared better, see, e.g. Gager (1975).
140 Jones (1966), p. 50; Sordi (1983), pp. 3–6, 23–5, 46–7.
141 Jones (1966), pp. 21–5.
142 Ibid., p. 50. Davies (1965), pp. 68–9, notes a revival of pagan religions during the second century CE.
143 For an attempt to 'place' gnosticism in an economic and social context see Green (1985), who stresses the significance of colonial states in the formation of a gnostic 'anti-cosmic' ideology.
144 Augustine (1873), p. 216.
145 And not by the 'practical' but exclusive means of protected cults, such as the Essenes, or ascetic withdrawal. See especially Vööbus (1958), (1960), (1988); P. Brown (1989).
146 Augustine (1873), p. 88.
147 Blumenberg (1983).

3 BELIEF: HAPPINESS OBSCURED

1 MacMullen (1984), pp. 50–1. The growing respectability of Christianity depended on its misrepresentation as a cultic religion. Sordi (1983), p. 6, for example, in a careful study remarks that 'Constantine's choice of Christianity as the new religion for the empire was motivated by the desire to form an alliance with the strongest God of all'; see also Jones (1948), p. 111; and Alföldi (1948), p. 23, 'The Christianity of Constantine, then, was not wrapped in the glory of the true Christian spirit, but in the darkness of superstition'.
2 Pelikan (1974), vol.2, pp.26–9.
3 Sordi (1983), pp. 46–7.
4 Quoted in Kaegi (1968), p.3.
5 Pirenne (1939), p. 76.
6 Ibid., p. 62. Geary (1988), p. vi, goes even further, arguing that it was impossible for barbarian tribes 'to understand themselves and their past apart from Roman categories of ethnography, politics, and custom, just as it was impossible for them to prosper apart from Roman traditions of agriculture and commerce or to exercise power apart from Roman traditions of politics and law'.
7 Ibid., p. 140.

8 Herrin (1987), p. 31.
9 In particular the division between eastern 'Greek' and western 'Latin' Christianity was only glossed over. Pelikan (1974), vol.2, p. 31: 'Alongside the objectivity of the knowledge available through councils, fathers, and Scriptures, there arose a theology of subjective knowledge and of religious experience, which came to occupy a large place in Byzantine dogmatics'.
10 And its own 'unitarian' Christological conceptions, Nestorian, Monophysite and Chalcedonian. Young (1983); Pelikan (1974).
11 Augustine (1987), p. 17, the Symbol of faith (creed) 'briefly contained all that is necessary to believe to obtain salvation'. And, in this sense, the Christian Symbols are the obligatory preparation of all genuine knowledge; 'Unless you believe you shall not understand', ibid., p. 19.
12 A series of Oecumenical Councils (Constantinople 381, Ephesos 431, Chalcedon 451) reiterated the 'orthodoxy' of Nicaea which came to possess quasi-scriptural authority. See Herrin (1987), Young (1983). The Creed, claimed Isidore of Seville, contained in itself 'enough for salvation'; James (ed.) (1986), p. 26.
13 Pelikan (1974), vol.2; Atiya (1968), pp. 65–70.
14 Atiya (1968), p. 70. 'National' divisions rather than matters of doctrine were at the root of some of these 'heresies'. See, especially, Frend (1952).
15 Wallace-Hadrill (1983), p. 1.
16 Ibid., p. 24.
17 Gurevich (1985), pp. 40–5. Towards the end of the fourth century the Visigoths had been the first to be accepted en bloc into the empire, and had been the first barbarian tribe to be 'converted' to Christianity; see Thompson (1966).
18 As in north Africa it was 'not conversion from heathendom to a higher form of religion', so much as 'a transformed popular religion'; Frend (1952), p. 104.
19 Wallace-Hadrill (1983), p. 24.
20 Ibid., p. 33; James (1988), pp. 121–3.
21 Ibid., p. 36.
22 Ibid., p. 53.
23 Gelasius, quoted in Folz (1974), p. 76.
24 Ibid., p. 79.
25 Ibid., p. 84. Ganshof (1968), p. 11.
26 Ibid., p. 85. By anointing Pippin and his successors the pope effectively created them kings for the specific purpose of protecting the church. Thus, 'the empire under Charlemagne's rule was that entity which was held together by the Christian faith as expounded by the Roman church', and not a continuation of the 'Roman empire'; Ullmann (1955), p. 105. Indeed, 'Charlemagne's coronation was, so to speak, the final and solemn act by which the papacy emancipated itself from the constitutional framework of the Eastern empire'; ibid., p. 99.
27 Folz (1974), p. 93.
28 Ibid., p. 17; Knowles and Obolensky (1972), p. 53. In Visigothic Spain, Isidore observed, many became bishops in order to become rich;

Thompson (1969), p. 298.
29 Pelikan (1974), vol.2.
30 Ibid., p. 11. See also Eliade (1985), vol.3, p. 57.
31 Pelikan (1974), vol.2, p. 59.
32 Pseudo-Dionysius (1940); Louth (1989); Knowles and Obolensky (1972), pp. 86–91.
33 Herrin (1987), p. 308.
34 Ibid., p. 338.
35 Ibid.
36 Mango (1980), p. 32.
37 Pirenne (1939), p. 187.
38 See, for example, Havighurst (1969); Lyon (1972); Hay (1968).
39 Writing before Pirenne, Weber did not fully develop his analysis of the historical significance of Islam. For an attempt to highlight Weber's view of Islam with his comparative sociology of the world religions see Turner (1974).
40 Dix (1953).
41 Donner (1981), p. 8. Sweetman (1945), vol.1, p. 63, stresses the similarity between Islam and the Byzantine iconoclasts in insisting on a rigorous and simple monotheism, as the core of a politically potent religious creed.
42 Ibid., pp. 51–2.
43 Gurevich (1985), p. 160.
44 Donner (1981), p. 81.
45 Thompson (1969), pp. 298–302.
46 St Benedict (1960), p. 163; 'we hope to ordain nothing that is harsh or burdensome', ibid. p. 13. A spirit of moderation which inspired his follower, John Cassian, who introduced monasticism to western Europe. He argues that although 'purity of heart' requires 'loneliness, fasting, vigils, work, nakedness' as the 'means of perfection', excessive asceticism is positively dangerous; 'given the frailty of the flesh . . . Who will not be turned aside by the requirements and need of his own body?' He insists that 'one should take cognizance of the state of one's strength and body and age and allow oneself as much food as will sustain the flesh but not satisfy its longing'; Cassian (1985), pp. 41–6, 77. For the origins of rigorously ascetic monasticism and its continued significance in eastern Christianity see Vööbus (1958, 1960, 1988); Atiya (1968).
47 James ed. (1986), p. 13.
48 Ibid., p. 26.
49 Quoted in Folz (1974), p. 84.
50 The legal, political and religious theory of feudalism described an ideal world which was never replicated in practice. Bloch (1965), vol.1, p. 173, admits that 'it was never a perfect system', a view previously expressed by Weber (1978), vol.1, p. 257. See also Ganshof (1952); Ullman (1966); Critchley (1978).
51 Painter (1961), for a vigorous insistence on the distance between ideal and practice.
52 Duby (1977, 1980).

53 Bloch (1965), pp. 145–240. Glick (1979), p. 145, stresses the substitution of feudal relations for kinship organization.

54 Kantorowicz (1957); the king was, like the bishop, a *persona mixta* rather than the fully 'deified' being of the eastern Emperor. As Ullmann (1961) points out, feudalism supplanted any tendencies towards a genuinely theocratic state. On the cosmological significance of dependence in feudal society see particularly Gilson (1936); Lovejoy (1960), pp. 67–98; Haren (1985); Marenbon (1983).

55 Gurevich (1985), pp. 70–3.

56 Gilson (1936), p. 64, points out that as God is Being 'everything else is only partial being, hardly deserves the name of being at all'. And (1955), p. 83, he quotes Denis the Areopagite as an important source in medieval western theology: 'A being has the very nature defined by its degree of elongation from God; pure Intelligence is at the top, matter is at the bottom'.

57 An idea stressed by Augustine (1950), but coming into greater prominence as the anthropological foundation of *both* 'rational' scholastic and 'mystical' monastic theology during the medieval period.

58 Gilson (1936), p. 84: 'If God is Being, how can there be anything other than Himself?' The conception of God as a 'tranquil ocean of substance' seems to rule out the radical contingency of earthly experience.

59 Weber, viewing medieval Christianity from the perspective of the Reformation, paradoxically underestimates its capacity for 'rationalization'.

60 Aquinas (1955), pp. 86–96; (1911), pp. 24–5. 'By "motion" we mean nothing else than the reduction of something from a state of potentiality into a state of actuality'; Gilson (1924), pp. 46–59; Aertsen (1988), pp. 256–78.

61 Gilson (1924), 60–3.

62 Kantorowicz (1957).

63 Anselm (1974), vol.1. For the recent revival of the ontological argument see Hartshorne (1965), Plantinga (1974). For the development of the cosmological argument see Rowe (1975); Davies (1982), pp. 38–49.

64 Evans (1978) makes clear the 'internal' logic of Anselm's argument. This was, in fact, the common context of feudal reasoning. Le Goff (1988), for example, makes clear the extent to which nature was conceived as a 'vast reservoir of symbols', an insight developed in the pioneering work of Chenu (1968), pp. 99–145.

65 As, for example, in Mannheim (1936), pp. 9–11.

66 See particularly Vööbus (1958, 1960, 1988), who links world-rejecting practices to the popularity of 'dualistic' cosmologies, and to the conception of monasticism as 'the transformation of martyrdom'; ibid., vol.2, p. 99; and Leclerq (1978); Daniélou and Marrou (1978), pp. 269–77; more generally Decarreaux (1964).

67 Wallace-Hadrill (1983), pp. 70–4; Rousseau (1978).

68 Useful discussions are contained in Leyser (1984); Constable (1988); Cowdrey (1970); Hunt (1967, 1971); Knowles and Obolensky (1972); Southern (1970); Lawrence (1984); Hamilton (1986).

69 Hunt (1967); Cowdrey (1970).

70 It was the proneness to corruption which attracted the reformers' zeal; how the holy community should be occupied, and thus avoid laxity, was a central issue. St Peter Damian (1959), p.28, the most zealous advocate of religious renewal, writes: 'Our whole new way of life and our renunciation of the world has but one end: rest. But a man can only come to this state of rest if he stretches his sinews in many labours and strivings, so that when all the clamour and disturbance is at an end the soul may be lifted up by the grace of contemplation to search for the very face of truth'.

71 Constable (1988), V, pp. 239–43, notes the variety of intermediate forms between ideal-typical eremitic and coenobitic forms. And though Damian (1959), p. 25, praises the 'solitary cell' as the 'wonderful workshop of spiritual labour, in which the human soul restores to itself the likeness of its Creator and returns to its pristine purity', he argued powerfully for the advantage of the monastic community over the undisciplined pursuit of solitary holiness. Since the human mind, he argues 'cannot be utterly empty, but must always be concerned with love of something, it must be completely surrounded with (the) wall of virtue' which is the disciplined religious community; ibid., p. 85.

72 Southern (1970), p. 269, 'by the end of the thirteenth century most Cistercian houses were distinguished exponents of the very qualities which they had come into existence to denounce'. Duby (1977), p. 4, 'But because the Cistercians refused to live off rents, insisted on gaining their daily bread by their own toil, chose to live in the wilderness among pasture and forest, and conformed to the archaic rule of life they had rashly adopted, they found themselves, in spite of their vow of poverty, in the forefront of economic activity'.

73 Duby (1980); Southern (1970), p. 38.

74 Hunt (1967), p. 106. A practice that was enthusiastically imitated by other orders, see Knowles (1949), p. 149.

75 St Bernard (1940), pp. 197–225.

76 Thus St Benedict (1960), p. 33, had declared 'The first degree of humility is obedience without delay'.

77 The theme of encountering God 'face to face' was particularly prominent in Cistercian spirituality, and nowhere more beautifully expressed than in the works of William of St Thierry. See, for example, William (1971), pp. 37–9; (1979), (1974); McGinn (1977).

78 William of St Thierry (1979), p. 71; and (1971), p. 56, 'everyone possesses you just insofar as he loves you'.

79 Bynum (1979); Lawrence (1984), pp. 137–42. Between these two notions of the religious life – inward rational thought, and the contemplative life – an intermediate stage was formed. Regular canons, ecclesiastical officials attached to a particular cathedral, lived together in a community under a *Rule*, usually the somewhat less specific *Rule* of St Augustine. They did not abandon their property or other wealth on entering the community; indeed, they qualified for a portion of ecclesiastical revenues on a personal basis. Their search for the *vita apostolica*

embraced a more immediately social doctrine of edification. By 'word and example' they engaged in teaching and learning. The canonical notion of 'example' was taken in a more literal fashion than the monk's metaphor of 'mirror of God' allowed. Service, and particularly service in teaching, was held to be an essential aspect of the religious vocation.

80 Duby (1980), p. 181.
81 An ever increasing cost which, as it could neither be avoided nor afforded, ultimately destroyed feudalism.
82 Lynch (1976), p. 25, points out that 'Places in religious houses were a moderately scarce commodity'.
83 Bouchard (1987), p. 56–60. Though, frequently, entry to the order was incidental to, rather than a good purchased by, a transfer of land or other resources; Lynch (1976), pp. 14–15.
84 Aquinas (1969), vol.16, p. 23, 'all man's desires are on account of his love for an ultimate end'. Sin, therefore, is desire wrongly aroused; 'when men sin they turn away from that in which the idea of the ultimate end is truly realized, not from the intention of reaching it, which mistakenly they seek elsewhere', ibid., p. 27.
85 Ibid., p. 25.
86 Duby (1980), pp. 296–9; Bumke (1977), p. 89.
87 Aquinas (1969), vol.16, p. 45. And thus, 'Man's happiness cannot consist in natural riches. For they are sought for the sake of something else, namely the support of human life, and so are subordinate to its ultimate end, not the end itself', ibid., p. 33.
88 Ibid., p. 117.
89 Boase (1972); Brooke and Brooke (1984); Russell (1984); Emmerson (1981). Le Goff (1984) brilliantly documents the new significance of Purgatory in medieval religious life and argues that it introduces a new and more complex way of thinking about sin and redemption. The simple opposition between Heaven and Hell was mediated through a third term which stood mid-way, but above the human world, between them. See also Gurevich (1988).
90 Ariès (1981), pp. 5–94.
91 Brown (1981), Gurevich (1988). For an empirical survey of medieval sainthood see Weinstein and Bell (1982). Popular piety was largely responsible for the medieval transformation of Mary, from 'mother' to 'bride' of Christ; see Gold (1985), pp. 45–50.
92 Bakhtin (1968).
93 Ferguson (1990), pp. 106–11.
94 Christianity, for the medieval world, was 'sacred' in the sense of being the 'rule' through which the possibility of that kind of society was arbitrarily established.

4 MORALITY: HAPPINESS POSTPONED

1 For a survey of sociological theories of the transition see Holton (1985). The best introduction to the intellectual context is still Koyré (1957),

and Cassirer (1963). On the relation of religion and magic, especially in the context of popular beliefs, during the latter part of the transition see Thomas (1971). On the emergence of a new 'moral' universe see particularly Huizinga (1965) and Elias (1978).

2 Morris (1972). A view implicit in Haskins (1927), and restated in Stiefel (1985).

3 Cusanus (1928, 1954), and Cassirer (1963).

4 Cusanus (1954), p. 8.

5 Ibid., pp. 74–5. And in Cusanus (1928), p. 43, we are told that God is 'beyond even the highest ascent of intellect'. The strict interdict on natural theology was ignored as, for example, Montaigne's famous *Apology for Raymond Sebond*, written in the following century, which re-asserts the belief that 'God has given us two books: the Book of the Universal Order of Things (or, of Nature) and the book of the Bible'. The former, moreover, is the primary source of our knowledge of God, for it 'cannot be corrupted nor effaced nor falsely interpreted . . . from this Book no one becomes a heretic'. Montaigne (1987), p. xliii.

6 Cusanus (1928), p. 43, is typical: 'Hence I observe how needful it is for me to enter into the darkness, and to admit the coincidence of opposites, beyond all the grasp of reason, and there to seek the truth where impossibility meeteth me'.

7 Cassirer (1963); Ferguson (1990), ch.7.

8 Cusanus (1954), p. 107. For early *astronomical* interpretations of this doctrine see Johnson (1937).

9 Thus, in Copernicus, we can find the *religious* assumptions of feudalism co-existing with new astronomical insights. In *De revolutionibus*, for example, the universe is held to be spherical because it is 'the most perfect shape' (p. 36), circular motion retains its privileged status and with consistent Aristotelian–Christian logic he argues that 'nothing is more repugnant to the whole pattern and form of the universe than for something to be out of its own place' (p. 45).

10 Written about 1500, see editor's Introduction to Erasmus (1936).

11 Erasmus (1936), p. 189.

12 Ibid., p. 148.

13 Ibid.

14 Ibid., p. 160.

15 Ibid., p. 150.

16 Erasmus (1905), p. 6.

17 Ibid., p. 112.

18 Aldridge (1966), p. 41, remarks that 'The *philosophia Christi* places piety above theology. The important feature for Erasmus was religion and not theology . . . The ethical aspect is of prime importance'. Christ is viewed, therefore, as the incarnation of a specific ethical ideal of 'love, simplicity and purity'. Ibid., p. 38.

19 Erasmus (1905), p. 157.

20 Ibid., p. 141 (emphasis added).

21 Ibid., p. 117.

22 Siirala (1970) provides a clear exposition of their mutual misunder-

standing. Luther's admiration of *Praise of Folly* was tempered by the suspicion that it was not quite serious; it was 'so jocund, so learned, and so ingenious, that is, so entirely Erasmian, that it makes the reader laugh at the vices of the Church, over which every true Christian ought rather to groan'; Williams (1969), p. 20.

23 Erasmus (1971), especially pp. 201–11; and for a careful and insightful exposition Screech (1980).

24 Erasmus (1971), p. 202, the phrase 'a certain kind' was added to later editions; see Screech (1980).

25 Erasmus (1971), p. 201; 'the biggest fools of all appear to be those who have been wholly possessed by zeal for Christian piety. They squander their possessions, ignore insults, submit to being cheated, make no distinction between friends and enemies, shun pleasure, sustain themselves on fasting, vigils, tears, toil and humiliations, scorn life and desire only death – in short they seem to be dead to any normal feelings, as if their spirit dwelt elsewhere than in their body. What else can that be but madness'. A theme taken up in masterly fashion, of course, in Dostoevsky's *The Idiot*.

26 Ibid., p. 206.

27 Ibid., p. 207.

28 The secular Platonism of Ficino, and the revival of the hermetic tradition which it inspired, was, from this point of view, markedly less 'progressive'. See Walker (1958); Yates (1964).

29 Erasmus (1936), p. 160.

30 In the medieval world knightly virtue is 'exemplary' and active; see Auerbach (1968), ch. 6. The bourgeois revolution was, therefore, not simply a shift in the content of human values, but in their locus.

31 Erasmus (1936), p. 188.

32 Erasmus (1971), pp. 164–73. It is the practical squalor, and general lack of 'civilized' manners, that strikes him most about such people, 'their filth and ignorance, their boorish and shameless behaviour'.

33 Elias (1978), Huizinga (1924).

34 Bodily functions, in particular, become the objects of new moral regulation. Elias (1978), pp. 129–31.

35 This is not to imply that, at an earlier period or in other societies, the body is a wholly 'natural' phenomenon. It is simply that the conventions which constitute bodily experience are individuated and interiorized. The body becomes the 'natural' expression of the self which, as the primary moral phenomenon, acquires an essentially religious meaning.

36 Hinnebusch (1965), vol.1, pp. 55–7, 119–20.

37 Hamilton (1981), pp. 31–9. Ironically the spur to heresy was often, as with the Waldensians, the demand that the church should demonstrate 'moral' restraint and leadership. See, e.g., Lambert (1977), p. 65.

38 Lambert (1977) for a comprehensive survey. Loos (1974) on the significance of eastern European movements, Ladurie (1980) and Ginzburg (1980) for detailed local studies. The revival of heresy was frequently viewed as a 'disease' visited upon human society, in part at least, as a punishment, see Moore, in Lourdaux and Verhelst (1976).

39 Cohn (1970).
40 Ladurie (1981) for the political dimensions of Carnival. Hamilton (1981).
41 Hamilton (1981), pp. 40–8.
42 As revealed particularly by Ladurie (1980) and Ginzburg (1980).
43 The Inquisition had no 'forces' of its own; its victims were 'relaxed' to the secular arm for punishment.
44 Ginzburg (1980), p. 120. Equally, it should be noted, the most popular movements of heresy conceived their rejection of orthodoxy to be based on moral, rather than strictly theological, grounds. See Lambert (1977).
45 Loos (1974), pp. 151–2.
46 And to overestimate the reliability of contemporary evidence; Lerner (1972).
47 Luther (1952), p. 33.
48 Notable also in e.g. Vives (1979), Norena (1970), pp. 154–61.
49 Luther (1952), vol.1, p. 35.
50 Ibid., p. 33.
51 Ibid., p. 40.
52 Ibid., p. 33.
53 Ibid., p. 36 (emphasis added).
54 Ibid., p. 32.
55 Ibid., p. 37.
56 Ibid., p. 47.
57 Ibid., p. 113; 'For all Christians whatsoever really and truly belong to the religious class, and there is no difference among them except in so far as they do different work'.
58 Ibid., p. 114.
59 Ibid., p. 71.
60 Ibid.
61 Ibid., p. 76.
62 Ibid., p. 77.
63 Ibid., p. 78.
64 Ibid., p. 78.
65 Ibid., p. 82.
66 Ibid., p. 231.
67 Ibid., p. 244.
68 Ibid., p. 247.
69 Ibid.
70 Luther, in this regard, is close to the mystical tradition. He would, presumably, have agreed with Eckhart (1979), vol.1, p. 4; 'inwardly the soul is free and void of all means and all images'. The immediate context of Luther's theological thought is the mysticism of Johannes Tauler, see Ozment (1969).
71 Luther (1952), vol.1, p. 273.
72 Viewed 'objectively' it is the distinction between 'use' and 'exchange' value.
73 Luther, ibid., p. 369.
74 Ibid.

75 Ibid.
76 Ibid. Both Erasmian Folly and Lutheran Faith are *beyond* categories and moral rules cannot, therefore, be *deduced* from them. This is why their religious radicalism can be linked to political and social conservatism.
77 Calvin (1986), p. 15.
78 Ibid.
79 Ibid., p. 16.
80 Ibid.
81 Ibid.
82 Ibid., pp. 16–17.
83 Ibid., p. 43.
84 Ibid.
85 Ibid., p. 39.
86 Ibid., p. 47.
87 Ibid., p. 59.
88 Ibid., p. 61.
89 Ibid.
90 Ibid., p. 62.
91 Ibid.
92 Augustine (1987).
93 Calvin (1986), p. 125.
94 Ibid., p. 88.
95 Ibid., p. 99.
96 Ibid., p. 70.
97 Ibid., p. 74.
98 Ibid., p. 86; this again is worth comparing with Eckhart's view of religiosity as 'silence and waiting', Eckhart (1979), vol.1, p. 6.
99 Calvin (1986), p. 179.
100 Ibid., p. 180.
101 Melanchthon, in Pauck (ed.) (1969), p. 23.
102 Ibid.
103 Ibid., p. 24.
104 Ibid., p. 29.
105 Ibid., p. 27.
106 Luther (1952), vol.1, p. 360.
107 Ibid.
108 Ibid., p. 83.
109 Ibid.
110 Melanchthon, in Pauck (ed.) (1969), p. 89.
111 Ibid., p. 91.
112 Zwingli (1984), vol.2, p. 6.
113 Ibid., p. 7.
114 Miller and Johnson (1963), vol.1, p. 52.
115 Pelikan (1984), vol.4, pp. 1–9, reaffirms the centrality of doctrine, rather than organization and authority, to the Reformation.
116 Williams (1962) remains the fundamental study. Thomas Muntzer, rejecting the 'Magisterial Reformation's' alternative views of the Church as the 'fellowship of all believers' or as an 'elect of saints',

insisted on the separation of the Church from all national and territorial authority. His religious radicalism was an ideal vehicle for the expression of new social aspirations; consequently, he was 'considered the personification of the social and religious unrest to which the new evangelical ideas could lead without the support and constraint of reform-minded princes'. Williams (1962), p. 44.

117 Weber (1930), p. 104; 'In its extreme inhumanity this doctrine must above all have had one consequence for the life of a generation which surrendered to its magnificent consistency. That was a feeling of unprecedented inner loneliness of the single individual'.

118 This is particularly evident in New England. The non-traditional, 'rational' attitude to everyday life quickly gave way to new forms of scriptural legalism. For example, Increase Mather inveighs against *gynicandrical dancing* (mixed or 'promiscuous' dancing), citing the Seventh Commandment as his ultimate authority, and arguing 'whenever any sin is forbidden, not only the highest acts of that sin, but all degrees thereof, and all occasions leading thereto are prohibited'; Miller and Johnson (1963), vol.3, pp. 411–12. And Solomon Stoddard, in the light of Ezekial 44.20 – 'Neither shall they shave their heads, nor suffer their locks to grow long' – is equally severe on long hair; ibid., p. 455.

119 Hill (1964).

120 Weber (1930), p. 181.

121 Ibid.

5   PASSION: DESIRE FOR HAPPINESS

1 This is the strength of classical political economy, which was fully recognized by Marx (1976, p. 169); 'The categories of bourgeois economics consist precisely in forms of this kind. They are forms of thought which are socially valid, and therefore objective'. For a contemporary statement see Abercrombie, Hill and Turner (1986). This is not to say, of course, that 'individualism' is the *real* foundation of capitalist society, or that its relations can be fully specified as contract, only that these relations must *appear* so.

2 Gay (1966, 1969) significantly subtitles his study *The Rise of Modern Paganism*.

3 Rowe (1975) for a detailed consideration. Its modern variant – the principle of sufficient reason – did not really survive the scientific revolution.

4 Glacken (1973).

5 Boyle's *Disquisition about the Final Causes of Natural Things*, using the subsequently famous analogy of the Strasbourg clock, argues that in many cases the nature of things cannot be deduced from their 'final cause' or 'function'. But, in a key example, he assumes it foolish to deny that the perfect adaptation of the structure of the eye to its final cause of envisioning can be explicated other than by reference to a Divine

fabricator. See Boyle (1979); Jacob (1976).
6 Cohen (1980), p. 131; Westfall (1977), pp. 139–45.
7 On Pascal's achievements in mathematics and physics see Broome (1965), pp. 46–74.
8 Goldmann (1964), p. 27.
9 Quoted in ibid., p. 56.
10 Ibid.
11 Pascal (1966), 114 (throughout refers to numbered entries not pages).
12 Ibid., 200.
13 Ibid., 131. Melzer (1986) argues that it is at this point that Pascal cuts himself off from all previous 'cosmological' arguments. He uses the 'argument from wretchedness' to save himself from the solipsism of a world of self-reflecting and self-multiplying signifiers; 'God speaks to humans not through the signs of the order of creation but through the message of his punishment which he inscribes in their souls', ibid. p. 87. Significantly, the *Pensées* classifies pain *and* pleasure under 'Misère'.
14 Ibid.
15 Ibid., 427.
16 Ibid., 134.
17 Ibid., 133.
18 Ibid., 136.
19 Ibid.
20 Ibid.
21 Ibid.
22 Ibid., 143.
23 Ibid., 131.
24 Ibid., 143.
25 Ibid., 148. Thus, Grimsley (1969), p. 79, points out that 'withdrawal from society was not simply a means of retreating from others but also of finding an opportunity for recovering the freedom and independence he deemed necessary for true self-affirmation'.
26 Ibid.
27 Ibid., 418.
28 Ibid., 686.
29 Ibid.
30 Ibid., 423.
31 Ibid., 424.
32 Ibid., 373; 'If the foot had never known it belonged to the body, and that there was a body on which it depended, if it had only known and loved itself, and if it then came to know that it belonged to a body on which it depended, what regret, what shame it would feel for its past life, for having been useless to the body which poured life into it, and would have annihilated it if it had rejected and cut it off as the foot cut itself off from the body!'
33 Ibid., 201.
34 Pascal (1850), vol.2, p. 240.
35 Ibid.
36 Pascal (1966), 564.

37 Ibid.
38 Ibid. And ibid., 978; 'The nature of self-love and of this human self is to love only self and consider only self'. This is quite distinct from a 'social' passion. Society can be constituted only on the basis of vanity and false self-representation; 'Human relations are only based on this mutual deception; and few friendships would survive if everyone knew what his friend said about him behind his back, even though he spoke sincerely and dispassionately. Man is therefore nothing but disguise, falsehood and hypocrisy, both in himself and with regard to others'.
39 Pascal (1850), vol.2, p. 247.
40 Pascal (1966), 131.
41 Pascal (1850), vol.2, p. 132.
42 Ibid.
43 Ibid.
44 Ibid., p. 133. And, similarly (689) 'It is not in Montaigne but in myself that I find everything I see there'.
45 Ibid., p. 209.
46 Pascal (1966), 688.
47 Ibid. Qualities, that is, are always qualities of the *ego* rather than of an, absolutely simple, selfhood. Yet a portion of the ego carries with it an echo of authentic being, thus, 'The Christian's hope of possessing an infinite good is mingled with actual enjoyment as well as with fear, for, unlike people hoping for a kingdom of which they will have no part because they are subjects, Christians hope for holiness, and to be free from unrighteousness, and some part of this is already theirs'; 917.
48 Ibid., 919.
49 And the only legitimate form of consumption is a wholly internalized process of self-reference, i.e. it is transformed into an ascetic withdrawal from the world of objects.
50 Coleman (1986), 194–7.
51 Evident in the fashionable revival of Stoicism among the Scottish *philosophes*; see, for example, Ferguson (1973).
52 Ferguson (1990), p. 176–92. Hume's (1888), Book I, Section VI, pp. 251–63, scepticism, unusually extending to the notion of the 'self', looked forward to 'modern' psychology rather than to the completion of the Enlightenment project of scientific rationalism.
53 Rousseau (1911), p. 6.
54 Ibid.
55 Ibid., p. 7.
56 Ibid.
57 Rousseau (1953), p. 337. A project fraught with 'quite incredible difficulties'. It was the relations of greatest apparent 'value' that proved to be the greatest obstacle; 'If I had shaken off the yoke of friendship as well as that of public opinion, I should have accomplished my purpose', ibid., p. 338.
58 Ibid., p. 332.
59 Rousseau (1911), p. 249. Rules of conduct cannot be 'deduced' from our knowledge of God; 'I do not derive these rules from the principles

from the higher philosophy, I find them in the depths of my heart, traced by nature in characters which nothing can efface'. Ibid.

60 Ibid., p. 30; 'All children are afraid of masks'.
61 Ibid., p. 330.
62 Rousseau (1953), pp. 29–30; 'I had not yet sufficient reasoning power to realize the extent to which appearances were against me . . . There ended the serenity of my childish life'.
63 Starobinski (1988), p. 27. Rousseau (1984), p. 40; '*Amour de soi-meme* is a natural sentiment, which prompts every animal to watch over its own conservation, and which, directed in man by reason and modified by piety, produces humanity and virtue. *Amour-propre* is only a relative, artificial sentiment, born in society, prompting every individual to attach more importance to himself than to anyone else and inspiring all the injuries men do to themselves and to others; it is the true source of honour'. And, thus, Rousseau (1911), p. 56: 'The only natural passion is self-love'.
64 Starobinski (1988), p. 27.
65 Quoted in Starobinski p. 28.
66 Ibid. 'Since men no longer seek to satisfy their "true needs" but only the needs created by vanity, they are never at one with themselves but always estranged – one another's slaves.'
67 Rousseau (1911), p. 298.
68 Starobinski (1988), p. 41.
69 Rousseau (1979), p. 88. Consequently 'I doubt whether any of us knows the meaning of lasting happiness'.
70 Ibid.
71 Ibid., p. 89.
72 Ibid.
73 Ibid., p. 107.
74 Ibid., p. 108.
75 Ibid.
76 Ibid., p. 112.
77 Ibid.
78 Ibid., p. 123.
79 Ibid., p. 126.
80 Ibid., p. 124.
81 Ibid., p. 137.
82 Starobinski (1988), p. 69.
83 Rousseau (1979), p. 137.
84 Ferguson (1990) for an attempt to distinguish types of cosmology *within* the bourgeois world view.
85 Rousseau (1911), p. 242.
86 Ibid., p. 242.
87 Ibid., p. 249.
88 Ibid.
89 Ibid.
90 Ferguson (1990), pp. 27–46.
91 Lowith (1964), pp. 31–52; Taylor (1975), pp. 3–75.

92 Kierkegaard (1975), vol.3, 3072 (references to Kierkegaard's *Journals and Papers* are to numbered entry, and not to page number). See also (1967), vol.1, 484, 'Christianity is not a doctrine . . . but an existential-communication . . . Consequently (since Christianity is not a doctrine), it is not a matter of indifference . . . Christ has not appointed assistant-professors'.

93 Kierkegaard (1967), vol.1, 484.

94 Expressions which completely lack the *innocence* of Erasmian Folly, e.g. Kierkegaard (1967), vol.1, 491, 'really to stick to Christianity a man must be brought to madness by suffering'.

95 A view he shared with the youthful Marx and other 'young Hegelians'. Lowith (1964), pp. 65–120; Taylor (1980), pp. 23–69; Thulstrup (1980).

96 Kierkegaard (1970), vol.2, 1605. 'If Hegel had written his whole logic and had written in the preface that it was only a thought-experiment, in which at many points he still steered clear of some things, he undoubtedly would have been the greatest thinker who has ever lived. As it is he is comic.'

97 Kierkegaard (1970), vol.2, 1986. 'There is really only one single quality – individuality'; and 1997, 'The whole development of the world tends towards the absolute significance of the single individual (*den Enkelte*), which is the very principle of Christianity'; 2086, 'Is it the infinite which unites men? No, it is the infinite which makes them into individuals (*Enkelte*)'. The distinction between the phenomenal 'ego' and the existentially authentic 'self' makes Kierkegaard's 'single individual' quite unlike Stirner's 'absolute ego', see Stirner (1971).

98 Kierkegaard (1962), pp. 109–36. And for his critique of 'mass society' see *The Present Age* (1962).

99 Kierkegaard (1941), p. 126. As for Rousseau, Christ remains heroically transparent.

100 Kierkegaard (1959), vol.2, p. 171.

101 Ibid., p. 185, 'Personality immediately determined is not spiritual but physical'.

102 Ibid. p. 215, and 'doubt is a despair of thought'.

103 Ibid. p. 216–17. 'Despair is a far deeper and more complete expression, its movement much more comprehensive than that of doubt. Despair is precisely an expression for the whole personality, doubt only an expression for thought . . . One cannot despair at all without willing it, but to despair truly one must truly will it, but when one truly wills it one is truly beyond despair; when one has truly willed despair one has truly chosen that which despair chooses, i.e., oneself in one's eternal validity.'

104 Kierkegaard (1965). Indeed he may be trapped in a purely 'aesthetic' form of despair. 'For no intoxication is so beautiful as despair', Kierkegaard (1959), vol.2, p. 199, his entire personality 'anaesthetized by despair', ibid., p. 226.

105 Ibid., p. 262.

106 Ibid., p. 218. 'I choose the absolute. And what is the absolute? It is I myself in my eternal validity.' And, ibid., p. 226, 'when you choose

yourself absolutely you easily discover that this self is not an abstraction or a tautology'.

107 Kierkegaard (1941), p. 473.

108 Although the whole intention of the authorship is to 'edify' the reader, only the later works are explicitly Christian in orientation, Kierkegaard (1962), p. 92.

109 The transition to Christian 'categories' must, in principle, remain incommunicable. Thus (1978) vol.5, 6131, 'My whole nature is changed. My concealment and inclosing reserve are broken', and, 6132, 'Now, by the help of God, I shall become myself', is followed at once by, 6133, 'No, no, my inclosing reserve still cannot be broken, at least not now'.

110 Kierkegaard (1941), pp. 64–77 and (1985), pp. 83–95.

111 Kierkegaard (1972), p. 104.

112 Ibid., p. 109.

113 Ibid., p. 85, and, e.g. (1975), vol.3, 3084, 'Christianity does not want to be understood . . . Christianity entered into the world not to be understood but to be existed in. This cannot be expressed more strongly than by the fact that Christianity itself proclaims itself to be a paradox'.

114 Kierkegaard (1972), p. 89.

115 Ibid.

116 Pascal (1966), 641.

117 An insight due, particularly, to Meyerson (1930).

118 Kierkegaard (1972), p. 89.

119 Ibid., p. 174.

120 Ibid., p. 139.

121 Ibid., p. 124.

122 Ibid., p. 126.

123 Ibid.

124 Ibid., p. 160.

125 Ibid., p. 38.

126 Ibid., p. 151. Kierkegaard's view has, through the writings of Bultmann, been enormously influential. Significantly, although unwilling to separate 'faith' from the historical circumstances of the life of Jesus, Schillebeeckx (1979), p. 150, concurs; 'Jesus' deliberate focus on the future entails no doctrine, no theory about it'.

127 Ibid., p. 64.

128 Ibid., p. 67.

129 Kierkegaard (1957), pp. 37–41. Dread is 'different from fear and similar concepts which refer to something definite, whereas dread is freedom's reality as possibility for possibility'; (1980), pp. 41–6.

130 Most notably in Durkheim (1933), pp. 111–32.

6 SENSUOUSNESS: HAPPINESS RECLAIMED

1 The 'objectivity' of things is 'created' through acts of self-alienation. 'Things' therefore 'mediate' between an original, inward, unspoilt 'dreaming' subjectivity, and a redeemed self-consciousness.

2 Durkheim clearly sees this, but at various points seems to lose the courage of his convictions. Modern society is 'solidary' by virtue of its intricate division of labour, and has nothing to fear from the emergent 'pathologies' of individualism which, in fact, become normative for 'advanced' capitalism. Durkheim (1952), pp. 297–325.

3 The characteristic public face of modern subjectivity is seen in the *flâneur*, see Baudelaire (1964), Frisby (1985) pp. 15–16, and the cosmopolitan *blasé* attitude, see Simmel (1971). Bely's novel of fantasy, *Petersburg*, provides the most comprehensive ethnography.

4 Williams (1982) describes the consumer revolution in late nineteenth century France, a potent 'conjunction of banking and dreaming', which appealed directly 'to the fantasies of the consumer'. Some of the general implications are discussed in Ferguson (1990), pp. 239–57.

5 Schutz (1976), vol. 2.

6 'Wholeness', 'unity' and 'the centred self' have remained, in spite of the influence of Nietzsche, the explicit goal of much modern theological writing. See, e.g. Tillich (1957) and Brunner (1939). Pohier (1985) is an interesting exception. His book is revealingly titled *God-in-Fragments*, and even more revealingly he has been forbidden to preach.

7 Turner (1974).

8 Meyerson (1930), p. 31; Bergson (1911b), p. 31, expresses a similar thought; 'Science can work only on what is supposed to repeat itself – that is to say, on what is withdrawn, by hypothesis, from the action of real time. Anything that is irreducible and irreversible in the successive moments of a history eludes science . . .'

9 Nietzsche (1974), pp. 172–3.

10 Boltzmann (1974), p. 30.

11 Holton (1973).

12 Pagels (1982), p. 144; and more generally Polkinghorne (1983, 1986), Heisenberg (1959).

13 Baudelaire's description of modern painting is applicable as a general characterization of modern culture in general.

14 De Broglie (1939), p. 47.

15 This is not to say, of course, that we have simply abandoned the search for personal identity. The 'classical model' is, for many everyday purposes (as in science), assumed to be accurate and realistic. Much of our activity remains 'comprehensible' within the framework of 'ego' psychology. For a recent sophisticated defence see Taylor (1989).

16 Bakhtin (1973), 4–7.

17 Raskolnikov's 'conversion' is an inessential and arbitrary postscript to *Crime and Punishment*, see Mochulsky (1967), p. 312.

18 The most limiting of experiences can become 'infinite', see Ferguson (1983).

19 Bergson (1911a), p. 275.

20 Ibid., p. 261.

21 Ibid., p. 262. Identity is always a differentiation within a relational totality. Thus (1911b), 'Life does not proceed by the association and addition of elements, but by dissociation and division'.

22 Bergson (1911a), p. 170.
23 Expressed, for example, by Alexander (1934); Whitehead (1978), pp. 342–52. See, particularly, Mascall (1971).
24 The argument from design, however, remains the most popular defence of theism from a 'scientific' perspective. See Polkinghorne (1986), p. 80.
25 Collingwood (1946).
26 Bergson (1911b), p. 3. Our attention constructs 'objects' from the flux of impressions and imagines 'a formless *ego*, indifferent and unchangeable, on which it threads the psychic states which it has set up as independent entities'.
27 Ibid., p. 2. Scheler (1987) describes human being as a 'continuous movement and a *transition itself*'; an idea that had been characteristically taken much further by Nietzsche, e.g. (1961) pp. 43–4, 'What is great in man is that he is a bridge and not a goal . . . a rope between man and superman'. Scheler, protective of an 'ethical' religious world-view, remained suspicious of Nietzsche's and Bergson's affirmative philosophies, and their acceptance of 'that thrusting, covetous, demonic power, throwing out new forms of existence in ever greater profusion'; Scheler (1960), p. 116.
28 Bergson (1911a), p. 102.
29 Nietzsche (1968), p. 49. And Nietzsche (1910), vol.2, p. 7, 'I am convinced of the phenomenalism of the *inner* world also: everything that reaches our consciousness is utterly and completely adjusted, simplified, schematised, interpreted, – the *actual* process of inner "perception", the *relation of causes* between thoughts, feelings, desires, between subject and object, is absolutely concealed from us, and may be purely imaginary'.
30 Proust (1966), vol.1, pp. 56–62, for the most celebrated illustration.
31 The ego died from multiple wounds. Already weakened and unsure of itself the proximity of God drained it of its residual energy.
32 Dostoevsky (1958), pp. 288–311.
33 Ibid., pp. 299–300.
34 Ibid., p. 299. Nietzsche (1909), vol.1, p. 197, criticizing rather than defending the church, similarly remarks that Christianity has 'lost its terrible nature', so that, 'even if it were a mistake, it nevertheless provides the greatest advantages and pleasures for its adherents throughout their lives: – it therefore seems that this belief should be upheld owing to the peace and quiet it ensures – not owing to the terror of a threatening possibility, but rather out of fear of a life that has lost its charm . . . People are satisfied with a Christianity which is an *opiate*, because they no longer have the strength to seek, to struggle, to dare, to stand alone . . . But a Christianity the chief object of which is to soothe diseased nerves, does *not require* the terrible solution consisting of a "God on the cross"'.
35 See Moltmann (1988); Rahner (1978); Pannenberg (1970, 1985); and for a useful overview Brown (1987).
36 Feuerbach (1957).
37 Wartofsky (1977) for a comprehensive exposition and successful vindication of the originality of Feuerbach's philosophy.

38 Bergson (1911a), pp. 74–5; 'The *actuality* of our perception thus lies in its *activity*'.
39 Nietzsche (1909), vol.1, p. 72. This 'irritability' is the 'consequence of an extreme capacity for suffering and irritation which no longer wants to be "touched" at all because it feels every contact too deeply', Nietzsche (1968), p. 143.
40 Nietzsche (1909), vol.1, p. 58.
41 Nietzsche (1973), p. 97.
42 Nietzsche (1973), p. 140.
43 Nietzsche (1909), vol.1, p. 150.
44 Nietzsche (1973), pp. 132–3.
45 Bergson (1911b), p. 27.
46 On the development of a bodily *order* see Foucault (1977), pp. 135–70.
47 Bergson (1911a), p. 177.
48 Schilder (1964) claims that we know nothing of the inside of our own bodies, which we treat as an undifferentiated 'heavy mass'.
49 Ibid., p. 46.
50 Nietzsche (1973), p. 115.
51 Ibid.
52 Ibid., p. 116.
53 Ibid. One is reminded, of course, of Musil's great novel.
54 Kretschmer (1936), p. 161.
55 And internal, normally unconscious, organic processes are perceived with tormenting acuteness. See, for example, Schreber (1955), Bleuler (1950) pp. 91–5. The limiting condition is explored by Kafka in his *Metamorphosis*.
56 The neurotic suffers, that is to say, from a failure in repression. This often manifests itself as a paradoxical inactivity, loss of vitality or local paralysis.
57 Nietzsche (1909), vol.1, pp. 63–4, describes the process of 'adaptation to the accumulation of impressions' as an 'artificial *modification* of one's own nature in order to make it resemble a "mirror"; one is interested, but only epidermally: this is systematic coolness, equilibrium, a steady *low* temperature just beneath the thin surface on which warmth, movement, "storm" and undulation ply'. This is quite distinct from the classical bourgeois interest in the medical topology of the body, which organizes and differentiates its organic *interior*, see Foucault (1973).
58 Schilder (1964) remains the most subtle and complete phenomenological account.
59 Simmel (1971) draws attention to the necessity, in the modern city, of assuming an attitude of indifference to the overwhelming variety of external stimuli.
60 Schilder (1964), in particular, stresses the multiplicity and shifting outline of the body image. For a useful review of modern philosophical discussions of the body see Zaner (1971).
61 Uexküll (1926) makes the morphology of body-type the main task of theoretical biology. Each species 'constructs' its own world as an aspect of the subjective relations established in its particular body-type; 'around

each living being an appearance-world of its own lies spread', p. 71. 'Every animal is a subject, in virtue of the structure peculiar to it, selects stimuli from the general influences of the outer world, and to these it responds in a certain way', p. 126. Some of the more sinister implications are brought out beautifully in Michel Tournier's extraordinary novel *The Erl-King*.

62 Claude Bernard (1957) established the internal stability and relative independence of organic processes from environmental stimuli; a *milieu interieur*. See Hirst (1975).

63 Bergson (1911b), pp. 32–3. Schilder (1964), p. 16, 'the postural model of the body is in perpetual inner self-construction and self-destruction'.

64 Schilder (1964), p. 237, 'One may be enshrouded by various body images. They cannot form a unit, but they may form a sum'.

65 Proust (1966), vol.1, pp. 58–62, describes the 'vast structure of recollection' that constitutes the body: ' . . . the smell and taste of things remain poised a long time, like souls, ready to remind us, waiting and hoping for their moment, amid the ruins of all the rest'. And in *Time Regained*, vol.1, p. 2, 'Our legs and our arms are full of torpid memories'.

66 Nietzsche (1973), p. 134.

67 Nietzsche (1909), vol.1, p. 327.

68 Tillich (1957), vol.2, p. 170, 'There is no divine nature which could be abstracted from his eternal creativity'. See generally Ward (1982); Mascall (1971).

69 And allows him to value the body in a completely new way. Thus, (1961), p. 60, 'There is more reason in your body than in your wisdom'. It is the body which 'enraptures the spirit with its joy'. An idea enthusiastically embraced by, for example, Powys (1920, 1930, 1935).

70 Nietzsche (1968), p. 91.

71 Dostoevsky (1958), p. 89.

72 Ibid., p. 76. Dmitry is the central actor in 'a revel to end all revels', when he 'seemed to be in a delirium, feeling that his "happiness" was now assured . . . In short, what followed was utterly fantastic and chaotic, but Mitya seemed to be in his natural element, and the more fantastic it all became, the more his spirits rose', ibid., pp. 508–9.

73 Ibid., p. 268.

74 Ibid., p. 201.

75 Ibid.

76 Breuer and Freud (1955), Freud, Standard Edition, vol.2.

77 Nietzsche (1968), p. 143.

78 Jaspers (1963), p. 309. Tillich (1957), vol.2, pp. 51–90.

79 Buber (1970), p. 27, quoting Nietzsche.

80 Schleiermacher, quoted in Brunner (1939), p. 42.

81 Barth (1933), p. 36. Barth's insistence on the unknownness of God as the starting point of theology forces him, in spite of everything, to adopt an anthropological perspective. On this see Pannenberg (1985), pp. 11–23.

82 Moltmann (1988), pp. 55–6. Pannenberg (1970), pp. 6–7, 'Initially, and repeatedly, man is so taken by the exciting strangeness of the things

around him that he learns from them to view himself with completely different eyes as a strange entity. Man experiences himself only in terms of the world, by coming across his own body in particular relations with other things'. Rahner (1978), p. 41, 'Rather the subject's self-alienation is precisely the way in which the subject discovers himself and affirms himself in a definite way'.

83 Tillich (1953), vol.1, p. 17, 'Man is infinitely concerned about the infinity to which he belongs, from which he is separated, and for which he is longing . . . Man is unconditionally concerned about that which conditions his being beyond all the conditions in him and around him'.

84 Kierkegaard (1954), p. 146.

85 Pannenberg (1988) thus contrives to place the 'secular' anthropology of Gehlen (1988) alongside that of Tillich (1957).

86 Buber (1970), p. 137.

87 Brunner (1939), p. 45. As early as 1911 Rudolf Eucken provided a religious view of modernity. He viewed 'the whole history of modern times as a progressive transference of life from a world of belief . . . into the world of immediate existence' (1911) p. 40. He argues, however, that 'man does not seem willing to be merged in the fleeting lapse of the moment'. Ibid., p. 54. Man, he insists, 'does not belong to the domain of flux'. Ibid., p. 55. And, therefore, modern man has 'discovered in the midst of incessant joy and pleasure the absence of genuine happiness'. Ibid., p. 61. The immediate cannot ever be the bearer of spiritual value, which lies in the inward transformation of 'the turbid evanescence of ordinary commonplace life'. Ibid., p. 243. For many similar statements see also Eucken (1909, 1909a, 1912).

88 Dostoevsky (1958), p. 268.

89 Pannenberg (1970), pp. 6–7.

90 Schmidt (1971), Ferguson (1990), pp. 158–75.

91 Marx (1975), pp. 322–34.

92 Marx (1976), p. 163.

93 The endurance of the commodity world is the 'eternal recurrence of the ever same'.

CONCLUSION: THE END OF *HAPPINESS*

1 Rahner (1978), p. 140. He makes clear the radical nature of this historicity; 'man realizes his transcendental subjectivity neither unhistorically in a merely interior experience of unchanging subjectivity, nor does he grasp this transcendental subjectivity by means of an unhistorical reflection and interpretation which is possible in the same way at every point in time', ibid. Schillebeeckx (1989), p. 55, similarly, argues that 'transcendence lies *in* human experience, but in such a way that this experiential content contains an intrinsic reference to what makes this experience possible and is not constituted by the experience itself'.

2 Berger (1961, 1969, 1970) has made a particular virtue of discovering the transcendental structure of human activity in traditionally 'non-

religious' contexts. His analysis depends, however, on social actors themselves treating some activities in a 'special' way, that is as 'sacred'. Rahner's point goes much further; human activity as such, and quite irrespective of its subjective 'meaning', is implicated in transcendence. Thus, Schillebeeckx (1989), p. 61, 'We do not find salvation primarily by means of a correct interpretation of reality, but by acting in accordance with the demands of reality'.

3 We can, of course, imagine another (though not *any* other) society. That possibility, as Ernst Bloch has so perfectly demonstrated, is part of our present reality. A number of theologians, notably Moltmann and Metz, have been inspired by Bloch's work. Together with 'death of god' theologians they expressed in a rather striking fashion the groundless optimism of faith. The presence of the future, as possibility, however, can repress as much as it might liberate. Hope is always oriented towards the future, but the future need not be, and usually is not, hopeful. Moltmann (1965); Altizer (1967); Altizer and Hamilton (1966); MacIntyre and Ricoeur (1969); Dean (1975); and from a somewhat different perspective Cox (1969); Berger (1970).

4 This is why 'post-axial' religion is not simply a continuation (and already a partial 'secularization') of the 'elementary forms' of primitive religion.

5 Aquinas (1967) vol.10, p. 119, argues that 'In the hierarchy of being man cannot surpass the angels, who by nature are of a higher order. Yet a man can pass beyond them in his knowing, as when he understands there is a being above them who can make him blessed and when quite possessed will give complete bliss'. The 'ascent' to God is in the 'perfection of the soul' through contemplation of God. He can be 'possessed' only in mind. Popular mystical Christianity, especially in the later medieval period was more emotional and fervent. Its leading exponents, however, such as Ruusbroec, were as careful as Bonaventure or Bernard to introduce a mediating hierarchy of 'steps' between man and God, and, when that was finally surmounted, to preserve in a transformed state, rather than to annihilate, the human structure of consciousness. See, generally, Underhill (1911); Ruusbroec (1985), and especially Screech (1980); Zaehner (1957).

BIBLIOGRAPHY

Abercrombie, N., Hill, S. and Turner, Bryan S. (1980) *The Dominant Ideology Thesis*, London.
—— (1986) *Sovereign Individuals of Capitalism*, London.
Acquaviva, S. S. (1979) *The Decline of the Sacred in Industrial Society*, Oxford.
Aertsen, Jan (1988) *Nature and Creature: Thomas Aquinas's Way of Thought*, Leiden and New York.
Aldridge, John William (1966) *The Hermeneutics of Erasmus*, Richmond, Va.
Alexander, Paul J. (1978) *Religious and Political History and Thought in the Byzantine Empire*, London.
Alexander, S. (1934) *Space, Time, and Deity*, 2 vols., London.
Alföldi, Andrew (1948) *The Conversion of Constantine and Pagan Rome*, trans. Harold Mattingly, Oxford.
Altheim, Franz (1938) *A History of Roman Religion*, trans. Harold Mattingly, London.
Altizer, Thomas J. J. (1967) *The Gospel of Christian Atheism*, London.
Altizer, Thomas J. J. and Hamilton, William (1966) *Radical Theology and the Death of God*, Indianapolis.
Anderson, Perry (1974) *Passages from Antiquity to Feudalism*, London.
Anselm, St (1974) *Anselm of Canterbury*, ed. and trans. J. Hopkins and H. Richardson, 4 vols., London.
Aquinas, St Thomas (1911–25) *Summa Theologiae*, London.
—— (1955) *On the Truth of the Catholic Faith*, New York.
—— (1964–81) *Summa Theologiae*, Latin/English, London.
Ariès, Philippe (1983) *The Hour of Our Death*, trans. H. Weaver, London.
Armstrong, A. H. (1967) *The Cambridge History of Later Greek and Early Medieval Philosophy*, Cambridge.
Atiya, Aziz S. (1968) *A History of Eastern Christianity*, London.
Auerbach, Erich (1968) *Mimesis: The Representation of Reality in Western Literature*, trans. Willard R. Trask, Princeton, NJ.
Augé, Marc (1982) *The Anthropological Circle: Symbol, Function, History*, Cambridge.
Augustine, St (1873) *The Works of Aurelius Augustine*, Edinburgh.
—— (1950) *The Greatness of the Soul/The Teacher*, trans. Joseph M. Colleran, Westminster, Maryland and London.

—— (1951) *St Augustine Against the Academics*, trans. John O'Meara, Westminster, Maryland and London.

—— (1958) *On Christian Doctrine*, trans. and intr. D. W. Robertson, Jr., Indianapolis.

—— (1961) *Confessions*, trans. and intr. R. S. Pine-Coffin, Harmondsworth, Middx.

—— (1972) *City of God*, trans. Henry Bettenson, intr. John O'Meara, Harmondsworth, Middx.

—— (1987) *Augustine: De Fide et Symbolo*, trans., intr. and commentary E. P. Meijering, Amsterdam.

Aune, David Edward (1972) *The Cultic Setting of Realized Eschatology in Early Christianity*, Leiden.

Avineri, Shlomo (1968) *The Social and Political Thought of Karl Marx*, Cambridge.

Bakhtin, Mikhail (1968) *Rabelais and His World*, trans. H. Iswolsky, Cambridge, MA.

—— (1973) *Problems of Dostoevsky's Poetics*, trans. R. W. Rostel, New York.

Barnes, Timothy D. (1981) *Constantine and Eusebius*, Cambridge, MA and London.

Barth, Karl (1933) *The Epistle to the Romans*, trans. Edwyn C. Haskyns, Oxford.

—— (1972) *Protestant Theology in the Nineteenth Century*, London.

Baudelaire, Charles (1964) *The Painter and Modern Life and Other Essays*, trans. and ed. J. Mayne, London.

Bauer, Walter (1971) *Orthodoxy and Heresy in Earliest Christianity*, ed. Robert A. Kraft and G. Krodel, Philadelphia.

Beidelman, T. O. (1974) *W. Robertson Smith and the Sociological Study of Religion*, Chicago and London.

Bellah, Robert N. (1970) *Beyond Belief: Essays on Religion in a Post-Traditional World*, New York and London.

Benedict, St (1960) *The Rule of Saint Benedict*, trans. and ed. Justin McCann, London.

Berger, Peter L. (1961) *The Precarious Vision*, New York.

—— (1969) *The Social Reality of Religion*, London.

—— (1970) *A Rumour of Angels: Modern Society and the Rediscovery of the Supernatural*, London.

Bergson, Henri (1911a) *Matter and Memory*, New York.

—— (1911b) *Creative Evolution*, London.

—— (1935) *The Two Sources of Morality and Religion*, London.

Bernard, Claude (1957) *An Introduction to the Study of Experimental Medicine*, New York.

Bernard, St (1940) *The Steps of Humility*, ed. G. B. Burch, Cambridge, MA.

Black, M. (1961) *The Scrolls and Christian Origins*, London.

Bleuler, Eugene (1950) *Dementia Praecox or the Group of Schizophrenias*, trans. Joseph Zirkin, New York.

Bloch, Ernst (1986) *The Principle of Hope*, trans. Neville Plaice, Stephen Plaice and Paul Knight, 3 vols., Oxford.

Bloch, Marc (1965) *Feudal Society*, trans. L. A. Manyon, 2 vols., London.

Blum, Owen J. (1947) *St Peter Damian: His Teaching on the Spiritual Life*, Washington, D.C.

Blumenberg, Hans (1983) *The Legitimacy of the Modern Age*, trans. and intr. Robert M. Wallace, Cambridge, MA.

—— (1987) *The Genesis of the Copernican World*, trans. and intr. Robert M. Wallace, Cambridge, MA.

Blumenthal, H. J. (1971) *Plotinus' Psychology*, The Hague.

Boase , T. S. R. (1972) *Death in the Middle Ages*, London.

Boethius (1969) *The Consolation of Philosophy*, trans. and intr. V. E. Watts, Harmondsworth, Middx.

Bolton, Brenda (1983) *The Medieval Reformation*, London.

Boltzmann, Ludwig (1974) *Theoretical Physics and Philosophical Problems*, Brian McGuinness (ed.), Dordrecht and Boston.

Bonaventure, St (1953) *Works of Saint Bonaventure*, New York.

Bonner, Gerald (1986) *St Augustine of Hippo: Life and Controversies*, Norwich.

Boring, M. Eugene (1982) *Sayings of the Risen Jesus*, Cambridge.

Bouchard, Constance Brittain (1987) *Sword, Miter and Cloister: Nobility and the Church in Burgundy, 980–1198*, Ithaca and London.

Bowker, John (1978) *The Religious Imagination and the Sense of God*, Oxford.

Boyle, Robert (1979) *Selected Philosophical Papers of Robert Boyle*, ed. and intr. M. A. Stewart, Manchester.

Braudel, Fernand (1981) *The Structure of Everyday Life*, trans. Siân Reynolds, London.

—— (1983) *The Wheels of Commerce*, trans. Siân Reynolds, London.

—— (1984) *The Perspective of the World*, trans. Siân Reynolds, London.

Broglie, Louis de (1939) *Matter and Light: The New Physics*, London.

Broome, J. H. (1965) *Pascal*, London.

Brooke, Rosalind and Brooke, Christopher (1984) *Popular Religion in the Middle Ages*, London.

Brown, David (1987) *Continental Philosophy and Modern Theology: An Engagement*, Oxford.

Brown, Peter (1967) *Augustine of Hippo: A Biography*, London.

—— (1981) *The Cult of the Saints*, London.

—— (1989) *The Body and Society: Men, Women and Sexual Renunciation in Early Christianity*, London.

Brubaker, Roger (1984) *The Limits of Rationality: An Essay on the Social and Moral Thought of Max Weber*, London.

Brunner, Emil (1939) *Man in Revolt: A Christian Anthropology*, trans. Olive Wyon, London.

—— (1944) *The Divine-Human Encounter*, trans. Amandus W. Loos, London.

Buber, Martin (1970) *I and Thou*, trans. Walter Kaufmann, Edinburgh.

Bultmann, Rudolf (1935) *Jesus and the Word*, trans. Louise Pettibone Smith and Erminie Huntress, London.

—— (1952) *Theology of the New Testament*, trans. Kendrick Grobel, 2 vols., London.

—— (1956) *Primitive Christianity: In Its Contemporary Setting*, trans. R. H. Fuller, London and New York.

Bumke, Joachim (1977) *The Concept of Knighthood in the Middle Ages*, trans.

W. T. H. and Erika Jackson, New York.

Burkert, Walter (1985) *Greek Religion: Archaic and Classical*, trans. John Raffan, Oxford.

Burrow, J. W. (1966) *Evolution and Society: a Study in Victorian Social Theory*, Cambridge.

Bynum, Caroline Walker (1979) *Docere Verbo et Exemplo: An Aspect of Twelfth-Century Spirituality*, Missoula, Montana.

—— (1987) *Holy Feast and Holy Fast: The Significance of Food to Medieval Women*, Berkeley, Los Angeles and London.

Calvin, John (1986) *Institutes of the Christian Religion: 1536 edition*, trans. and annotated Ford Lewis Battles, London.

Cassian, John (1985) *John Cassian: Conferences*, trans. Colm Luibheid, New York.

Cassirer, Ernst (1963) *The Individual and the Cosmos in Renaissance Philosophy*, Oxford.

Chenu, M.-D. (1968) *Nature, Man, and Society in the Twelfth Century*, trans. and ed. Jerome Taylor and Lester K. Little, Chicago and London.

Clement of Alexandria (1867) *The Writings of Clement of Alexandria*, trans. William Wilson, ed. Alexander Roberts and James Donaldson, Edinburgh.

Cohen, I. Bernard (1980) *The Newtonian Revolution*, Cambridge.

Cohn, Norman (1970) *The Pursuit of the Millenium*, London.

Coleman, Francis X. J. (1986) *Neither Angel Nor Beast: The Life and Work of Blaise Pascal*, New York and London.

Collingwood, R. G. (1946) *The Idea of History*, Oxford.

Constable, Giles (1988) *Monks, Hermits and Crusaders in Medieval Europe*, London.

Cowdrey, H. E. J. (1970) *The Cluniacs and the Gregorian Reform*, Oxford.

Cox, Harvey (1969) *The Feast of Fools: A Theological Essay on Festivity and Fantasy*, Cambridge, MA.

Critchley, J. S. (1978) *Feudalism*, London.

Cumont, Franz (1956), *Oriental Religions in Roman Paganism*, New York.

Cusanus, Niocolas (1928) *The Vision of God*, intr. Evelyn Underhill, London and New York.

—— (1954) *Of Learned Ignorance*, London.

Cyprian, Saint, Bishop of Carthage (1868) *The Writings of Cyprian*, trans. Robert Ernest Wallis, Ante-Nicene Christian Library, vols. 8 & 9, Edinburgh.

Damian, St Peter (1959) *St Peter Damian: Selected Writings on the Spiritual Life*, trans. and intr. Patricia McNulty, London.

Daniélou, Jean (1964, 1973, 1977) *A History of Early Christian Doctrine*, trans. and ed. John A. Baker and David Smith, 3 vols., London.

Daniélou, Jean and Marrou, Henri (1978) *The Christian Centuries: The First Six Hundred Years*, trans. Vincent Cronin, London.

Davies, Brian (1982) *An Introduction to the Philosophy of Religion*, Oxford.

Davies, J. G. (1965) *The Early Christian Church*, London.

Davies, Paul (1984) *God and the New Physics*, Harmondsworth, Middx.

Davis, Charles (1976) *Body as Spirit: The Nature of Religious Feeling*, London.

Dean, Thomas (1975) *Post-Theistic Thinking*, Philadelphia.

Decarreaux, Jean (1964) *Monks and Civilization: From the Barbarian Invasions to the Reign of Charlemagne*, trans. Charlotte Haldane, London.

Derrett, J. Duncan M. (1970) *Law in the New Testament*, London.

Dewick, E. C. (1912) *Primitive Christian Eschatology*, Cambridge.

Dillon, John (1977) *The Middle Platonists*, London.

Dilthey, Wilhelm (1988) *Introduction to the Human Sciences*, trans. and intr. Ramon J. Betanzos, Detroit.

Dix, Gregory (1953) *Jew and Greek: A Study in the Primitive Church*, London.

Dodds, E. R. (1965) *Pagan and Christian in an Age of Anxiety*, London.

Donner, Fred McGraw (1981) *The Early Islamic Conquests*, Princeton, NJ.

Dostoevsky, Fyodor (1953) *The Devils*, trans. David Magarshack, Harmondsworth, Middx.

—— (1955) *The Idiot*, trans. David Magarshack, Harmondsworth, Middx.

—— (1958) The Brothers Karamazov, trans. David Magarshack, 2 vols., Harmondsworth, Middx.

—— (1966) *Crime and Punishment*, trans. David Magarshack, Harmondsworth, Middx.

—— (1972) *Notes from Underground/The Double*, trans. Jessie Coulson, Harmondsworth, Middx.

Duby, George (1977) *The Chivalrous Society*, London.

—— (1980) *The Three Orders: Feudal Society Imagined*, Chicago.

—— (1984) *The Knight, The Lady, And The Priest*, trans. Barbara Bray, Harmondsworth, Middx.

Durkheim, Emile (1933) *The Division of Labour in Society*, trans. George Simpson, London.

—— (1952) *Suicide: A Study in Sociology*, trans. John A. Spaulding and George Simpson, London.

—— (1915) *The Elementary Forms of the Religious Life*, trans. Joseph Ward Swain, London.

—— (1975) *Durkheim on Religion: A Selection of Readings with Bibliographies*, ed. W. S. F. Pickering, London.

Durkheim, Emile and Mauss, Marcel (1963) *Primitive Classification*, trans. Rodney Needham, London.

Eckhart, Meister (1979, 1981) *Meister Eckhart: German Sermons and Treatises*, trans., intr. and notes M. O'C. Walshe, London.

Eliade, Mircea (1959) *The Sacred and the Profane: The Nature of Religion*, trans. Willard R. Trask, New York.

—— (1979, 1982, 1985) *A History of Religious Ideas*, Chicago and London.

Elias, Norbert (1978) *The Civilizing Process: The History of Manners*, trans. Edmund Jephcott, Oxford.

Emmerson, Richard Kenneth (1981) *Antichrist in the Middle Ages*, Manchester.

Erasmus, Desiderius (1905) *Enchiridion Militis Christiani*, London.

—— (1936) *The Education of a Christian Prince*, trans. and intr. Lester K. Born, New York.

—— (1970) *The Praise of Folly*, trans. with essay and commentary Hoyt Hopewell Hudson, Princeton NJ.

250

—— (1971) *Praise of Folly and Letter to Martin Dorp 1515*, trans. Betty Radice, intr. and notes A. H. T. Levi, Harmondsworth, Middx.

—— (1975) *Christian Humanism and The Reformation: Selected Writings of Erasmus*, ed. John C. Olin, New York.

Eucken, Rudolf (1909) *The Life of the Spirit*, trans. F. L. Pogson, London and New York.

—— (1909a) *The Problem of Human Life*, trans. Williston S. Hough and W. R. Bryce Gibson, London.

—— (1911) *The Truth of Religion*, trans. W. Tudor Jones, London and New York.

—— (1912) *Life's Basis and Life's Ideal*, trans. Alban G. Widgery, London.

Evans, G. R. (1978) *Anselm and Talking about God*, Oxford.

Ferguson, Adam (1973) *Principles of Moral and Political Science*, 2 vols., New York.

Ferguson, Everett (1987) *Backgrounds of Early Christianity*, Grand Rapids, Michigan.

Ferguson, Harvie (1983) *Essays in Experimental Psychology*, London.

—— (1990) *The Science of Pleasure: Cosmos and Psyche in the Bourgeois World View*, London.

Feuerbach, Ludwig (1957) *The Essence of Christianity*, trans. George Eliot, New York and London.

Filoramo, Giovanni (1990) *A History of Gnosticism*, trans. Anthony Alcock, Oxford.

Foerster, Werner (1972, 1974) *Gnosis: A Selection of Gnostic Texts*, trans. R. McL. Wilson, Oxford.

Folz, Robert (1974) *The Coronation of Charlemagne*, trans. J. E. Anderson, London.

Foucault, Michel (1973) *The Birth of the Clinic*, trans. A. M. Sheridan Smith, London.

—— (1977) *Discipline and Punish: the Birth of the Prison*, trans. Alan Sheridan, London.

—— (1978) *The History of Sexuality Volume 1: An Introduction*, trans. Robert Hurley, Harmondsworth, Middx.

—— (1987) *The Use of Pleasure: The History of Sexuality Vol. 2*, trans. Robert Hurley, Harmondsworth, Middx.

—— (1990) *The Care of the Self: The History of Sexuality Vol. 3*, trans. Robert Hurley, Harmondsworth, Middx.

Fox, Robin Lane (1986) *Pagans and Christians*, Harmondsworth, Middx.

Frazer, Sir James (1900) *The Golden Bough: A Study in Magic and Religion*, London.

Frend, W. H. C. (1952) *The Donatist Church*, Oxford.

—— (1980) *Town and Country in the Early Christian Centuries*, London.

Freud, Sigmund (1953–74) *The Standard Edition of the Complete Psychological Works of Sigmund Freud*, trans. and ed. James Strachey, Alix Strachey, and Alan Tyson, 24 vols., London.

Frisby, David (1985) *Fragments of Modernity*, Cambridge.

Gager, John G. (1975) *Kingdom and Community: The Social World of Early Christianity*, Englewood Cliffs, NJ.

Ganshof, F. L. (1952) *Feudalism*, London.

Ganshof, F. L. (1968) *Frankish Institutions Under Charlemagne*, Providence, Rhode Island.

Gay, Peter (1966, 1969) *The Enlightenment: An Interpretation*, 2 vols., London.

Geary, Patrick J. (1988) *Before France and Germany: The Creation and Transformation of the Merovingian World*, Oxford.

Gehlen, Arnold (1988) *Man: His Nature and Place in the World*, trans. Clare McMillan and Karl Pillener, New York.

Gilkey, Langdon (1981) *Society and the Sacred: Toward a Theology of Culture in Decline*, New York.

Gilson, Etienne (1924) *The Philosophy of St Thomas Aquinas*, Cambridge.

—— (1936) *The Spirit of Medieval Philosophy*, London.

—— (1955) *History of Christian Philosophy in the Middle Ages*, London.

—— (1961) *The Christian Philosophy of Saint Augustine*, London.

Ginzburg, Carlo (1980) *The Cheese and the Worms: The Cosmos of a Sixteenth-Century Miller*, trans. John and Anne Tedeschi, London.

Glacken, J. (1973) *Traces on the Rhodian Shore: Nature and Culture in Western Thought from Ancient Times to the End of the Eighteenth Century*, Berkeley.

Glick, Thomas F. (1979) *Islamic and Christian Spain in the Early Middle Ages*, Princeton, NJ.

Goguel, Maurice (1964) *The Primitive Church*, trans. H. C. Snape, London.

Gold, Penny Schine (1985) *The Lady and the Virgin: Image, Attitude, and Experience in Twelfth-Century France*, Chicago and London.

Goldmann, Lucien (1964) *The Hidden God*, London.

Gould, Stephen Jay (1977) *Ontogeny and Phylogeny*, London and Cambridge, MA.

Grant, Robert M. (1958) *Gnosticism and Early Christianity*, New York and London.

—— (1971) *Augustus to Constantine: The Thrust of the Christian Movement into the Roman World*, London.

—— (1978) *Early Christianity and Society: Seven Studies*, London.

Greeley, Andrew M. (1973) *The Persistence of Religion*, London.

Green, Henry A. (1985) *The Economic and Social Origins of Gnosticism*, Atlanta, Georgia.

Grimsley, Ronald (1969) *Jean-Jacques Rousseau: A Study in Self-Awareness*, Cardiff.

Gurevich A. (1985) *Categories of Medieval Culture*, London.

—— (1988) *Medieval Popular Culture*, London.

Haeckel, Ernst (1879) *The Evolution of Man; a Popular Exposition of the Principal Points of Human Ontogeny and Phylogeny*, London.

Hamilton, Bernard (1981) *The Medieval Inquisition*, London.

—— (1986) *Religion in the Medieval West*, London.

Haren, M. (1985) *Medieval Thought: The Western Intellectual Tradition from Antiquity to the Thirteenth Century*, London.

Harnack, Adolf von (1894–99) *History of Dogma*, 7 vols., London.

—— (1957) *Outlines of the History of Dogma*, trans. Edwin Knox Mitchell, intr. Philip Rieff, London.

Hartshorne, Charles (1965) *Anselm's Discovery*, Lasalle, Illinois.

Haskins, Charles Homer (1927) *The Renaissance of the Twelfth Century*, Cambridge, MA.

Havighurst, Alfred F. ed. (1969) *The Pirenne Thesis: Analysis, Criticism and Revision*, Lexington, MA.

Hay, Denys (1968) *Europe: The Emergence of an Idea*, Edinburgh.

Hedrick, Charles W. and Hodgson Jr, Robert (1986) *Nag Hammadi, Gnosticism and Early Christianity*, Peabody, MA.

Hegel, Georg Wilhelm Friedrich (1948) *Early Theological Writings*, trans. T. M. Knox, Chicago.

—— (1977) *Phenomenology of Spirit*, trans. A. V. Miller, Oxford.

—— (1988) *Lectures on the Philosophy of Religion*, ed. Peter C. Hodgson, Berkeley.

Heisenberg, Werner (1959) *Physics and Philosophy: The Revolution in Modern Science*, London.

Herberg, W. (1960) *Protestant, Catholic, Jew*, New York.

Herrin, Judith (1987) *The Formation of Christendom*, Oxford.

Hick, John (1989) *An Interpretation of Religion: Human Responses to the Transcendent*, London.

Hill, Christopher (1965) *Intellectual Origins of the English Revolution*, Oxford.

—— (1966) *Society and Puritanism in Pre-Revolutionary England*, London.

(1975) *The World Turned Upside Down: Radical Ideas During the English Revolution*, Harmondsworth, Middx.

Hinnebusch, William A. (1965) *The History of the Dominican Order*, 2 vols., Staten Island, N.Y.

Hirst, Paul Q. (1975) *Durkheim, Bernard and Epistemology*, London.

Holton, Gerald (1973) *Thematic Origins of Scientific Thought: Kepler to Einstein*, Cambridge, MA.

Holton, R. J. (1985) *The Transition from Feudalism to Capitalism*, London.

Huizinga, Johan (1965) *The Waning of the Middle Ages*, trans. F. Hopman, London.

Hume, David (1888) *A Treatise of Human Nature*, ed. L. A. Selby-Bigge, Oxford.

—— (1963) *Hume on Religion* ed. Richard Wollheim, London.

Hunt, Noreen (1967) *Cluny under Saint Hugh, 1049–1109*, London.

—— ed. (1971) *Cluniac Monasticism in the Central Middle Ages*, London.

Hyppolite, Jean (1969) *Studies on Marx and Hegel*, London.

Irenaeus of Lyon (1868) *The Writings of Irenaeus*, trans. Alexander Roberts and W. H. Rambaut, 2 vols., Edinburgh.

Jacob, Margaret C. (1976) *The Newtonians and the English Revolution 1689–1720*, Hassocks.

James, Edward (1988) *The Franks*, Oxford.

—— ed. (1986) *Visigothic Spain: New Approaches*, Oxford.

James, William (1960) *The Varieties of Religious Experience*, London and New York.

Jaspers, Karl (1963) *General Psychopathology*, trans. J. Hoenig and Marion W. Hamilton, Manchester.

Johnson, Francis R. (1937) *Astronomical Thought in Renaissance England*, London.

Jonas, Hans (1958) *The Gnostic Religion: The Message of the Alien God and the Beginning of Christianity*, Boston.
Jones, A. H. M. (1948) *Constantine and the Conversion of Europe*, London.
—— (1966) *The Decline of the Ancient World*, London.
Justin (1861) *The Works of Justin the Martyr*, Oxford.
Kaegi Jr, Walter Emil (1968) *Byzantium and the Decline of Rome*, Princeton, NJ.
Kamen, Henry (1985) *Inquisition and Society in Spain*, London.
Kames, Lord (Henry Home) (1813) *Sketches of the History of Man*, Edinburgh.
Kantorowicz, Ernst H. (1957) *The King's Two Bodies: A Study in Medieval Political Theory*, Princeton, NJ.
Kautsky, K. (1925) *The Foundations of Christianity*, London.
Kee, Alistair (1985) *The Way of Transcendence: Christian Faith Without Belief in God*, London.
Kierkegaard, Søren (1939) *Christian Discourses*, trans. Walter Lowrie, London and New York.
—— (1941) *Concluding Unscientific Postscript*, trans. David F. Swenson and Walter Lowrie, Princeton, NJ.
—— (1944) *Attack upon 'Christendom'*, trans. and ed. Walter Lowrie, Princeton, NJ.
—— (1948) *The Gospel of Suffering*, trans. David F. Swenson and Lillian Marvin Swenson, Minneapolis.
—— (1954) *Fear and Trembling and The Sickness unto Death*, trans. Walter Lowrie, Princeton, NJ.
—— (1957) *The Concept of Dread*, trans. Walter Lowrie, Princeton, NJ.
—— (1959) *Either/Or*, trans. David F. Swenson and Lillian Marvin Swenson, 2 vols., Princeton, NJ.
—— (1962) *The Point of View of my Work as an Author: A Report to History*, trans. Walter Lowrie, ed. Benjamin Nelson, New York.
—— (1964) *Repetition: an Essay in Experimental Psychology*, trans. Walter Lowrie, New York and London.
—— (1967) *Stages on Life's Way*, trans. Walter Lowrie, New York.
—— (1972) *Training in Christianity*, trans. Walter Lowrie, Princeton, NJ.
—— (1978) *Two Ages*, ed. and trans. Howard V. Hong and Edna H. Hong, Princeton, NJ.
—— (1967–78) *Søren Kierkegaard's Journals and Papers*, ed. and trans. Howard V. Hong and Edna H. Hong, 6 vols., Bloomington, IN., and London.
King, John H. (1892) *The Supernatural: Its Origin, Nature and Evolution*, London.
Klibansky, Raymond (1982) *The Continuity of the Platonic Tradition During the Middle Ages*, London and New York.
Knowles, David (1949) *The Monastic Order in England*, Cambridge.
—— (1969) *Christian Monasticism*, 1969.
Knowles, David and Obolensky, Dimitri (1972) *The Christian Centuries: The Middle Ages*, London and New York.
Koester, Helmut (1986) *Introduction to The New Testament*, 2 vols., Philadelphia, Berlin and New York.
Kolakowski, Leszek (1978) *Main Currents in Marxism*, 3 vols., Oxford.

—— (1982) *Religion*, Oxford.

Koyré, Alexandre (1957) *From the Closed World to the Infinite Universe*, Baltimore.

Kretschmer, Ernst (1936) *Physique and Character: An Investigation of the Nature of Constitution and of the Theory of Temperament*, trans. W. J. H. Sprott, London.

Ladurie, Emmanuel Le Roy (1980) *Montaillou*, Harmondsworth, Middx.

—— (1981) *Carnival in Romans*, Harmondsworth, Middx.

Lambert, M. D. (1977) *Medieval Heresy: Popular Movements from Bogomil to Hus*, London.

Lawrence, C. H. (1984), *Medieval Monasticism: Forms of Religious Life in Western Europe in the Middle Ages*, London and New York.

Leclerq, Jean (1978) *The Love of Learning and the Desire for God*, London.

—— (1979) *Monks and Love in Twelfth-Century France*, Oxford.

Leeuw, G. van der (1963) *Religion in Essence and Manifestation*, trans. J. E. Turner, New York.

Le Goff, Jacques (1980) *Time, Work, and Culture in the Middle Ages*, Chicago and London.

—— (1984) *The Birth of Purgatory*, London.

—— (1988) *Medieval Civilization: 400–1500*, Oxford.

Lenski, Gerhard (1966) *The Religious Factor*, New York.

Lerner, Robert E. (1972) *The Heresy of the Free Spirit in the Later Middle Ages*, Berkeley.

Levi-Strauss, Claude (1968), *Structural Anthropology*, trans. Claire Jacobson and Brooke Grundfest Schoepf, London.

Leyser, Henrietta (1984) *Hermits and the New Monasticism: A Study of Religious Communities in Western Europe 1000–1150*, London.

Ling, T. (1980) *Karl Marx and Religion in Europe and India*, London.

Logan, A. H. B. and Wedderburn, A. J. M. (1983) *The New Testament and Gnosis*, Edinburgh.

Loos, Milan (1974) *Dualist Heresy in the Middle Ages*, trans. Iris Lewitova, The Hague and Prague.

Lourdaux, W. and Verhelst, D. eds. (1976) *The Concept of Heresy in the Middle Ages*, The Hague.

Louth, Andrew (1989) *Denys the Areopagite*, Wilton, CT.

Lovejoy, Arthur O. (1960) *The Great Chain of Being: A Study of the History of an Idea*, New York.

Lowith, Karl (1949) *Meaning in History: The Theological Presuppositions of the Philosophy of History*, Chicago.

—— (1964) *From Hegel to Nietzsche: The Revolution in Nineteenth-Century Thought*, trans. David E. Green, London.

—— (1982) *Max Weber and Karl Marx*, London.

Luckmann, Thomas (1967) *The Invisible Religion: the Problem of Religion in Modern Society*, New York and London.

Luibheid, Colm and Rorem, Paul eds. (1987) *Pseudo-Dionysius: The Complete Works*, London.

Lukes, Steven (1973) *Emile Durkheim, His Life and Work*, London.

Luther, Martin (1952) *Reformation Writings of Martin Luther*, trans., intro. and notes by Bertram Lee Woolf, 2 vols., London.

Lynch, Joseph H. (1976) *Simoniacal Entry into Religious Life from 1000 to 1260*, Columbus, Ohio.

Lyon, Bryce D. (1972) *The Origins of the Middle Ages: Pirenne's Challenge to Gibbon*, New York.

McGill, V. J. (1967) *The Idea of Happiness*, New York and London.

McGinn, Bernard ed. (1977) *Three Treatises on Man: A Cistercian Anthropology*, Kalamazoo, Michigan.

MacIntyre, A. (1967) *Secularization and Moral Change*, London.

—— (1969) *Marxism and Christianity*, London.

MacIntyre, A. and Ricoeur, P. (1969) *The Religious Significance of Atheism*, New York and London.

McLellan, David (1969) *The Young Hegelians and Karl Marx*, London.

MacMullen, Ramsay (1981) *Paganism in the Roman Empire*, New Haven and London.

—— (1984) *Christianizing the Roman Empire : A.D.100–400*, New Haven and London.

Malherbe, Abraham J. (1977) *Social Aspects of Early Christianity*, Baton Rouge and London.

Mango, Cyril (1980) *Byzantium: The Empire of New Rome*, London.

Mannheim, Karl (1936) *Ideology and Utopia*, London.

Marcuse, Herbert (1955) *Reason and Revolution: Hegel and the Rise of Social Theory*, London.

Marenbon, John (1983) *Early Medieval Philosophy 480–1150*, London.

Marshall, Gordon (1982) *In Search of the Spirit of Capitalism: An Essay on Max Weber's Protestant Ethic Thesis*, New York and London.

Martin, David (1969) *The Religious and the Secular: Studies in Secularization*, London.

—— (1978) *A General Theory of Secularization*, London.

Marx, Karl (1970) *The German Ideology*, ed. C. J. Arthur, London.

—— (1973) *Grundrisse: Foundations of the Critique of Political Economy*, trans. Martin Nicolaus, Harmondsworth, Middx.

—— (1975) *Early Writings*, trans. Rodney Livingstone and Gregor Benton, intr. Lucio Colletti, Harmondsworth, Middx.

—— (1976) *Capital*, vol. 1, trans. Ben Fowkes, Harmondsworth, Middx.

—— (1959) *Marx and Engels: Basic Writings on Politics and Philosophy*, ed. Lewis S. Feuer, New York.

Marx, Karl and Engels, Friedrich (1955) *On Religion*, Moscow.

Mascall, E. L. (1971) *The Openness of Being: Natural Theology Today*, London.

Mauss, Marcel (1954) *The Gift*, trans. Ian Cunnison, London.

Meeks, Wayne E. (1983) *The First Urban Christians: the Social World of the Apostle Paul*, New Haven and London.

Melzer, Sara E. (1986) *Discourses of the Fall: A Study of Pascal's Pensées*, Berkeley and London.

Meyerson, Emile (1930) *Identity and Reality*, trans. Kate Loewenberg, London and New York.

Miller, Perry and Johnson, Thomas H. (1963) *The Puritans*, 2 vols., New York.

Mitzman, Arthur (1970) *The Iron Cage: An Historical Interpretation of Max Weber*, New York.
Mochulsky, Konstantin (1967) *Dostoevsky: His Life and Work*, trans. Michael A. Minihan, Princeton, NJ.
Moltmann, Jurgen (1965) *The Theology of Hope*, New York.
—— (1971) *Man: Christian Anthropology in the Conflicts of the Present*, trans. John Sturdy, London.
—— (1973) *Theology and Joy*, intr. David E. Jenkins, London.
—— (1988) *Theology Today*, trans. John Bowden, London.
Mommsen, Wolfgang J. (1974) *The Age of Bureaucracy*, Oxford.
Montaigne, Michel de (1987) *An Apology for Raymond Sebond*, trans. and ed. with intr. and notes by M. A. Screech, Harmondsworth, Middx.
Morris, Colin (1972) *The Discovery of the Individual*, London.
Muller, F. Max (1898), *Lectures on the Origin and Growth of Religion*, London.
Musil, Robert (1968) *The Man Without Qualities*, trans. Eithne Wilkins and Ernst Kaiser, London.
Nietzsche, Friedrich (1909–10) *The Will to Power*, ed. Oscar Levy, 2 vols., Edinburgh and London.
—— (1961) *Thus Spoke Zarathustra*, trans. R. J. Hollingdale, Harmondsworth, Middx.
—— (1967) *On the Genealogy of Morals/Ecce Homo*, trans. Walter Kaufmann and R. J. Hollingdale, New York.
—— (1968) *Twilight of the Idols/The Antichrist*, trans. R. J. Hollingdale, Harmondsworth, Middx.
—— (1973) *Beyond Good and Evil*, trans. R. J. Hollingdale, Harmondsworth, Middx.
—— (1974) *The Gay Science*, trans. Walter Kaufmann, New York.
—— (1986) *Human, All Too Human*, trans. R. J. Hollingdale, Cambridge.
Nock, A. D. (1933) *Conversion: The Old and the New in Religion from Alexander the Great to Augustine of Hippo*, Oxford.
—— (1972) *Arthur Darby Nock: Essays on Religion and the Ancient World*, ed. Zeph Stewart, 2 vols., Oxford.
Norena, Carlos G. (1970) *Juan Luis Vives*, The Hague.
Nygren, Anders (1953) *Agape and Eros*, London.
Ollman, Bertell (1971) *Alienation: Marx's Conception of Man in Capitalist Society*, Cambridge.
Onians, R. B. (1951) *The Origins of European Thought about the Body, the Mind, the Soul, the World, Time, and Fate*, Cambridge.
Origen (1869) *The Writings of Origen*, trans. Frederick Crombie, 2 vols., Edinburgh.
—— (1973) *On First Principles*, trans., intr. and notes G. W. Butterworth, Gloucester, MA.
Otto, Rudolph (1959) *The Idea of the Holy*, trans. John W. Harvey, Harmondsworth, Middx.
Ozment, Steven E. (1969) *Homo Spiritualis: A Comparative Study of the Anthropology of Johannes Tauler, Jean Gerson and Martin Luther (1509–16) in the Context of their Theological Thought*, Leiden.
Pagels, Elaine (1975) *The Gnostic Paul*, Philadelphia.

257

Pagels, Elaine (1979) *The Gnostic Gospels*, London.

Pagels, Heinz R. (1982) *The Cosmic Code*, New York.

Painter, Sidney (1961) *Feudalism and Liberty: Articles and Addresses*, Baltimore, MD.

Pannenberg, Wolfhart (1970) *What is Man? Contemporary Anthropology in Theological Perspective*, trans. Duane A. Priebe, Philadelphia.

—— (1985) *Anthropology in Theological Perspective*, trans. Matthew J. O'Connell, Philadelphia.

Parsons, Talcott (1937) *The Structure of Social Action*, New York and London.

Pascal, Blaise (1850) *The Thoughts on Religion and Evidences of Christianity*, trans. and ed. M. P. Faugere and George Pearce, London.

—— (1966) *Pensées*, trans. A. J. Krailsheimer, Harmondsworth, Middx.

Pauck, Wilhelm (1968) *Harnack and Troeltsch: Two Historical Theologians*, New York.

—— ed. (1969) *Melanchthon and Bucer*, London.

Pelikan, Jaroslav (1971–89) *The Christian Tradition: A History of the Development of Doctrine*, 5 vols., Chicago and London.

Perkins, Pheme (1980) *The Gnostic Dialogue: The Early Church and the Crisis of Gnosticism*, New York.

Philo (1981) *Philo of Alexandria*, ed. David Winston, London.

Pickering, W. S. F. (1975) *Durkheim on Religion*, London.

—— (1984) *Durkheim's Sociology of Religion: Themes and Theories*, London.

Plantinga, Alvin (1974) *The Nature of Necessity*, Oxford.

Plotinus (1969) *The Enneads*, trans. Stephen MacKenna, London.

Poggi, Gianfranco (1983) *Calvinism and the Capitalist Spirit: Max Weber's 'Protestant Ethic'*, London.

Pohier, Jacques (1985) *God-in-Fragments*, trans. John Bowden, London.

Polkinghorne, John (1983) *The Way the World is: The Christian Perspective of a Scientist*, London.

—— (1986) *One World: The Interaction of Science and Theology*, London.

Powys, John Cowper (1920) *The Complex Vision*, London.

—— (1930) *In Defence of Sensuality*, London.

—— (1935) *The Art of Happiness*, London.

Pirenne, Henri (1936) *Economic and Social History of Medieval Europe*, London.

—— (1939) *Mohammed and Charlemagne*, trans. Bernard Miall, London.

Proust, Marcel (1966–70) *Remembrance of Things Past*, trans. C. K. Scott Moncrieff and Andreas Mayor, London.

Pseudo-Dionysius (1940) *The Divine Names and the Mystical Theology*, trans. C. E. Rolt, London.

Radcliffe-Brown, A. R. (1952) *Structure and Function in Primitive Society*, London.

Rahner, Karl (1978) *Foundations of Christian Faith: An Introduction to the Idea of Christianity*, trans. William V. Dyck, London.

Reitzenstein, Richard (1978) *Hellenistic Mystery-Religions*, trans. John E. Steely, Pittsburgh.

Rist, John M. (1964) *Eros and Psyche: Studies in Plato, Plotinus and Origen*, Toronto.

—— (1967) *Plotinus: The Road to Reality*, Cambridge.

—— (1982) *Human Value: A Study in Ancient Philosophical Ethics*, Cambridge.

Roberts, Alexander and Donaldson, James (1867) *Ante-Nicene Christian Library: Volume One, The Apostolic Fathers*, Edinburgh.

Robinson, James M. ed. (1988) *The Nag Hammadi Library in English*, Leiden and New York.

Robinson, James M. and Koester, Helmut (1971) *Trajectories Through Early Christianity*, Philadelphia.

Rostovtzeff, M. (1957) *Social and Economic History of the Roman Empire*, 3 vols., Oxford.

Rousseau, Jean-Jacques (1911) *Emile: or Education*, trans. Barbara Foxley, London.

—— (1953) *The Confessions of Jean-Jacques Rousseau*, trans. J. M. Cohen, Harmondsworth, Middx.

—— (1979) *The Reveries of a Solitary Walker*, trans., intr. and notes Peter France, Harmondsworth, Middx.

—— (1981) *Discours sur les sciences et les arts*, Paris.

—— (1984) *A Discourse on Inequality*, trans., intr. and notes Maurice Cranston, Harmondsworth, Middx.

Rousseau, Philip (1978) *Ascetics, Authority, and the Church: In the Age of Jerome and Cassian*, Oxford.

Rowe, William L. (1975) *The Cosmological Argument*, Princeton, NJ.

Rowley, H. H. (1947) *The Relevance of Apocalyptic*, London.

Rudolph, Kurt (1983) *Gnosis: The Nature and History of an Ancient Religion*, trans. and ed. Robert McLachlan Wilson, Edinburgh.

Russell, Jeffrey Burton (1984) *Lucifer: The Devil in the Middle Ages*, Ithaca and London.

Ruusbroec, John (1985) *John Ruusbroec: The Spiritual Espousals and Other Works*, trans. and intr. James Wiseman, New York and Toronto.

Ste Croix, G. E. M. de (1983) *The Class Struggle in the Ancient Greek World*, London.

Scheler, Max (1954) *The Nature of Sympathy*, trans. Peter Heath, London.

—— (1960) *On The Eternal in Man*, trans. Bernard Noble, London.

—— (1961) *Ressentiment*, trans. William W. Holdheim, New York.

—— (1987) *Person and Self-Value*, ed. M. S. Frings, Dordrecht and Boston.

Schilder, Paul (1964) *The Image and Appearance of the Human Body:Studies in the Constructive Energies of the Psyche*, New York.

Schillebeeckx, Edward (1979) *Jesus: An Experiment in Christology*, trans. Hubert Haskins, London.

—— (1989) *Christ: The Experience of Jesus as Lord*, trans. John Bowden, New York.

Schleiermacher, Friedrich (1928) *The Christian Faith*, ed. H. R. Mackintosh and J. S. Stewart, Edinburgh.

Schluchter, Wolfgang (1981) *The Rise of Western Rationalism: Max Weber's Developmental History*, Berkeley, CA.

Schmidt, Alfred (1971) *The Concept of Nature in Marx*, trans. B. Fowkes, London.

Schmidt, W. (1931) *The Origin and Growth of Religion: Facts and Theories*, London.

Scholem, Gershom G. (1941) *Major Trends in Jewish Mysticism*, New York.

Scholem, Gershom (1971) *The Messianic Idea in Judaism*, London.

Schreber D. P. (1955) *Memoirs of my Nervous Illness*, trans., ed., intr. and notes Ida Macalpine and Richard A. Hunter, London.

Schutz, Alfred (1976) *Collected Papers*, 3 vols., The Hague.

Screech, M. A. (1980) *Ecstasy and the Praise of Folly*, London.

Shapin, Stevin and Schaffer, Simon (1985) *Leviathan and the Air-Pump: Hobbes, Boyle, and the Experimental Life*, Princeton, NJ.

Siirala, Aarne (1970) *Divine Humanness*, trans. T. A. Kantonen, Philadelphia.

Simmel, Georg (1971) *On Individuality and Social Forms*, ed. D. N. Levine, Chicago.

—— (1978) *The Philosophy of Money*, trans. Tom Bottomore and David Frisby, London.

Smith, W. Robertson (1907) *Lectures on the Religion of the Semites*, London.

Sohn-Rethel, Alfred (1978) *Intellectual and Manual Labour: a Critique of Epistemology*, London.

Sordi, Marta (1983) *The Christians and the Roman Empire*, trans. Annabel Bedini, London.

Southern, R. W. (1970) *Western Society and the Church in the Middle Ages*, London.

Stanbaugh, John E. and Balch, David L. (1986) *The New Testament in its Social Environment*, Philadelphia.

Starobinski, Jean (1988) *Jean-Jacques Rousseau: Transparency and Obstruction*, trans. Arthur Goldhammer, Chicago and London.

Stevenson, J. (1987) *A New Eusebius: Documents Illustrating the History of the Church to AD 337*, revised by W. H. C. Frend, London.

Stepelevich, Lawrence S. ed. (1983) *The Young Hegelians*, Cambridge.

Stiefel, Tina (1985) *The Intellectual Revolution in Twelfth Century Europe*, London.

Stirner, Max (1971) *The Ego and His Own*, ed. John Carroll, London.

Sweetman, J. Windrow (1945–67) *Islam and Christian Theology*, 4 vols., London.

Tatarkiewicz Wladyslaw (1976) *Analysis of Happiness*, trans. E. Rothert and D. Zielinskn, The Hague and Warsaw.

Taylor, Charles (1975) *Hegel*, Cambridge.

—— (1989) *Sources of the Self: The Making of the Modern Identity*, Cambridge.

Taylor, Mark (1980) *Journeys to Selfhood: Hegel and Kierkegaard*, Berkeley and London.

Telfer, Elizabeth (1980) *Happiness*, London.

Theissen, Gerd (1978) *The First Followers of Jesus*, trans. John Bowden, London.

Thomas, Keith (1971) *Religion and the Decline of Magic*, London.

Thompson, E. A. (1966) *The Visigoths in the Time of Ulfila*, Oxford.

—— (1969) *The Goths in Spain*, Oxford.

Thompson, George (1961) *The First Philosophers*, London.

Thompson, Geraldine (1973) *Under Pretext of Praise: Satiric Mode in Erasmus' Fiction*, Toronto and Buffalo.

Thulstrup, Niels (1980) *Kierkegaard's Relation to Hegel*, trans. George L. Stengren, Princeton, NJ.

Tillich, Paul (1953, 1957, 1964) *Systematic Theology*, London.

Tournier, Michel (1972) *The Erl-King*, trans. Barbara Bray, London.

Towler, R. (1974) *Homo Religiosus: Sociological Problems in the Study of Religion*, London.

Troeltsch, Ernst (1931) *The Social Teachings of the Christian Churches*, trans. Olive Wyon, 2 vols., London and New York.

—— (1972) *The Absoluteness of Christianity and the History of Religions*, London.

—— (1977) *Ernst Troeltsch: Writings on Theology and Religion*, trans. and ed. Robert Morgan and Michael Pye, London.

Turner, Bryan S. (1974) *Weber and Islam*, London.

—— (1983) *Religion and Social Theory*, London.

—— (1984) *The Body and Society: Explorations in Social Theory*, London.

Turner, Denys (1983) *Marxism and Christianity*, Oxford.

Turner, Frank Miller (1974) *Between Science and Religion: The Reaction to Scientific Naturalism in Late Victorian England*, New Haven and London.

Tylor, Edward B. (1871) *Primitive Culture*, 2 vols., London.

Uexküll, J. von (1926) *Theoretical Biology*, London.

Ullmann, Walter (1955) *The Growth of Papal Government in the Middle Ages*, London.

—— (1966) *The Individual and Society in the Middle Ages*, London.

Underhill, Evelyn (1911) *Mysticism: A Study in the Nature and Development of Man's Spiritual Consciousness*, London.

Vermes, G. (1973) *Jesus the Jew*, London.

—— (1974) *Jesus and the World of Judaism*, Philadelphia.

Vives, Juan Luis (1979) *Juan Luis Vives Against the Pseudodialecticians: A Humanist Attack on Medieval Logic*, trans. and intr. Rita Guerlac, Dordrecht and Boston.

Vööbus, Arthur (1958, 1960, 1988) *History of Asceticism in the Syrian Orient: A Contribution to the History of Culture in the Near East*, Louvain.

Walker D. P. (1958) *Spiritual and Demonic Magic from Ficino to Campanella*, London.

Wallace-Hadrill, J. M. (1952) *The Barbarian West 400–1000*, London.

—— (1983) *The Frankish Church*, Oxford.

Ward, Keith (1974) *The Concept of God*, Oxford.

—— (1982) *Rational Theology and the Creativity of God*, Oxford.

Wartofsky, Marx W. (1977) *Feuerbach*, Cambridge.

Weber, Max (1930) *The Protestant Ethic and the Spirit of Capitalism*, trans. Talcott Parsons, London.

—— (1948) *From Max Weber*, ed. Hans H. Gerth and C. Wright Mills, London.

—— (1951) *The Religion of China: Confucianism and Taoism*, trans. Hans H. Gerth, New York.

—— (1952) *Ancient Judaism*, trans. Hans H. Gerth and Don Martindale, New York.

—— (1958) *The Religion of India*, trans. Hans H. Gerth and Don Martindale, New York.

—— (1965) *The Sociology of Religion*, trans. Ephraim Fischoff, London.

Weber, Max (1978) *Economy and Society*, ed. Guenther Roth and Claus Wittich, 2 vols., Berkeley, Los Angeles and London.

Weinstein, Donald and Bell, Rudolph M. (1982) *Saints and Society: The Two Worlds of Western Christendom, 1000–1700*, Chicago and London.

Weizsacker, Carl von (1894) *The Apostolic Age of the Christian Church*, trans. James Millar, 2 vols., New York.

Westfall, Richard S. (1977) *The Construction of Modern Science: Mechanism and Mechanics*, Cambridge.

Whitehead, Alfred North (1978) *Process and Reality: An Essay in Cosmology*, eds. David Ray Griffin and Donald W. Sherburne, New York and London.

Wilken, Robert L. ed. (1975) *Aspects of Wisdom in Judaism and Early Christianity*, Notre Dame and London.

William of St Thierry (1971) *On Contemplating God*, Shannon.

—— (1974) *The Enigma of Faith*, Washington, DC.

—— (1979) *The Mirror of Faith*, Kalamazoo, Michigan.

Williams, George Huntston (1962) *The Radical Reformation*, London.

Williams, Kathleen (1969) *Twentieth Century Interpretations of the Praise of Folly*, Englewood Cliffs, NJ.

Williams, Rosalind H. (1982) *Dream Worlds: Mass Consumption in Late Nineteenth-Century France*, Berkeley, CA.

Wilson, Bryan (1966) *Religion in a Secular Society*, London.

Wilson, Robert McLachlan (1958) *The Gnostic Problem*, London.

Yates, Frances (1964) *Giordano Bruno and the Hermetic Tradition*, London.

Young, Frances (1983) *From Nicaea to Chalcedon*, London.

Zaehner, R. C. (1957) *Mysticism: Sacred and Profane*, Oxford.

Zaner, Richard M. (1971) *The Problem of Embodiment: Some Contributions to a Phenomenology of the Body*, The Hague.

Zeitlin, Irving M. (1984) *Ancient Judaism: Biblical Criticism from Max Weber to the Present*, Cambridge.

—— (1988) *Jesus and the Judaism of His Time*, Cambridge.

Zwingli, Huldrych (1984) *Huldrych Zwingli: Writings*, 2 vols., Allison Park, Pennsylvania.

NAME INDEX

Abraham 162
Abu Bakhr 80
Alaric 70
Albert of Mainz 115
Alexander the Great 35, 61, 62
Alexandria 52
Anselm 88
Aquinas, Thomas x, 87, 94, 103
Augustine, Bishop of Hippo, ix, x,
    26, 57–61, 66, 69, 71, 72, 81,
    89, 123, 199

Baxter, Richard 131
Benedict 80, 90
Bergson, Henri 180, 182, 186–90
Bernard of Clairveaux 92
Bethlehem 20
Boethius x
Bohr, Niels 180
Boltzmann, Ludwig 176
Boniface 74
Boyle, Robert 136
Brothers Karamazov 179

Calvin, John 26, 121–4, 128, 129,
    133, 142, 146, 166
Cassian, John 80
Celsus 48
Chalcedon 72, 76
Charlemagne 74, 82
Charles the Great 74
Christ 46, 49, 50, 54, 58, 75, 76,
    106, 122, 126, 153, 159, 164
Clement of Alexandria 52, 53, 55, 57

Clovis 73
Cluny 90, 91
Confessions (Augustine) 57, 58
Confessions (Rousseau) 156
Constantine, Emperor 64, 69–71, 73
Constantine, Pope 74
Constantinople 70, 74, 77
Copernicus, Nicholas 104
Crime and Punishment 179
Cyprian, Bishop of Carthage 54, 58

Daniélou, Jean 43
Dead Sea Scrolls 43
Denys the Aeropagite
    (PseudoDionysius) 76
Devils 179
Dostoevsky, Fyodor 178, 179, 196,
    197
Durkheim, Emile 1–12, 20, 22, 28,
    31, 33, 45, 68, 82, 92, 97, 131,
    166, 208

Edifying Discourses 161
Either/Or 158, 159, 161, 162, 178
Elementary Forms of the Religious Life
    7, 8, 10
Enchiridion Militis Christiani 106
Encomium Moriae 107
Erasmus 106–9, 114, 116, 125
Eriugena, John Scotus 86
Essence of Christianity 14
Exhortation to Virtue 106

Fear and Trembling 162

Feuerbach, Ludwig 14, 15, 17–19, 21, 186, 189
Filippovna, Nastasya 197
Frankfurt 77
Freud, Sigmund 183, 188–99

General Psychopathology 198
God x, xi, xii, 25–7, 39, 40, 42, 43, 49, 51, 55, 56, 58–60, 76, 79, 84–9, 91, 92, 95, 98, 100, 101, 108, 117–19, 121–5, 127, 129, 136, 137, 140–5, 147, 151, 154, 155, 163, 168, 181, 184, 195, 199, 200, 204, 207, 210
Goethe, Johann Wolfgang von 192
Gregory of Tours 73

Hadrian I 74
Harnack, Adolf von 43, 51, 61
Hegel, Georg Wilhelm Friedrich xiii, 12–18, 157, 163, 186, 199
Hilary of Poitiers 58, 73
Hobbes, Thomas 144
Hume, David 183

Isidore of Seville 81

Jaspers, Karl 198
Jerome 70, 71
Jesus 43, 46–9, 145
John 50
John the Baptist 48
John of Chrysostom 58
Judge William 160
Justin the Martyr 52

Karamazov, Dmitry 196
Karamazov, Ivan 184, 201
Kautsky, Karl 34
Kelvin, Lord 178
Kierkegaard, Søren 138, 156–65, 167, 178, 195, 197, 200
Koran 43

Learned Ignorance 103
Leo the Great 74
Lombard, Peter 264
Luther, Martin 114–20, 122, 128

Mach, Ernst 177
Marcion 44, 46, 70
Marseilles 80
Marx, Karl 12–22, 31, 33, 67, 68, 163, 166, 186, 201, 202
Mather, Cotton 131
Mecca 79
Melanchthon, Philip 125, 126
Montaigne, Michel de 146
Montaillou 111
More, Sir Thomas 114
Muhammad 78, 79
Myshkin, Prince 197

Nag Hammadi 43
Newton, Sir Isaac 137
Nicaea 71, 81
Nicholas of Cusa 103–5, 115
Nietzsche, Friedrich 63, 176, 184, 187, 188, 190, 193, 196
Notes from Underground 178, 179

On the Trinity 60
Origen 52, 53, 55, 56

Pascal, Blaise 138–43, 145–8, 154, 156, 157, 160, 162, 163, 174, 175, 199
Paul 49, 50, 57, 69
Pensées 143
Phenomenology of Spirit xiii, 157
Philo of Alexandria 39, 40
Pippin 74
Pirenne, Henri 71, 77, 78
Planck, Max 178
Plato 38, 39
Plotinus 40, 41, 61, 86
Poincaré, Henri 177
Porphyry 40
Powys, John Cowper 201
Proust, Marcel 180, 183, 188, 196, 201

Ravenna 70, 71
Regine 159
Rome 70, 74
Rostovtzeff, M 63
Rousseau, Jean-Jacques 138, 148–57,

NAME INDEX

159, 160, 162, 164, 165, 174

Saint-Pierre 151
Schleiermacher, Friedrich 199
Scholem, Gershom 43
Sentences 125
Socrates 37
Solent, Wolf 201
Southern R.W. 99
Stages on Life's Way 179, 197

Tertullian 58
Theses on Feuerbach 15
Time Regained 194

Torah 43
Troeltsch, Ernst 34

Ulfila 71

Valentinus 70
Vives, Juan Luis 125

Weber, Max 1, 21–31, 33, 42, 44,
    45, 47, 48, 51, 61, 64, 67, 68,
    102, 128–34, 166

Zossimov 197

SUBJECT INDEX

abstraction 15, 23, 24, 65, 157, 158
actuality 13
aesthetic 159, 160
agape 65, 67, 155
alienation 17, 18, 21
antinomian 44, 112, 113
apocalypse 43, 50
apologetics 52–7
artisan 28, 64
asceticism 26, 27, 45, 92, 109, 130,
133, 135, 142, 143
axial age 6

barbarian society 70–5, 80
being 41, 59, 60, 86, 87, 95, 98, 180
belief xv; in feudal society 85–7,
93–5: in primitive society 5–7;
synthetic union of 100
biogenetic law 8
body 36, 40, 110, 188–93; of
Christ 50
boredom 159
bourgeoisie 28
bureaucratic 28, 30
Byzantium 75–7

capitalism 12, 19, 131, 135, 136,
145, 166–9
Catharism 110
charisma 47
Christian philosophy 106–7
Christianity xi, xii, xiv, xv; in
barbarian society 71–5; development of 23; division between

eastern and western 75; and
history of subjectivity xiii;
origins of 46–51; in relation to
Islam 78
Christology 75, 76
church 69, 71, 72
civil society 16, 103
civilization 22
classification 3, 4
commodity 18, 20, 21, 64, 115,
173, 199–203
communication 118, 159, 160, 164
community 8, 28, 37, 45, 46, 65,
79, 80, 91, 97
conformity 109–21
conscience 103, 149
conscience collective 8, 11
consciousness 181
consolation 16, 163
consumption 32, 33, 60, 66, 99,
145, 176
contemplation 42
convention 5, 9, 149
conversion 64, 69
cosmological argument 87, 103,
104
cosmology 56, 85, 86, 102, 133,
135, 138, 139, 154, 176–8, 181
covenant 42
creation 41, 56, 195
creed 72
cult 35, 36; of saints 73

desire 144, 150, 153

266

despair 156–65
dialectic 34, 35
doctrine 24
dread 165
dualism 25, 26, 112
duration 180–5

ego 108, 145, 157
Enlightenment xii, xiv, 18, 30, 136, 148, 167
entropy 176
epiphany 193–9
eros 39
eschatology 47, 101
estrangement 15, 20, 21
ethical 25, 115, 160–2
evil 59
exchange 20, 65
excitement 173, 196

faith xv, 53, 117, 118, 121, 125
feudal society 82–4, 93, 102
folly 107, 108
forgiveness 114
form 38
fragmentation 195
functionalism 7, 9

gnosticism 43–6, 57, 67, 112
god x; as creator xi; early theological conceptions of 55, 56; and goodness 25, 59; gnostic view of 44; and happiness xi; in medieval thought 87–9; and modern theology 140; and perfection 25, 98; and personal salvation xi; in Reformation theology 119, 120
good 41
good works 116, 117, 122
goodness 38, 39
grace 59, 121
guilt 161

happiness xiv, 6; Augustine's view of ix, x; definitions of, ix–xi; and God xi; and history of Christianity xiii–xv; and human

ends xiii, 1; illusion of 16; and selfhood 108
heresy 35, 110–13
hierarchy 83, 84, 89, 97, 102
humility 91, 92

iconoclasm 76, 77
image 85
immanence 13
immediacy 150, 153
individual 6, 11, 15, 26, 57, 144, 149, 158, 159, 170
individualism 106, 166–8, 171
indulgences 114, 115, 117
infinity 103, 104, 143, 144–6
Inquisition 111
Islam 77–80

Jesus movement 48, 49, 66
Judaism 39, 42, 43
justice 34

Kabbalistic 43
karma 26
kerygma 46, 47
kinship 4, 5, 28, 82

labour 18, 19, 21
law 42, 43
legitimation 28, 29, 73, 74, 83
liturgy 90, 91
logos 37–41, 47, 51
loneliness 138–47

macrocosm 99
magic 3, 23, 24, 73, 97, 128
Manichaeism 25
martyrdom 54
materialism 142, 144
meaning 22, 23
mediation 18, 58, 119, 157, 158
memory 182, 183, 194
methodology xiv, 34
microcosm 99, 190
Mithraism 36
modern society 11, 16, 18, 171–5
monasticism 80, 90
monotheism xi, 2, 23

morality xv, 102, 103, 105;
   bourgeois 132–4; in
   Reformation 114–16, 128
mysticism 27, 39, 42, 43, 76, 104

nature 19, 28, 58, 59, 136, 137,
   139, 151, 152, 175, 178, 182

obedience 59, 91, 92, 119
objectification 14, 18, 20
obligation 121–6
offence 162, 163
omniscience 26
ontological argument 88, 89
organic society 7
orthodoxy 35, 60

paganism 69, 81
papacy 74, 77
paradox 157, 158, 163, 164
passion xv
philosophy 37, 38, 39, 41, 51, 52,
   65, 157, 158
piety 127–32
pleroma 43
pneuma 44, 45
polis 34
polytheism 36
popular religion 96, 110–12, 127
poverty 91
prayer 123–4
predestination 123, 129
profane 3, 10
proletariat 17
prophecy 24, 25
prophet 37, 79
psychology 144, 146, 172
psychopathology 191, 192, 198
Puritanism 130, 131, 134

rationalization 23–5, 27, 29, 42,
   91, 210
reason 13, 60, 139
recollection 39
reductionism 34
Reformation 30, 114–32, 147
relativity 104, 105, 175–80
religion 2, 3, 6, 7, 9, 15, 35–7

repetition 160, 161
representation 5, 8, 9, 10
ressentiment 63
Resurrection 53
rites 36
ritual 92, 97
Roman Empire 61–7, 70

sacred 3, 5, 10
salvation xi, 13, 26, 31, 39, 91, 94,
   115, 121, 152
scholasticism 84
science 137, 175–8
secularization xv, 84, 135–8, 166, 208
self 108, 138, 147, 161, 183, 184
self-analysis 57, 150
self-control 109, 110, 164
self-indulgence 124
self-love 150, 155
sensations 185–8
sensitivity 187, 191, 196
sensuousness xv, 15, 20, 97, 98,
   113, 174, 175, 186, 192, 195–7
sin 57, 58, 125
slavery 62
sociology of religion xiii, xvi,
   2–31, 67, 68
solitude 147–56
soul 38, 39, 40, 57, 124
spirit 12, 13, 50
state 16
structuralism 7
subjectivity xiii, 22, 154, 174, 178,
   179
symbols 72, 84, 96, 101, 103, 123
Syriac culture 36, 37, 42, 44, 48, 61

theodicy 26
theology 12, 27, 28, 49, 51–7,
   136–7
Torah 43
totemism 4, 5, 12
transcendence 11, 12, 14, 20, 21,
   23, 29, 44, 98, 115, 122, 141,
   164, 170, 204

umma 79
urban 28, 64

SUBJECT INDEX

utilitarian 9, 10, 148

value 23, 29, 32, 65, 99, 100
vassalage 83
virtue 105–9, 112

wisdom 37–9, 46

Zoroastrianism 25, 37